WALL
STREET
JOURNAL
BOOKS

PRESIDENTIAL LEADERSHIP

Rating the Best and the Worst in the White House

EDITED BY

JAMES TARANTO, *The Wall Street Journal,*
AND LEONARD LEO, THE FEDERALIST SOCIETY

A WALL STREET JOURNAL BOOK
PUBLISHED BY FREE PRESS
NEW YORK   LONDON   TORONTO   SYDNEY

A WALL STREET JOURNAL BOOK
Published by Free Press
Rockefeller Center
1230 Avenue of the Americas
New York, NY 10020

FREE PRESS and colophon are trademarks
of Simon & Schuster, Inc.

The Wall Street Journal and the Wall Street Journal Book colophon
are trademarks of Dow Jones & Company, Inc.

For information about special discounts for bulk purchases,
please contact Simon & Schuster Special Sales: 1-800-456-6798 or
business@simonandschuster.com

Designed by Karolina Harris

Manufactured in the United States of America

1 3 5 7 9 10 8 6 4 2

The Library of Congress has cataloged the hardcover edition as follows:
Presidential leadership : rating the best and the worst in the White House / edited
by James Taranto and Leonard Leo
p.   cm.
Includes bibliographical references and index.
1. Presidents—United States—Biography. 2. Presidents—United States—History.
3. Political leadership—United States—History. 4. United States—Politics and
government. I. Taranto, James. II. Leo, Leonard
E176.1.P74 2004
973'.09'9—dc22
[B]
2004040945

ISBN 978-0-743-27408-1

CONTENTS

FOREWORD: Presidents, Greatness, and History
by William J. Bennett   1
INTRODUCTION: The Presidency, *Federalist No. 10*, and the
Constitution *by Steven G. Calabresi*   5
THE RANKINGS   11

The Presidents

1. George Washington (1789–97) *by Richard Brookhiser*   15
2. John Adams (1797–1801) *by Matthew Spalding*   20
3. Thomas Jefferson (1801–09) *by Forrest McDonald*   25
4. James Madison (1809–17) *by Lynne Cheney*   30
5. James Monroe (1817–25) *by David B. Rivkin, Jr., and Mark
   Wendell DeLaquil*   34
6. John Quincy Adams (1825–29) *by Richard Norton Smith*   39
7. Andrew Jackson (1829–37) *by H. W. Brands*   44
8. Martin Van Buren (1837–41) *by John Steele Gordon*   48
9. William Henry Harrison (1841) *by Glenn Harlan Reynolds*   52
10. John Tyler (1841–45) *by John S. Baker, Jr.*   55
11. James Knox Polk (1845–49) *by Douglas G. Brinkley*   60
12. Zachary Taylor (1849–50) *by Brendan Miniter*   64
13. Millard Fillmore (1850–53) *by Melanie Kirkpatrick*   67
14. Franklin Pierce (1853–57) *by Cynthia Crossen*   71
15. James Buchanan (1857–61) *by Christopher Buckley*   75

16. Abraham Lincoln (1861–65) *by Jay Winik*   80

17. Andrew Johnson (1865–69) *by Jeffrey K. Tulis*   88

18. Ulysses Simpson Grant (1869–77) *by Michael Barone*   94

19. Rutherford Birchard Hayes (1877–81) *by Ari Hoogenboom*   99

20. James Abram Garfield (1881) *by Allan Peskin*   104

21. Chester Alan Arthur (1881–85) *by John J. DiIulio, Jr.*   107

22. & 24. Stephen Grover Cleveland (1885–89, 1893–97)
    by Suzanne Garment   111

23. Benjamin Harrison (1889–93) *by Jessica King*   115

25. William McKinley (1897–1901) *by Fred Barnes*   119

26. Theodore Roosevelt (1901–09) *by John S. McCain*   125

27. William Howard Taft (1909–13) *by Theodore B. Olson*   130

28. Thomas Woodrow Wilson (1913–21) *by Max Boot*   135

29. Warren Gamaliel Harding (1921–23) *by Jeremy Rabkin*   141

30. John Calvin Coolidge (1923–29) *by John O. McGinnis*   146

31. Herbert Clark Hoover (1929–33) *by Robert H. Ferrell*   151

32. Franklin Delano Roosevelt (1933–45) *by Robert H. Bork*   155

33. Harry S. Truman (1945–53) *by Terry Eastland*   159

34. Dwight David Eisenhower (1953–61) *by Edwin Meese III*   163

35. John Fitzgerald Kennedy (1961–63) *by Peggy Noonan*   168

36. Lyndon Baines Johnson (1963–69) *by Robert Dallek*   173

37. Richard Milhous Nixon (1969–74) *by Kenneth W. Starr*   178

38. Gerald Rudolph Ford, Jr. (1974–77) *by Thomas J. Bray*   183

39. James Earl Carter, Jr. (1977–81) *by Joshua Muravchik*   188

40. Ronald Wilson Reagan (1981–89) *by Harvey C. Mansfield*   193

41. George Herbert Walker Bush (1989–93) *by Pete du Pont*   198

42. William Jefferson Clinton (1993–2001) *by Paul Johnson*   202

43. George Walker Bush (2001–   ) *by Paul A. Gigot*   208

Issues in Presidential Leadership

Presidential Leadership in Economic Policy
    by Robert L. Bartley   217

Presidential Leadership During Wartime
   by *Victor Davis Hanson*   226
Presidential Leadership and the Judiciary
   by *Robert P. George*   234
Presidential Leadership After Disputed Elections
   by *James Taranto*   241

Appendixes

1. Methodology of Rankings *by James Lindgren*   249
2. Survey Participants   273
3. Election Data, 1789–2004   276

Acknowledgments   287
Index   289

PRESIDENTIAL
LEADERSHIP

FOREWORD
Presidents, Greatness, and History

by William J. Bennett

"Be not afraid of greatness," William Shakespeare wrote. "Some are born great, some achieve greatness, and some have greatness thrust upon 'em." As a proud country that once taught our youth the importance of heroes and the importance of leadership, we used to venerate all our presidents and esteem them as "great." Some of our presidents came from humble means, some from quasi-aristocratic backgrounds; but they were our presidents, our leaders, and we celebrated them and taught their greatness—however they achieved it.

I write this as our forty-third president, George W. Bush, is waging a war against terrorism and the states, regimes, and cells that sponsor and perpetrate it. Just prior to the attack upon our country on September 11, 2001—another "date which will live in infamy"—the newspaper headlines seemed to have our president bogged down in things that now seem distant and unfamiliar to us. I believe, in time, barring the September Slaughter, President Bush could very well have achieved greatness. But, instead, the opportunity for greatness was thrust upon him. Yet the question remains: Will history give George W. Bush his due? Will it remember him primarily for his accomplishments, or for the unusual circumstances of his election—a disputed vote that left some in the other party denying his legitimacy?

This will depend in part on his continued success. But it also may depend on the political biases of historians. The politicization of American colleges and universities, combined with the dumbing-down of elementary and secondary education, has corrupted our history, and the understanding of it—including our presidents.

Once upon a time, President Washington was known as "first in war, first in peace, first in the hearts of his countrymen." Today he is almost exclusively known for being a slave owner. It is common for a fourth-grader today, when asked what he learned of President Lincoln, to say, "We learned he didn't actually free the slaves." President Grant is now known for being a drunk and having a scandal-ridden presidency. He was once known, however, as the man Frederick Douglass supported, turning down a third party ticket in order to campaign for him; as a man who stipulated that at his death an equal number of Confederate and Union soldiers carry his body to its resting place; as a man whose memoir sales broke all previous records.

Our nation's presidents have their warts, to be sure. But they have far more than warts. Whatever is said of the worst of them, it must also be remembered that, at the very least, they submitted them-selves—and their character—to public scrutiny and public service. They were men in the arena—a valor outlined by Theodore Roosevelt, a valor worth remembering today as we seem, at times, to be inundated with the study of their faults.

If a monument to character in leadership is needed, I cannot think of a better example than Mount Rushmore. How many other coun-tries have Mount Rushmores or leaders worthy of a Mount Rushmore? I do not know how the decision was made to portray the four presidents depicted on that colossal sculpture: Washington, Jefferson, Lincoln, and Theodore Roosevelt. I will say this about the monument, though: They are well chosen. Some might argue that Benjamin Franklin or James Madison should have joined the quartet. Others would say that Franklin D. Roosevelt or John F. Kennedy or Ronald Reagan should be presented to the people of the world and to posterity. Yet in these four leaders who served in the presidential chair, we have examples to offer of the leaders whom a democratic people have selected through reflection and choice. In their charac-ter and deeds, these leaders deserve to be held up. Each of the four demonstrated a willingness to assume power only through constitu-tional means. Three of the four stepped down from power voluntar-ily. Lincoln, of course, was removed by the willful act of an assassin.

Our students and our country need to relearn why we once celebrated leaders such as these—as well as their predecessors and successors. In his farewell address, President Reagan warned the
American people—and the world—of a whirlwind we would reap by
not studying our history, our history of great events, great movements, and great people. He concluded his warning: "If we forget
what we did, we won't know who we are. I'm warning of an eradica-
tion of the American memory that could result, ultimately, in an ero-
sion of the American spirit. Let's start with some basics: more
attention to American history and a greater emphasis on civic ritual."

We are, indeed, losing our history of great men and women in this
country (and, with it, our great country's history) because too many
of those who honeycomb our academies, and who dominate the
writing of history, take a cynical or even hostile approach toward
America and the people who made it great. We must combat the
iconoclasm and false history with better history—better historical
writing, better historical analysis, and better historical honesty. One
theologian put it this way: "The best way to show that a stick is
crooked is not to argue about it or spend time denouncing it, but to
lay a straight stick alongside it."

This book, dedicated to the study of those who were not afraid to
attempt greatness, is a contribution toward that effort. It is a straight
stick.

*Mr. Bennett served as U.S. secretary of education, 1985–88, and direc-
tor of the U.S. Office of National Drug Control Policy, 1989–90. He is the
author of several books, including* The Book of Virtues, The Children's
Book of Heroes, Our Sacred Honor, *and* Why We Fight: Moral Clarity and
the War on Terrorism.

INTRODUCTION
The Presidency, Federalist No. 10, and the Constitution

by Steven G. Calabresi

Americans are fascinated by the presidency and have been ever since George Washington became our first president in 1789. The presidency plays many of the symbolic roles for us that the monarchy plays for the British, and for that reason alone it has always been the object of mixed feelings of admiration, awe, and fear. Every age defines itself by its heroes, and in the United States our foremost heroes (and villains) are our presidents. It is for this reason that the Federalist Society set out together with *The Wall Street Journal* to do a current turn-of-the-millennium look at who are America's most admired presidents. The results of that survey, which appear on pages 11 to 12 and 249 to 272 of this book, are of great interest because of what they tell us about our own age.

There are, however, two other reasons why I personally thought it important to launch the survey of the presidents that this book reproduces. These reasons also explain why I have devoted much of my time as a law professor to writing about the presidency. First, I think the presidency is an important moderating force in American life for reasons my hero, James Madison, set out in *Federalist No. 10*. Second, the presidency plays a vital role in maintaining the Constitution, a subject I am inherently interested in as a law professor.

The presidency is and almost always has been an important moderating force in American public life. This is in part because the president and the vice president are the only two officers of the national government who are elected by a nationwide constituency. Senators and representatives are elected to office by small constituencies consisting of a state or a congressional district. As Madison argued in his brilliant essay in *Federalist No. 10,* it is comparatively easy for small factions to dominate congressional districts or states. Some states and districts may be dominated by farmers while others may be dominated by manufacturers. The senators or representatives elected from those constituencies will all too often be very attentive to the interests of the farmers or the manufacturers they represent. The president and vice president, however, must win a nationwide election, and to do that they will have to appeal to both farmers and manufacturers, and to a whole host of other interests besides. Because of that, the president and vice president are less likely to be "captured" by special interests than are senators and representatives.

Madison offered *Federalist No. 10* as a cure to an ancient problem of democracy, evident to the Framers in the turbulent history of the Greek city-states. The Framers knew that democracy had failed there because all too often it degenerated into mob rule and violent contest between vicious factions. In addition to this sorry history, the Framers feared democracy could never work in a continental-size republic because the representatives of the people would not follow the popular will. Madison, however, argued that this way of conceiving things was exactly backward. He pointed out that if you extend the size of a democracy you take in an ever-larger number of factions or interest groups. In a large democracy, Madison noted, no one faction would ever be big enough to always dominate the national political process. This would mean that national politics would have to be dominated by ever-shifting coalitions of factions rather than by one majority and one minority faction. As a result, a large democracy would be less prone to interest group capture and majority tyranny than were the Greek city-states. Thus, the expansive size of the proposed new United States was not a problem for American democracy. Rather, it was the cure to the ancient problem of factional turbulence that had doomed the Greek city-states.

Madison's argument is widely known, but few people appreciate its implications for the presidency. The president and the vice president are the only elected officers of our national government whose constituency is a national majority coalition. Representatives and senators may be able to get reelected by pleasing a few powerful local or state interests, but presidents can get reelected (or see an ideologically sympathetic successor elected) only if they please a whole national coalition of interests. This means that presidents are less likely than senators or representatives to be captured by any one interest, and they are more likely to take positions that are vague and are calculated to appeal to the moderate middle, which decides most national elections.

What this means is that American presidents, both Republicans and Democrats, tend to have a moderating effect on our body politic, even when they are leading us in some new direction. This point can easily be illustrated by the examples of just a few recent presidents.

Ronald Reagan charted a bold new course in foreign and domestic policy in a host of ways, but it was clear to me as a political appointee in his administration that he always worked hard to pull together a broad national coalition. Reagan forged an alliance of economic conservatives, social conservatives, anti-communists, and moderate and even liberal Republicans, as well as many conservative Democrats. He kept this coalition happy by having different officials in his administration to appeal to different constituencies. Conservatives looked to Ed Meese, Cap Weinberger, Bill Casey, Bill Bennett, and Donald Hodel, while moderates looked to Jim Baker, George Shultz, and later Howard Baker. The whole enterprise was a balancing effort, and different factions were represented in the administration in different ways.

Reagan's policies too were more balanced and nuanced than many appreciated at the time. His anti-communism was balanced by the stunning and fateful rapprochement he achieved with Mikhail Gorbachev. His tax cuts were balanced by the 1986 tax reform bill and by some unfortunate but necessary tax increases. His social conservatism was tempered by an instinct for appealing to younger, more libertarian suburban Republicans. In sum, Ronald Reagan was nothing less than a genius at tending to the needs of the broad Madisonian coalition that elected him. And in the process of tending to the needs of that broad coalition he emerged as a far more moderate *and effective* president than anyone would have expected when he challenged Gerald Ford in the primaries of 1976.

Now fast-forward to Bill Clinton. He began his career as an unabashed McGovernite liberal. (He was also, in my judgment, corrupt and pathologically dishonest, and I thus advocated his impeachment.) Nonetheless, he was a surprisingly moderate president in a few notable respects. He signed landmark welfare reform legislation and a capital gains tax cut. He signed the Defense of Marriage Act, albeit at midnight when no press could record the event. He committed U.S. troops to war in the Balkans, even though in his youth he sympathized with those who "had come to loathe the military." He signaled to the American people that "the era of big government" was over, thus legitimizing the Reagan Revolution in much the same way that Dwight Eisenhower legitimized the New Deal. His two Supreme Court nominees, Ruth Bader Ginsburg and Stephen Breyer, were relative moderates who attracted little Republican opposition. He repositioned the Democrats as being tough on crime.

Why would a politician with basically left-wing instincts do all of these things? Because he was tending to his reelection and to the hope that his vice president would be picked to succeed him, and that meant he had to keep a Madisonian coalition happy. The genius of the American political system forced Clinton to be a moderate president even though his ideology tugged him constantly in the other direction.

James Madison's argument for extended, continental democracy in *Federalist No. 10* was as right and as influential as any essay in political science could ever hope to be. Critically for this book, however, it explains why the presidency is so often and so surprisingly a force for moderation in our national life. In an era when most House seats are redistricted to be safely Republican or safely Democratic, the presidency remains an institution that neither party can quite permanently capture. The moderation and centrism of our presidents are features of the presidency that make it an admirable institution and that have served this country well.

A second feature of the presidency that is underappreciated is the role the president plays in the development and exposition of our constitutional law. We all know that every new president takes a special oath of office when he assumes the presidency in which he swears to "preserve, protect, and defend the Constitution of the United States," but few of us know that the Framers in Philadelphia put more stock in the president as a defender of the Constitution than they did in the Supreme Court. What was it about the presidency that made the Framers think that the president would play a bigger role in preserving our constitutional order than the Supreme Court?

To begin with, the Framers rightly thought that the major threat to our constitutional order was foreign invasion or domestic insurrection, and since 1789 the presidency has been a stalwart backstop against both of those two threats. More broadly, the presidency has an almost unchallenged role to play in the foreign affairs area, where the Supreme Court tends almost always to defer to presidential judgments about issues of constitutional meaning. In the whole critical area of foreign policy and domestic security, therefore, the president is the dominant interpreter of the Constitution.

In domestic affairs, the president is the chief law enforcement officer of the nation, and he sets the policy priorities that largely determine whether the laws are faithfully executed. Moreover, the president is the font of constitutional law because he nominates new justices of the Supreme Court and new judges of the one-thousand-member lower federal judiciary. Two-term presidents can expect to name, on average, three or four Supreme Court justices and some 40 percent of lower-court judges. That is almost always enough to "tip the balance" on the federal courts in some new direction. While senatorial advice and consent sometimes slows the president down, the fact is that each new president gets to move the courts decisively in some new direction and two-term presidents can almost always change the direction of the courts, unless they face a Senate controlled by the opposite party.

The net result, as Mr. Dooley famously said, is that "the Supreme Court follows th' iliction returns," and the returns it mainly follows are those of *presidential* elections. That is why it matters so much for domestic policy who wins presidential elections even though the president does not have much leverage over Congress aside from the veto power. The Supreme Court is basically a caboose on the train of government with the presidency functioning as the locomotive. Whichever direction the president goes, the Supreme Court will eventually follow, even if there is a bit of a lag. The president is, thus, as the Framers expected he would be, the font of our constitutional law. Anyone interested in constitutional law or the Supreme Court must also be interested in the presidency because that is where constitutional law gets made in the first instance.

These two underappreciated features of the presidency help explain why Americans are right to be fascinated by this uniquely important American institution. The presidency *is* as important as Americans think it is, and we are justified in making our quadrennial presidential elections the big national town meeting of our democracy. It is my hope that this book, with its study of the forty-two men who've served as president, and with the reproduced survey ranking of the presidents, will contribute to a better and deeper understanding of this incredibly vital, distinctively American, institution.

Mr. Calabresi is George C. Dix Professor of Constitutional Law at Northwestern University and co-founder of the Federalist Society. He would like to thank Gary Lawson for helpful comments and suggestions.

THE RANKINGS

In February and March 2005, the Federalist Society and *The Wall Street Journal* asked an ideologically balanced group of 130 prominent professors of history, law, political science, and economics to rate the presidents on a 5-point scale, with 5 meaning highly superior and 1 meaning well below average. Eighty-five scholars responded, and the presidents are ranked in order of mean score, adjusted to give equal weight to Democratic- and Republican-leaning respondents. For more details, see Appendix I, page 249.

GREAT

1. George Washington	4.94
2. Abraham Lincoln	4.67
3. Franklin Roosevelt	4.41

NEAR GREAT

4. Thomas Jefferson	4.23
5. Theodore Roosevelt	4.08
6. Ronald Reagan	4.03
7. Harry Truman	3.95
8. Dwight Eisenhower	3.67
9. James Polk	3.59
10. Andrew Jackson	3.58

ABOVE AVERAGE

11. Woodrow Wilson	3.41
12. Grover Cleveland	3.34
13. John Adams	3.33
14. William McKinley	3.32

15. John Kennedy	3.25
16. James Monroe	3.24

AVERAGE

17. James Madison	3.07
18. Lyndon Johnson	3.05
19. George W. Bush	3.01
20. William Taft	2.97
21. George H. W. Bush	2.95
22. Bill Clinton	2.93
23. Calvin Coolidge	2.77
24. Rutherford Hayes	2.73

BELOW AVERAGE

25. John Quincy Adams	2.66
26. Chester Arthur	2.65
27. Martin Van Buren	2.63
28. Gerald Ford	2.61
29. Ulysses Grant	2.57
30. Benjamin Harrison	2.54
31. Herbert Hoover	2.50
32. Richard Nixon	2.40
33. Zachary Taylor	2.30
34. Jimmy Carter	2.24
35. John Tyler	2.23

FAILURE

36. Millard Fillmore	1.85
37. Andrew Johnson	1.75
38. Franklin Pierce	1.73
39. Warren Harding	1.64
40. James Buchanan	1.31

Note: Because of the short duration of their tenures, William Henry Harrison and James Garfield were excluded from the rankings.

The Presidents

1.
GEORGE
WASHINGTON

SURVEY RANKING: I

BORN: February 22, 1732 (February 11, old style), Westmoreland County, Virginia

WIFE: Martha Dandridge Custis

RELIGION: Episcopalian

PARTY: Federalist

MILITARY EXPERIENCE: Virginia militia (colonel), Continental Army (general and commander in chief)

OTHER OFFICES HELD: Member of Virginia House of Burgesses (1759–74), delegate to Continental Congress (1774–75), president of Constitutional Convention (1787)

TOOK OFFICE: April 30, 1789

VICE PRESIDENT: John Adams

LEFT OFFICE: March 4, 1797

DIED: December 14, 1799

BURIED: Mount Vernon, Virginia

by Richard Brookhiser

In February 1789 presidential electors met in the capitals of their states to cast the first ballots ever to fill the office of president. Every one of them voted for George Washington (a sweep that would be repeated when he won reelection, and never since). Congress, meeting in New York City, the nation's capital, counted the ballots in March, and informed the victor in early April. Washington's trip north from Mount Vernon was a pageant of acclaim, marked in every town and city he passed by banquets, songs, and parades, and culminating in a ceremonial barge trip across New York Harbor that was accompanied by booming cannon and leaping porpoises. He was not elated by his triumph, however. Before he set off, he wrote that he felt like "a culprit who is going to the place of his execution."

Thomas Jefferson believed that Washington was naturally "inclined to gloomy apprehensions." Yet there was much to apprehend in the spring of 1789. Two serious problems faced the Washington administration, and another was in the offing.

The first problem was unique to the first presidency: What exactly does the president do? The Constitution had given him "the executive power," and defined certain aspects of it, chiefly diplomatic and military. But many details were still fluid. The president could make treaties, "with the advice and consent of the Senate." Did that mean he should formally consult them before negotiating with foreign powers? In August 1789 Washington appeared before the Senate to tell them what he proposed to offer the Creek Indians. The senators began asking questions, which carriages rattling on the street outside made inaudible. The discussion bogged down, and Washington, showing rare public irritation, left. Though he returned on a later day, he vowed never to submit his bargaining positions to the Senate—one bystander recalled him saying "he would be damned if he ever went there again"—a precedent his successors have followed.

Washington also had to establish presidential etiquette. His behavior at weekly receptions struck some guests as stiff. Yet he was accessible and peripatetic, making a point of visiting all thirteen states (most of the ubiquitous "Washington Slept Here" signage on eighteenth-century American buildings is probably accurate). In a world of divine right, he had to define the manners of republican authority. Once he defined them, he had to enact them with conviction. Americans, well versed in ancient history, knew that many aspiring tyrants had honored republican forms on their way up. But, as Tacitus wrote, "grand sentiments of this kind sounded unconvincing." Washington had to get etiquette right, and he had to mean it.

The second problem Washington faced was America's shaky finances. This was an old story. As commander in chief during the Revolution, he had struggled with faltering supplies and chronic arrears in soldiers' pay. Postwar efforts to pay off the debt had led to crushing state taxes and severe rural discontent. Even so, the government could not pay its bills. By 1789 American obligations were trading as low as 25 percent of face value on European money markets.

Most of the Founding Fathers were planters and lawyers, with little understanding of commerce, and less of finance; reading what John Adams and Thomas Jefferson had to say about banks and banking is hair-raising. Washington shared their ignorance. But he knew, from his wartime experience, that the debt problem required bold solutions; and he had met, on his staff, a bold young colonel, Alexander Hamilton. Washington tapped Hamilton to be the first treasury secretary, and he let him work. Washington had the great gift of leadership: he knew what he knew (war and politics), and he knew when to rely on others.

When Hamilton's economic program, which included an excise tax on distilled spirits, provoked the Whiskey Rebellion on the Appalachian frontier in 1794, Washington had to rely on his own talents. The Whiskey Rebels thought they were justly defying an oppressive tax. But Washington saw their defiance of a legitimately passed law as a violation of republican government. "[If] a minority . . . is to dictate to the majority," he wrote, then "all laws are prostrate, and everyone will carve for himself." Washington sent troops to the scene, five times as numerous as the army he had led across the Delaware in 1776; the show of force prevented further bloodshed. Good government and sound finances were saved. When Hamilton stepped down in 1795, American public securities were trading at 110 percent of face value.

The third great problem of the Washington administration began three months after his first inauguration, with the fall of the Bastille.

Despite its bloody excesses, the French Revolution looked at first like an exercise in liberal constitutionalism. The Marquis de Lafayette, Washington's idealistic comrade-in-arms, was one of the early leaders, and Tom Paine, the author of *Common Sense,* was elected to the French legislature. By 1794, however, Lafayette was in exile, Paine was in jail, and the guillotines were doing their work.

The French Revolution began a quarter century of superpower conflict. The principal belligerents both had long-standing ties with the United States. Britain was the former colonial power, now a major trading partner. France was an ally in the throes of chaos, intent on exporting its ideology. Washington's guiding principle throughout the conflict was to keep the infant United States out of harm's way. He issued a proclamation effectively declaring neutrality, thus spurning America's obligations to France, though he softened the blow by avoiding the word. When a bumptious French diplomat, "Citizen" Edmond-Charles Genet, tried appealing over the president's head to the American people, Washington held his tongue until Genet overstepped himself, and then demanded his recall. He negotiated a new treaty with Britain, to resolve issues left unsettled by the Revolution, and pushed it through a reluctant Congress. In his farewell address, Washington looked forward to a time "when we may choose peace or war, as our interest guided by our justice shall counsel." But for the time being, he declared, it was "our true policy to steer clear of permanent alliances, with any portion of the foreign world."

Foreign war also became a topic of domestic strife. Like boxing fans with ringside seats, Americans chose sides. Jefferson, the first secretary of state, took a view of the French Revolution that was sanguine, in both senses of the word—hopeful, and bloodthirsty. "Rather than it should have failed," he wrote, "I would have seen half the earth devastated. Were there but an Adam and an Eve left in every country, and left free, it would be better than as it now is." Hamilton believed that U.S. prosperity depended on an understanding with Britain. "We think in English," he assured a British diplomat. Jefferson and Hamilton's disagreement and rivalry—they came to dislike each other personally—formed the nub of the first two-party system, the Republicans (ancestors of today's Democrats) and the Federalists. The Founding Fathers viewed political parties with distaste—James Madison wrote disdainfully of "factions"—yet they all joined one or the other.

Washington inclined to Federalism—in his view of the world, France, albeit a republic, was more aggressive and therefore more dangerous than monarchic Britain—yet he only inclined to it. He did not want Americans to take sides on foreign policy. In his farewell address, he warned Americans against both "inveterate antipathies" and "passionate attachments" to other countries. As president, he steered between contending pressures and weathered several ugly domestic storms. The United States finally slipped into the French revolutionary wars—by then the Napoleonic wars—in 1812, and the experience was disastrous. But the country was strong enough to weather it, thanks to Washington's early firm hand.

Washington performed his last service in March 1797 at another inauguration, when he witnessed John Adams taking the oath as second president. Americans had fought a revolution against a king, yet they were not completely weaned from royalist yearnings. Washington Irving makes the point comically in "Rip Van Winkle": Rip sleeps through the American Revolution to find, when he wakes, that the image of George III on the sign outside his favorite tavern has been changed, by painting in a cocked hat and a sword, to that of George Washington. Had he been a different man, the American George could easily have been reelected to a third term and died in office; had he been a very different man, he could have angled to become king or leader for life (the suggestion was made to him).

But Washington was who he was. When John Adams was an old man, he thought of poor mankind, so often "deceived and abused" by their leaders. "But such is their love of the marvelous . . . that they will believe [the most] extraordinary pretensions" to selflessness and public spirit. Adams quoted a cynical Renaissance pope: "If the good people wish to be deceived, let them be deceived." A dark thought. Then he added: "Washington, however, did not deceive them."

Mr. Brookhiser is a senior editor of National Review *and author of* Founding Father: Rediscovering George Washington *(Free Press, 1996) and, most recently,* Gentleman Revolutionary: Gouverneur Morris, the Rake Who Wrote the Constitution *(Free Press, 2003).*

2.
JOHN ADAMS

SURVEY RANKING: 13

BORN: October 30, 1735 (October 19, old
style), Braintree (now Quincy),
Massachusetts

WIFE: Abigail Smith

RELIGION: Unitarian

PARTY: Federalist

MILITARY EXPERIENCE: None

OTHER OFFICES HELD: Massachusetts colonial legislator (1770–71),
delegate to Continental Congress (1774–78),
vice president (1789–97)

TOOK OFFICE: March 4, 1797

VICE PRESIDENT: Thomas Jefferson

LEFT OFFICE: March 4, 1801

DIED: July 4, 1826

BURIED: Quincy, Massachusetts

by Matthew Spalding

An early advocate of American independence and a significant political and intellectual leader of the Revolution, John Adams was a weak

president. The descendant of three generations of farmers, Adams attended Harvard and taught grammar school before passing the bar and comfortably settling into the practice of law in Boston. But his abiding interest in constitutionalism, government, and history drew Adams to the brewing controversies of imperial rule and colonial self-government.

Adams's first prominent writing was *A Dissertation on the Canon and Feudal Law* (1765), opposing Parliament's recently enacted Stamp Act, the first direct tax levied on the colonies. Adams viewed it as an intrusion into local affairs that exposed the coercive and arbitrary character of English politics, and he advocated a renewed "spirit of liberty" in response. Yet his principled stands didn't always make him popular with fellow patriots. In his first high-profile case, in 1770, Adams defended the British soldiers who had fired on a Boston crowd in what came to be called the Boston Massacre—"as important a cause as ever was tried in any court or country of the world," he wrote.

By the summer of 1774, when he represented Massachusetts at the First Continental Congress, Adams—though never quite as radical as his cousin Samuel—was arguing that Parliament lacked the authority not only to tax but also to legislate for the colonies. But it was at the Second Continental Congress that Adams made his greatest contribution. He chaired the committee that drafted the Declaration of Independence and dominated the debate in the Congress during the first days of July 1776, defending the document and demanding unanimous support for a decisive break with Britain.

Thomas Jefferson called him "our colossus on the floor." Another delegate wrote, "The man to whom the country is most indebted for the great measure of independence is Mr. John Adams," and dubbed him "the Atlas of American Independence." That same July Adams also drafted the Plan of Treaties, which shaped American foreign policy over the next century. He was the unanimous choice to head the Board of War and Ordnance, making him a virtual one-man War Department responsible for raising and equipping the American army and creating an American navy.

In 1776, Adams wrote *Thoughts on Government* to counteract the "overly democratical" ideas advanced by the "disastrous meteor"

Thomas Paine in his book *Common Sense*. Whereas Paine proposed to concentrate all power in a single assembly, Adams proposed a complex government of representative assembly, council (or senate), and governor, each with a power to check the other.

During his time as ambassador in London, largely ignored by the English court, Adams studied the history of European politics for lessons that might help the new nation in its efforts to establish a stable republican form of government. The result was a massive three-volume collection of quotations, citations, and personal observations entitled *A Defence of the Constitutions of Government of the United States of America*. Adams defended representation based on consent over direct democracy, made a strong case for the structural separation of executive, legislative, and judicial powers, and argued that the "triple equipoise" of the one, the few, and the many—the classical categories of political rule—must be incorporated into republican constitutionalism.

In *Discourses on Davila* (1790), Vice President Adams denounced the French Revolution and concluded that "hereditary succession" produced "fewer evils" than frequent elections. Jefferson labeled the ideas "political heresies," and Adams's writings became a key piece of evidence in the growing split between Federalists and Republicans.

Taken together, these various writings contain Adams's distinctive insights as a political thinker. He opposed manifestos and movements that sought a fundamental break with the past and rejected the notion that a new age could be produced by transforming human nature. Such abstract theories were utopian, driven by what he called "ideology," the belief that imagined ideals, seemingly real and even seductive in theory, could be implemented in practice.

The role of government was to contain and control the passions of human nature by constructing a workable political system that balanced the ambitions of individuals and competing social classes for the sake of the common good. Although his arguments left him vulnerable to charges of opposing popular rule, his objective was to moderate democratic government and compensate for its leveling tendencies while preserving the principles of equal rights and the consent of the governed.

In 1789 Adams assumed the vice presidency, which he once described as "the most insignificant office that ever the Invention of man contrived or his Imagination conceived." Yet during his eight years in the office, Adams cast more tie-breaking votes than any subsequent vice president. In 1796, when President Washington decided to retire after two terms, Adams won a narrow electoral majority over Jefferson, who thereby became Adams's vice president.

Despite the extent of his studies of politics and history, Adams was not a strong president or political leader. Following Washington was challenge enough, but Adams's presidency was overwhelmed by intense partisan rivalry. Vice President Jefferson was the acknowledged head of the opposition party, and Adams unwisely decided to retain Washington's cabinet, whose highest loyalty was to Alexander Hamilton, a rival for the leadership of the Federalists. Where Washington could dominate a Jefferson and a Hamilton in his cabinet, Adams lacked the political skills to control lesser partisans.

Adams's administration was also dominated by a naval conflict in the Caribbean with France. The "Quasi-War" produced a bitter political argument between the pro-war Federalists, who opposed alienating Britain, and the Republicans, who viewed France as America's only European ally and the French Revolution as a continuation of the American Revolution. Adams did much to stir up the war fever, but he had sense enough to make peace over the objections of his own party. In the end, Adams remained consistent to his own principles of strategic independence, broke with the High Federalists and made peace with France, a move that ruined him politically and split his party but avoided a costly war that the infant American republic was ill-prepared to fight.

The election of 1800 again pitted Adams against Jefferson. The deft maneuvering of Aaron Burr shifted New York's electoral votes to Jefferson, giving Jefferson and Burr a tie electoral victory (which the House resolved in Jefferson's favor after thirty-six ballots). Adams thus has the honor of having won the first contested presidential election in American history, along with the dubious distinction of being the first president to lose his bid for reelection.

John Adams's life was blessed with two great friendships. The first was with Abigail Smith, whom John married in 1764 and with whom he raised four children, including John Quincy Adams, the sixth president. Between 1774 and 1784, when John was serving the young nation in the Continental Congress and later abroad, the Adamses exchanged some three hundred letters. John addressed Abigail as Diana, the Roman goddess of purity and love, while she called him Lysander, the great Spartan general.

John wrote about how Abigail had "always softened and warmed my heart [and] shall polish and refine my sentiments of life and manners"; Abigail's letters intermix stories about the children and the difficulties of managing the family farm with descriptions of battles and the domestic production of saltpeter to make gunpowder. Their voluminous writings not only give a vivid picture of the time, but also are a model of affection and marital devotion.

The other friendship was with Thomas Jefferson. Friends and fellow patriots since 1775, Adams and Jefferson did not speak or write after the bitter election of 1800. But in 1812, thanks to the prodding of Benjamin Rush, the two reconciled and began one of the greatest correspondences in the history of American letters. They discussed the role of religion in history, the tribulations of growing old, the emergence of an American language, the French Revolution, and the party battles of the 1790s.

"You and I ought not to die," Adams wrote Jefferson, "before we have explained ourselves to each other." Adams and Jefferson both died on July 4, 1826, the fiftieth anniversary of America's independence.

Mr. Spalding is director of the Heritage Foundation's B. Kenneth Simon Center for American Studies. He is author of A Sacred Union of Citizens: George Washington's Farewell Address and the American Character *(Rowman & Littlefield, 1996) and editor of* The Founders' Almanac *(Heritage, 2002).*

3.
THOMAS JEFFERSON

SURVEY RANKING: 4

BORN: April 13, 1743 (April 2, old style), Albemarle County, Virginia

WIFE: Martha Wayles Skelton

RELIGION: Deist

PARTY: Democratic-Republican

MILITARY EXPERIENCE: Virginia militia (colonel)

OTHER OFFICES HELD: Member of Virginia House of Burgesses (1769–74), delegate to Continental Congress (1775, 1776, 1783–84), governor of Virginia (1779–81), state delegate (1782), U.S. secretary of state (1790–93), vice president (1797–1801)

TOOK OFFICE: March 4, 1801

VICE PRESIDENTS: Aaron Burr (1801–05), George Clinton (1805–09)

LEFT OFFICE: March 4, 1809

DIED: July 4, 1826

BURIED: Monticello, Virginia

by Forrest McDonald

Despite his celebration as the author of the Declaration of Independence, and notwithstanding his following the best tradition of the Virginia gentry by spending more than a quarter of a century in public service, Thomas Jefferson had been a failure as a public man until he assumed the presidency in 1801. As wartime governor of Virginia he had confronted a British invasion with what many regarded as cowardice. His subsequent efforts as minister to France were unproductive, his conduct as secretary of state was futile, and his period as vice president was essentially meaningless.

The reason for this undistinguished record arose from the reality that in public life he had never been in a position with sufficient authority to carry out his responsibilities. Far more than the Father of his Country, George Washington, Jefferson was throughout his life the consummate paternalist. He took care of people—his daughters, their husbands, his halfwit brother, his slaves, and all manner of frail, needy, or defenseless persons he encountered—and managed their lives gently, considerately, and totally. What he sought from them was their devotion, and he got it. When dealing with his peers, he was inept; but when he was the master of his circumstances, he had no peers.

Moreover, as a thoroughly private man, he was never comfortable in large groups. He hated confrontation; disharmony was repugnant to him. He was therefore courteous, deferential, and placatory even in dealing with people he contemned. His enemies characterized him as indecisive, vacillating, and gutless, and when he acted differently in their absence than he did in their presence, they accused him of being duplicitous and hypocritical. The accuracy of their assessment aside, duplicity and hypocrisy—if combined, as they were in Jefferson, with charisma and a clearly conceived design—might be regarded as valuable political assets.

His enemies could also depict a wild-eyed radical, a belief given credibility by his penchant for suggesßting that a bloody revolution every generation was the best way to remove the oppressively dead hand of the past. But Alexander Hamilton insisted that the responsibilities of the presidential office would moderate his views, and Hamilton's judgment proved accurate. Jefferson's first inaugural address was the essence of moderation. "We have called by different names brethren of the same principle," he wrote. "We are all

Republicans, we are all Federalists." And he went on to recite his own republican credo, ranging from vague generalities ("Equal and exact justice to all men") to more policy-oriented matters such as paying off the public debt, economy by government, "the support of the State governments in all their rights," reliance upon the militias as the first line of defense, "encouragement of agriculture, and of commerce as its handmaiden," and freedom of the press (meaning the end of the 1798 Alien and Sedition Acts). To put it differently, Jefferson proposed to undo Hamiltonian Federalism, but not to cause any major cataclysm.

In two unrelated ways, Jefferson's personal attributes, in tandem with his intense hostility toward things that smacked of monarchy, might have weakened his performance as president, but they did not. The first involves a characteristic inherent in the presidency, namely that the office carries with it the need to be a sort of surrogate or symbolic king. Washington had played this role magnificently, carrying himself, as Abigail Adams gushed, "with a grace, dignity, and ease that leaves Royal George far behind him," and he made triumphal tours to greet the multitudes throughout the land. John Adams, more pompous than regal, nonetheless also toured much of the country. Jefferson refused to make monarchical showings, and he deported himself in such a simple, unpretentious way that people could count him as one of themselves, just far more gifted. He thereby completed the people's transition from thinking monarchically (a deep-seated habit among Americans) to thinking in republican terms.

The other attribute shaped his relations with Congress. Washington and Adams, like the state governors, had followed a ritual practice that had originated with the English Crown of appearing in person when the executive wished to communicate with the legislative branch. Jefferson did that but once, at his first inaugural. The inaugural address was a rhetorical and political masterpiece, but it was delivered in a voice so unprepossessing that few could hear it, much less be inspired by it. Thereafter, he communicated with Congress solely in writing. (Subsequent presidents until Woodrow Wilson followed Jefferson's example.)

Jefferson understood that his touch, to be effective, had to be personal. To that end, he wooed congressmen, in carefully selected groups, at a series of dinner parties where—in an atmosphere of artless grace—he enchanted them. Always unwigged, sometimes wearing frayed homespun and heelless carpet slippers, the president played the role of a country squire and put the guests at their ease by his open hospitality. The food (cuisine elegantly prepared by a French chef and washed down by superb French wines) was likely to be the finest the legislators had ever eaten. The conversation was doubtless the most fascinating they had ever heard. Jefferson dominated the conversation, dazzling his guests by talking with equal authority about architecture, art, history, mathematics, music, science, theology, or zoology—everything but current politics. Accounts of these occasions suggest that the talk was superficially brilliant rather than profound. But in any event, Jefferson's guests were usually overwhelmed; few congressmen were immune to the president's personality, and most returned to the congressional pit with renewed faith in his wisdom and virtue. And though he never mentioned specifically what he wanted them to do, they somehow understood and acted to give him what he wanted.

Thus Jefferson's personal qualities, together with the stroke of luck that made the Louisiana Purchase possible, equipped him to succeed in carrying out his program to an extent rarely rivaled by those who preceded or followed him in the office—at least throughout his first term and for most of his second. Two weaknesses, however, marred the way he conducted the presidency. First, his methods were effective only with a Thomas Jefferson in the White House, and thus far there have been no others. Second, his leadership style worked only when he was absolutely in command of himself and the tide of events. Beginning late in 1807 he lost control of both.

The occasion was his attempt to enforce an embargo on American shipping that Congress had adopted in response to the British Orders in Council and Napoleon's Berlin and Milan decrees, by which Britain and France attempted to blockade each other's trade. In December 1807 Congress prohibited Americans from trading with the belligerents on pain of confiscation. At the time the president was besieged by migraine headaches that rendered him virtually helpless. Recovering temporarily, he became obsessed with efforts to enforce the law, demanding ever more drastic authority. Civil liberties went by the board, and yet resistance was so strong that the most draconian measures could not subdue it. The headaches returned, and during Jefferson's last four months he all but abdicated (except in regard to trying to enforce the embargo), saying that he preferred being "but a spectator."

When his term finally and mercifully came to an end, Jefferson was enervated and embittered. As he wrote to the French statesman Dupont de Nemours (March 2, 1809), "Never did a prisoner, released from his chains, feel such relief as I shall on shaking off the shackles of power." He stood at James Madison's side on March 4, as Chief Justice John Marshall administered the presidential oath of office. He packed his effects and left for home about a week later. Then the sixty-five-year-old rode his horse through inclement weather, determined to regain the sanctuary of Monticello as quickly as possible; he never left his home country again. Toward the end of his life he indicated what he wanted his legacy to be: nothing having to do with his presidency, but as the author of the Declaration of Independence and the Virginia statute for religious freedom, and as the father of the University of Virginia.

Mr. McDonald is Distinguished Research Professor Emeritus in History at the University of Alabama and author of The American Presidency: An Intellectual History *(1994) and* States' Rights and the Union: Imperium in Imperio, 1776–1876 *(2000), both published by the University Press of Kansas.*

4.

JAMES MADISON

SURVEY RANKING: 17

BORN: March 16, 1751 (March 5, old
style), Port Conway, Virginia

WIFE: Dolley Payne Todd

RELIGION: Episcopalian

PARTY: Democratic-Republican

MILITARY EXPERIENCE: Virginia militia (colonel)

OTHER OFFICES HELD: Virginia state delegate (1776–77, 1784–86),
delegate to Continental Congress (1780–83, 1787–88), member of
Constitutional Convention (1787), U.S. representative (1789–97),
U.S. secretary of state (1801–09)

TOOK OFFICE: March 4, 1809

VICE PRESIDENTS: George Clinton (1809–12), Elbridge Gerry
(1813–14)

LEFT OFFICE: March 4, 1817

DIED: June 28, 1836

BURIED: Montpelier, Virginia

---

by Lynne Cheney

By the time James Madison, our fourth president, moved into the
White House in 1809, he had already changed the course of history.

Rightly known as the father of our Constitution, he was the prime mover behind that magnificent document as well as the primary author of the Bill of Rights.

The knowledge that enabled these achievements came in large part from reading, an occupation to which Madison dedicated himself from his youngest years. Even as a boy, he knew the power of the printed word to enlarge experience. He saw how books could teach about times and places that one could otherwise never know.

During his college years, which he spent at Princeton College, Madison encountered more books than he had ever seen before and well-trained minds to test himself against. He took a double class load and completed the required course of study in two years. He managed to find an excuse to stay an extra six months, but finally, in 1772, at age twenty-one, he returned home.

Back in Virginia, he fell into deep depression. Some scholars speculate that it was brought on by a seizure, others that he was troubled by the death of a college friend. It may also have been that he had trouble decompressing after Princeton. What use were his studies in history and philosophy? he may have asked himself as he considered his family's well-managed farm. What spur was there to probe deeper and learn more?

The American Revolution delivered him by involving him in an all-absorbing cause. He became a politician, though a more unlikely one is hard to imagine. He was small, no more than five foot six. He was shy and guarded around strangers. He was not a brilliant orator. But what he lacked in charisma, he made up for in brainpower—and in his willingness to study and prepare.

Once independence was won and the young country began to take stock of itself, many thoughtful people concluded that the Articles of Confederation did not provide a strong enough national government. As early as 1783, Madison began an intensive course of reading to assess the alternatives. He implored his friend Thomas Jefferson, then in Paris, to send him books. Jefferson responded by sending more than two hundred volumes across the Atlantic.

Madison read Plutarch, Polybius, and Montesquieu. He studied ancient governments and modern ones, and he pondered the lessons they taught: A republic was usually small, highly constricted in the area it covered. A republic was usually fragile, easy to tip over into despotism.

By the time of the Constitutional Convention in 1787, Madison had arrived at a plan for a republic that might both extend and endure. His theories took form in the Virginia Resolves, the plan that would become the basis for the convention's deliberations. Madison thus shaped the agenda for the delegates and then went on to steer their debates, speaking more than 160 times, "always . . . the best informed man at any point," as one of his fellow delegates wrote.

Madison's learning showed itself again after the Constitution had been signed and sent to the states for ratification. Working with Alexander Hamilton and John Jay, and writing at breakneck speed, Madison authored more than two dozen essays in *The Federalist*. Arguing for the Constitution, he helped to produce the most superb political commentary ever written on this continent—and to ensure the Constitution's ratification. He then went on to propose amendments enumerating freedoms that government must not abridge. And thus we have the Bill of Rights.

Douglass Adair, a scholar of the founding period, once called the course of study that Madison undertook before the Constitutional Convention "probably the most fruitful piece of scholarly research ever carried out by an American." It is a fair assessment, a modest one even. The Constitution, bearing Madison's mark more than any other, was crucial not just to this country, but to the history of the world. Nation after nation would use our Constitution as a model. Nation after nation would look to the freedom that our Constitution makes possible for inspiration in their own struggles for liberty.

Madison was not a forceful president. His way of making decisions was to examine every fact from every side, and he was not entirely happy with acting until everything pointed in one direction. The War Hawks in Congress, led by Henry Clay, ran roughshod over him and propelled the country into the War of 1812, a conflict that resulted in the burning of both the Capitol and the White House and ended in a peace treaty that left the situation after the war unchanged from what it had been before.

Still, Madison's influence was profound. His thoughts are part of the air we breathe, his ideas form the framework for almost every political discussion we have.

The astonishing thing about Madison's influence is that he exercised it without ever traveling very far from where he was born. He never saw Europe. He never saw most of North America. If one were to draw a rectangle six hundred or seven hundred miles long and four hundred or five hundred miles wide, it would encompass entirely the area of which Madison had firsthand knowledge.

Within that rectangle, he was born, lived, and died. And from within it, using books as his lever, he managed to move the world.

Mrs. Cheney, a senior fellow at the American Enterprise Institute, was chairman of the National Endowment for the Humanities, 1986–93. She is author, most recently, of When Washington Crossed the Delaware: A Wintertime Story for Young Patriots *(Simon & Schuster, 2004).*

5.

JAMES MONROE

SURVEY RANKING: 16

BORN: April 28, 1758, Westmoreland County, Virginia

WIFE: Elizabeth Kortright

RELIGION: Episcopalian

PARTY: Democratic-Republican

MILITARY EXPERIENCE: Continental Army (major)

OTHER OFFICES HELD: Virginia state delegate (1782, 1786, 1810–11), delegate to Continental Congress (1783–86), U.S. senator (1790–94), governor (1799–1802, 1811), U.S. secretary of state (1811–14, 1815–17), secretary of war (1814–15)

TOOK OFFICE: March 4, 1817

VICE PRESIDENT: Daniel Tompkins

LEFT OFFICE: March 4, 1825

DIED: July 4, 1831

BURIED: Richmond, Virginia

---

by David B. Rivkin, Jr., and Mark Wendell DeLaquil

It is ironic, but also somehow appropriate, that an Anti-Federalist ushered in the Era of Good Feelings. James Monroe's presidency was a time of comparative tranquillity, but also of transition. It saw both the end of the political and regional strictures that had governed the young republic for its first thirty-five years—symbolized by the death of the Federalist Party and the end of the "Virginia succession" of presidents—and the emergence of the political concerns that would dominate the United States for the next thirty-five years, embodied by the Missouri Compromise and the introduction of the American System. While Monroe did not handle gracefully many domestic issues during his presidency, he forged a lasting legacy through his foresight in foreign matters, most notably his eponymous doctrine that has long been the cornerstone of U.S. foreign policy.

Originally an opponent of the Constitution, Monroe became one of the Democratic-Republicans' most vigorous partisans. President Monroe's ideology mirrored the shift from the America of Washington and Jefferson to that of Jackson and Polk. Despite Jefferson's patronage of Monroe, which included training him in law, Monroe's republicanism was not consistently Jeffersonian. Indeed, it embodied the waning of Jeffersonian republicanism and the incorporation of Federalist ideas that would eventually be near-unanimously held. Monroe unsuccessfully recommended to Congress in 1819 a protective tariff and, in his first inaugural address, professed support for a standing army and navy, and inland and coastal fortifications. Monroe's residual Jeffersonian republicanism surfaced, however, in his otherwise strict construction of the Constitution, which caused him to limit executive engagement in domestic affairs. This strict construction is apparent in Monroe's conviction that the federal government should minimize economic intrusions, including support of domestic improvements, despite Monroe's recognition that they were "interests of high importance," and in his belief that the second Bank of the United States should not intervene in the economy to alleviate the Panic of 1819.

The phrase the Era of Good Feelings was coined by a Boston newspaper following Monroe's visit to that city in 1817. Over time it has come to describe the lack of partisan strife during Monroe's presidency. (Monroe was reelected almost unanimously in 1820, 231 electoral votes to one for John Quincy Adams.) America rapidly grew during Monroe's presidency, as five new states joined the Union.

Yet one could persuasively argue it was during Monroe's presidency that America's unity began to show fissures. The battle over whether Missouri would be a free or slave state reached a fever pitch during Monroe's first term, and, although it was Senator Henry Clay who finally brokered the Missouri Compromise, Monroe's inaction, largely caused by his long-held belief that the executive should not interfere in legislative affairs, did not counteract the slow boil toward the Civil War.

Monroe's attitudes toward race typified his genteel Virginian lineage. A slaveholder like Jefferson and Madison, Monroe too recognized the inherent evil of slavery, but, also like his two predecessors, Monroe was no abolitionist. Rather, he supported a combination of "colonization" and "diffusion" as a means for preventing the violence and turmoil he feared would inevitably accompany immediate abolition of slavery. His pro-colonization stance continues to affect the United States today: Monroe was a supporter of the American Colonization Society, which resettled freed blacks in Africa. It was during Monroe's presidency that the first settlers left for Africa, ending up in what is now Liberia; the settlement's capital was named Monrovia after the president.

Monroe's greatest accomplishments were in the sphere of foreign relations. Sometimes derided as a man of moderate talents and accomplishments, Monroe had amassed extensive experience, if uneven results, in the numerous foreign posts he held before his presidency. Although a dissatisfied President Washington recalled him after only two years from his post as minister to France, it was as special envoy to France in 1803 that he won acclaim for assisting Robert Livingston in executing the Louisiana Purchase. Under President Jefferson, Monroe served as minister to Britain, where he again experienced failure when Jefferson refused to submit to the Senate for ratification a commercial treaty Monroe had negotiated with Britain—a slight for which Monroe blamed Secretary of State James Madison.

These earlier experiences foreshadowed President Monroe's foreign policy, which, by emphasizing expansion and American resistance to European intrusions, set the climate of American foreign relations throughout the nineteenth century and, in the case of the

Monroe Doctrine, to this day. Monroe appointed John Quincy Adams secretary of state and, following General Andrew Jackson's invasion of Florida in pursuit of hostile Indians, they were able to force Spain to sign the Adams-Onis Treaty, acquiring Florida and settling the boundary of the Louisiana Purchase.

In 1823 Monroe announced his crowning achievement as president, which after his death would become known as the Monroe Doctrine. Following the Latin American revolutions of the early nineteenth century, the possibility of an alliance of European powers suppressing these revolutions or of Russia implementing its colonial desires in Oregon was omnipresent. Fearing that intervention would harm its burgeoning trade with the newly independent Latin American countries, Britain proposed that it and the United States jointly oppose any European intervention in the Americas. While initially receptive to Britain's overtures, Secretary Adams's forceful arguments that the United States unilaterally oppose European intervention won the day. Adams is largely credited with formulating the Monroe Doctrine, but it was Monroe who decided to announce the policy publicly in one of the most notorious ways possible: the president's annual message to Congress. The Monroe Doctrine emphasized American exceptionalism, noting the unique nature of a government that "has been achieved by the loss of so much blood and treasure, and matured by the wisdom of [the] most enlightened citizens."

The Monroe Doctrine has become the foundation of American foreign policy. By stating that the Western Hemisphere was no longer open to colonization, and that any attempt to do so would be viewed as an act of aggression toward the United States, Monroe served notice that the Western Hemisphere was no longer within the European zone of influence. Far from becoming a historical anachronism, the Monroe Doctrine remains an important component of modern American statecraft; for example, the 1962 Justice Department opinion concerning the legality of the Kennedy administration's naval blockade of Cuba cited the Monroe Doctrine as one of the key legal justifications. Moreover, and contrary to what many have come to believe, the Monroe Doctrine did not constitute a tocsin of American imperialism. American interventions in Latin

America, while frequent in the nineteenth and early twentieth centuries, never amounted to a coherent and determined colonization policy comparable to what the European powers were doing in Africa and Asia.

Instead, this ambitious statement, although unenforceable when announced, reflected the two core tendencies in American foreign policy—idealism and realpolitik. While much ink has been spilled arguing whether American foreign policy is or should be driven by idealistic or pragmatic imperatives, in reality, American statecraft has always reflected both of these impulses. It is only the relative balance of these two imperatives that is in play at any given time.

From an idealistic perspective, Monroe's statement manifested, in the best spirit of the American Revolution, the view that self-government was the norm and that people should be free to realize their destiny free from the undue involvement by outside powers. In this sense, even in arenas beyond the Western Hemisphere, the Monroe Doctrine can be considered the precursor of a uniquely American morality-driven foreign policy agenda.

On the realpolitik side, the Monroe Doctrine, by securing America's strategic rear, has for almost two centuries served as the basis of an engaged and assertive forward projection of American political, economic, and military power into Asia and Europe. Viewed through this historical prism, America's occasional bouts of isolationism are mere blips on the horizon.

Monroe's presidency is often thought of as the calm before the storm of struggles of the popular will against the post-Revolutionary elite, and the triumph of Jacksonian democracy. More than that, it served as a bridge between the two eras, with the relative lack of strife allowing Monroe to formulate an effective and ambitious foreign policy, the results of which still endure.

Mr. Rivkin, a partner in the Washington office of the law firm Baker & Hostetler LLP, served in the Reagan and George H. W. Bush administrations. Mr. DeLaquil is a member of Harvard Law School's Class of 2004.

6.
JOHN QUINCY ADAMS

SURVEY RANKING: 25

BORN: July 11, 1767, Braintree (now Quincy), Massachusetts

WIFE: Louisa Catherine Johnson

RELIGION: Unitarian

PARTY: Democratic-Republican

MILITARY EXPERIENCE: None

OTHER OFFICES HELD: Massachusetts state senator (1802), U.S. senator (1803–08), U.S. secretary of state (1817–25), U.S. representative (1831–48)

TOOK OFFICE: March 4, 1825

VICE PRESIDENT: John Calhoun

LEFT OFFICE: March 4, 1829

DIED: February 23, 1848

BURIED: Quincy, Massachusetts

by Richard Norton Smith

For John Quincy Adams, as for James Madison, William Howard Taft, and Herbert Hoover, life in the White House proved an unhappy interlude in an otherwise remarkable career. Adams grew up with the nation his family helped invent. As a boy, accompanied by his formidable mother, Abigail, he witnessed the Battle of Bunker Hill. At fourteen he followed in his father's diplomatic footsteps, serving as secretary to Francis Dana, American minister to Russia. Adams would go on to represent the infant republic in the Netherlands, Britain, and Prussia, before returning to Russia as minister in his own right. He earned further distinction as a Harvard professor, legislator, and chairman of the fractious American delegation that negotiated an end to the War of 1812.

Unprepossessing in appearance, of average height, Adams possessed intellectual gifts that were anything but average. As a scholar he could write English with one hand while translating Greek with the other. He demanded as much of his body as of his mind, rising before dawn each day to don a black cap, green goggles, and nothing else, before swimming ninety minutes in the Potomac. Being an Adams, he inevitably swam against the tide. "I was not formed to shine in company, nor to be delighted with it," Adams confided to his diary. An English diplomat who had the misfortune to sit across from him at a negotiating table called Adams "a bulldog among spaniels."

Yet this most undiplomatic of men ranks with the greatest of his country's diplomats. As James Monroe's secretary of state he gained Spanish Florida for the United States, and helped develop the doctrine immortalized under Monroe's name that declared the Western Hemisphere off-limits to Old World meddling. As Monroe prepared to hand off the baton in 1824, he found no shortage of contenders grasping for the prize. By then four of the nation's five presidents had come from lordly Virginia, and the dynasty was getting long in the tooth. Massachusetts-born, Adams was pure Yankee. He possessed a distinguished name, an impeccable résumé, and a high-minded attachment to the nationalist vision of George Washington.

What Adams singularly lacked was the political temperament. His ambition was at war with the disinterested ideals his parents had drilled into him. True to form, Adams initially refused to come down from his lofty perch and traffic in the dust. To an ally who urged him to take a more active part in pre-election jockeying, he replied with a quote from *Macbeth*: "If chance will have me king, why, chance may crown me, without my stir."

"This won't do," the friend told Louisa Catherine Adams, the reluctant candidate's wife. "Kings are made by politicians and newspapers; and the man who sits down waiting to be crowned, whether by chance or just right will go bareheaded all his life."

Not a good, or guileful, diplomat for nothing, Adams hoped to promote his rivals out of the race by sending them on missions abroad. Thus Adams pressed John C. Calhoun to become ambassador to France. He proposed Henry Clay as an emissary to South America's restive nations in the making. He even asked the president if he had thought of appointing the fiery Andrew Jackson to a foreign post. "Yes," replied Monroe, "but I am afraid he would get us into a quarrel." The four-way contest of 1824 touched off a quarrel of historic intensity. Jackson enjoyed a substantial lead, though not a majority, in both popular and electoral votes, yet this didn't prevent a bare minimum of state delegations in the House from selecting Adams over the Western champion.

At a subsequent White House reception the two men exchanged pleasantries, but behind the frozen smiles, Jackson and his supporters were already laying the groundwork to avenge what they saw as electoral grand larceny. When the president-elect announced his intention to make Henry Clay secretary of state—the three states Clay carried had provided the decisive margin for Adams's election by the House—the opposition cried foul. Shouts of "corrupt bargain" all but drowned out the feeble cheers accorded Adams on his inaugural day. The new president spoke almost apologetically, acknowledging his minority status and begging the indulgence of his countrymen. Like Rutherford B. Hayes and George W. Bush, he would have to earn his legitimacy.

This made all the more inexplicable Adams's decision to retain his predecessor's cabinet, several of whose members were openly hostile to his interests. Hoping to build on the pugnacious foreign policy he had promoted as secretary of state, Adams was thwarted in his attempt to send American representatives to a hemispheric conference in Panama. Southern Jacksonians took violent exception to the merest hint of U.S. recognition for Haiti as an independent black republic. (America didn't recognize Haiti until 1862.) They were no more favorably inclined toward the administration's relatively humane policies concerning the Creek Indians of Georgia—soon to be deposed of their lands by the old Indian fighter Andrew Jackson.

Adams made up in audacity what he lacked in political finesse. His first message to Congress was notable for its breathtaking program of internal improvements, an antebellum New Deal that would have Washington fund roads and canals, scientific expeditions, and a national astronomical observatory—the latter memorably, if ineptly, characterized as a "lighthouse of the sky." Proposals for a naval academy caused Senator William Smith of South Carolina to snort that neither Julius Caesar or Lord Nelson had attended such a school. To found such an institution would only lead to what another representative called "degeneracy and corruption of the public morality."

Henry Clay warned Adams that his planned economy was far in advance of public thinking. But the president refused to trim his sails, insisting that "the great object of . . . civil government is the improvement of those who are parties to the social compact." Today Adams's credo sounds commonplace, if hotly debatable; in the 1820s it was shockingly at odds with Jeffersonian notions of the best government as the least government.

Adams's presidency degenerated into a train wreck of embarrassments. On July 4, 1826, the president's father died in Quincy, Massachusetts. That fall private grief was reinforced by public misery, as the opposition reclaimed both houses of Congress. The man above party had become a man without a party.

Truth be told, Adams made little effort to enlist support for his program; in four years he delivered but a single public speech. On the other hand, it is questionable whether Demosthenes himself could have staved off the electoral humiliation visited on the hapless incumbent in 1828, climaxing a scandalous campaign in which opponents accused the stiff-necked New Englander of defiling the White House with a billiard table and of procuring American prostitutes for the czar of Russia. "The sum of my political life sets in the deepest gloom," Adams wrote.

Fresh tragedies beckoned. Within weeks of leaving the White House, the former president learned that his alcoholic son, George Washington Adams, had leapt to his death from a steamboat off Long Island. For years the perfectionist Adams had nagged and bullied his children. "One hour of the morning lamp is better than three of the evening taper," he reminded anyone who would listen. To which his son Charles responded, with more candor than consideration, that after rising at 5 A.M. and engaging in a vigorous round of exercise and twelve hours of business, it was not uncommon for the old man to fall asleep at the dinner table.

Events quickly roused him from his slumber. Overriding family protests, in 1831 Adams returned to Washington as a lowly representative from Massachusetts. For the next seventeen years he represented the Unionist cause, denouncing slavery (and in 1841 arguing the famous *Amistad* case before the Supreme Court) and insisting upon the right of every American citizen to petition his government. Angry colleagues voted to gag him, but the representative from Quincy would not be silenced. Adams was no literary gentleman, declared Ralph Waldo Emerson. "He is an old roué who cannot live on slops, but must have sulphuric acid in his tea."

Year after year Adams protested the gag rule as an infringement on liberty. Southerners called him the Madman from Massachusetts. Admirers called him Old Man Eloquent. Seventy-seven years old when the rule at last was repealed, Adams remained as harshly self-critical as ever. "I should have been one of the greatest benefactors of my country," he wrote a few days before his death. "But the conceptive power of mind was conferred upon me by my Maker, and I have not improved the scanty portion of His gifts as I might and ought to have done."

On February 21, 1848, Adams collapsed at his desk on the House floor. He was carried to a sofa in the speaker's office, where he died two days later. It fell to an old Jacksonian, Thomas Hart Benton, to deliver the most suitable benediction upon the First Son of the Republic, George Washington's political heir, whose lonely defiance of popular opinion would one day earn him a chapter in *Profiles in Courage,* the work of another Massachusetts congressman and president named John F. Kennedy.

"Where could death have found him but at the post of duty?" asked Benton. It was an epitaph even an Adams could appreciate.

Mr. Smith is executive director of the Abraham Lincoln Presidential Library and author, most recently, of The Colonel: The Life and Legend of Robert R. McCormick *(Houghton Mifflin, 1997).*

7.
ANDREW JACKSON

SURVEY RANKING: 10

BORN: March 15, 1767, Waxhaw, South Carolina

WIFE: Rachel Donelson

RELIGION: Presbyterian

PARTY: Democrat

MILITARY EXPERIENCE: U.S. Army (major general)

OTHER OFFICES HELD: U.S. representative from Tennessee (1796–97), U.S. senator (1797–98, 1823–25), state Supreme Court justice (1798–1804), governor of Florida Territory (1821)

TOOK OFFICE: March 4, 1829

VICE PRESIDENTS: John Calhoun (1829–32), Martin Van Buren (1833–37)

LEFT OFFICE: March 4, 1837

DIED: June 8, 1845

BURIED: Hermitage, Tennessee

by H. W. Brands

Andrew Jackson wasn't the greatest American president, but he may have been the most important. The United States had been a republic from its founding; under Jackson it became a democracy. Since the Revolution, the people had reigned; under Jackson they ruled. And in ruling, they conferred enormous power on the single office-holder who could speak in their collective name.

The arc of Jackson's ascendance made him the ideal embodiment of the popular will. A boy-soldier of the Revolutionary War, he grew up to lead American forces to victory in the Battle of New Orleans in 1815. His triumph won him the hearts of his countrymen, who soon began talking of a Jackson presidency. His first run for the White House, in 1824, confirmed his status as a man of the people, for in winning a plurality of the popular vote (in the first presidential election in which ordinary voters, rather than the state legislatures, chose presidential electors in three fourths of the states) but losing in the House, he gave his followers fresh reason to damn the politicians who frustrated the people's will.

With Jackson's 1828 election, American democracy came into its own. By now nearly all property tests for voting had fallen away, and the new states of the trans-Appalachian West almost balanced the old states of the seaboard. Westerners riotously installed Jackson as president in March 1829. Nervous conservatives fretted that "King Mob" was taking the capital city, but Jackson's partisans hailed the arrival of the people's president and looked to their hero to cure the ills that afflicted America.

After Jackson, reform—of one sort or another—would be the theme of nearly every presidential administration. But for the Jacksonians it meant something specific. Since the founding, they believed, American government had been corrupted by the self-interest of the wealthy and powerful. The rich and their friends monopolized public office, controlled the public purse, and dictated the public destiny.

To remedy the abuse of office, Jackson adopted the principle of democratic rotation, with new men replacing the old. His critics railed against the "spoils system," but Jackson defended it as a manifestation of democracy in action. If the people had wanted to keep the old officials, they could have reelected John Quincy Adams.

Regaining control of the public purse required a harder fight. The second Bank of the United States held the deposits of the federal government and issued notes—paper money—against them, giving its directors great influence over the American economy. Jackson distrusted banks in general, deeming them parasites on the common people, and he opposed the Bank of the United States in particular, despising its head, Nicholas Biddle, as the antithesis of everything America stood for. Jackson's enmity was reciprocated, leading Biddle to try to recharter the bank early and thereby damage the president politically. Jackson accepted the challenge. "The bank, Mr. Van Buren, is trying to kill me," he told his vice president, the man who would succeed him in the White House. *"But I will kill it!"* Jackson vetoed the recharter bill, then delivered the coup de grâce by removing the government's deposits from the bank. The result was a triumph for democracy—and a disaster for the economy, which lost one of its few stabilizing mechanisms and subsequently pitched into panic.

In other areas Jackson's wisdom better matched his resolve. He inherited a dispute with South Carolina over the 1828 "tariff of abominations," a squabble that grew into an angry test of states' rights. The South Carolinians contended that states might nullify federal laws they deemed to be unconstitutional. Jackson denounced nullification as akin to treason. The fight provoked a famously tense moment at a Jefferson's Birthday celebration. Robert Hayne of South Carolina toasted: "The *Union* of the States, and the *Sovereignty* of the States." Jackson answered with an icy stare and an ominous vow: "Our Union: *It must be preserved.*" The president persuaded Congress to pass a force bill expanding his authority as commander in chief, and he issued an unmistakable warning to the nullifiers. "Please give my compliments to my friends in your state," he told a South Carolina congressman. "And say to them, that if a single drop of blood shall be shed there in opposition to the laws of the United States, I will hang the first man I can lay my hand on engaged in such treasonable conduct, upon the first tree I can reach." The South Carolinians got the message and backed down.

Democracies don't elect saints, who make voters uncomfortable. Instead they elect candidates who share their prejudices, if sometimes in less virulent form. Jackson shared the prejudices of his day regarding race. He was a slaveholder who never questioned the morality of the peculiar institution. And he believed that Indians and whites could not live in peaceful proximity. Unlike many frontiers-men, he had no desire to destroy the Indians, and when he insisted that the Cherokees and other tribes be removed beyond the Mississippi, he did so from a conviction that the only alternative was genocide at the hands of grasping whites. He was doubtless correct, although this was cold comfort to the thousands who died on the Trail of Tears in the ethnic cleansing of the Southeast.

Jackson's enemies hated him as much as his friends loved him. One of the former tried to kill him (the first assassination attempt in American presidential history); only soggy powder on a misty day saved Jackson from two balls at close range. The hatred and love formed the basis of America's second party system, with the Jacksonphiles calling themselves Democrats and the Jacksonphobes Whigs. When Jackson left office in early 1837 to retire to the Hermitage, his plantation near Nashville, his journey took the form of a triumphal tour. His friends feared and his enemies hoped there would never be another like him.

But there were many like him. Indeed, every president after Jackson was like Old Hickory, or tried to be. After Jackson, every candidate claimed common roots; every candidate promised reform; every candidate pledged to put the interests of ordinary citizens above all else. And every president wielded the supreme power of American democracy: the power that comes from uniquely embody-ing the will of the people.

Mr. Brands is a professor of history at Texas A&M University and author, most recently, of Lone Star Nation: How a Ragged Army of Volunteers Won the Battle for Texas Independence—and Changed America *(Doubleday, 2004).*

8.

MARTIN VAN BUREN

SURVEY RANKING: 27

BORN: December 5, 1782, Kinderhook, New York

WIFE: Hannah Hoes

RELIGION: Dutch Reformed

PARTY: Democrat

MILITARY EXPERIENCE: None

OTHER OFFICES HELD: New York state senator (1813–20), state attorney general (1816–19), U.S. senator (1821–28), governor (1829), U.S. secretary of state (1829–31), vice president (1833–37)

TOOK OFFICE: March 4, 1837

VICE PRESIDENT: Richard Johnson

LEFT OFFICE: March 4, 1841

DIED: July 24, 1862

BURIED: Kinderhook, New York

---

by John Steele Gordon

As with comedy, so with politics: Timing is crucial to success. Just ask the eighth president of the United States, Martin Van Buren.

Van Buren was a consummate politician who enjoyed the game to the hilt and played it with immense skill. More, he was a principal creator of the Democratic Party. He developed many aspects of modern party politics and made parties the prime organizing mechanism of our democracy. He organized and dominated the first state political machine, the so-called Albany Regency. As a political maneuverer he was regarded as second to none, moving "as smoothly as oil and as silently as a cat" to advance himself and his agenda.

And advance himself he certainly did. Van Buren was born in 1782 into a relatively poor Dutch family in Kinderhook, New York, not far from Albany, where his father had a small farm and ran a tavern. Attending only the local schools, he entered a law office at fourteen and was admitted to the New York State bar when he was twenty-one. He soon proved an able and highly successful lawyer, but politics was his passion. And because he was very, very good at it, he moved steadily up through the ranks of public office, from county surrogate in 1808 to president twenty-nine years later.

Yet his presidency was a notable failure. Elected in 1836 with 170 electoral votes against 113 scattered among three opponents, he lost his reelection bid four years later when William Henry Harrison beat him badly, 234 to 60. What happened?

Timing.

First, Van Buren had the misfortune to have a very tough act to follow. Andrew Jackson, one of the most important figures in American history, had dominated the country's politics for more than a decade, changed them profoundly, and fascinated nearly everyone. Whether they loved him or loathed him, no one was indifferent to Old Hickory.

Van Buren, in contrast, preferred backroom deal making to the public brawls Jackson was so often involved in. This, of course, did not help his public reputation. Short in stature, he became known as "The Little Magician" and "The Red Fox of Kinderhook." But he also seemed a nonentity compared with his predecessor.

Other presidents have suffered similar fates, notably William Howard Taft, who couldn't begin to compete with Theodore Roosevelt's larger-than-life persona, and George H. W. Bush, who paled in comparison with the Gipper. Of all the presidents who have followed giants into the White House, only Harry S. Truman managed to escape his predecessor's shadow. And even Truman did it mostly in retrospect.

But far worse for Van Buren, Jackson's economic policies caused the first great depression in American history, just as Van Buren took over. Jackson sowed the wind, but it was his successor who was left to reap the whirlwind.

In the election of 1832, which he won in a landslide, Jackson had vowed to destroy the second Bank of the United States. Even before its twenty-year charter expired in 1836, Jackson began moving government deposits to the "pet banks" in Western states. These banks were booming. Speculators had increasingly been buying land from the federal government, financed by bank loans from local banks. The banks then issued ever larger quantities of banknotes, backed by the loans, greatly increasing the money supply and in turn fueling a bubble.

With the second Bank of the United States crippled, the federal government had no mechanism to control the growing frenzy in land speculation. Although many of his cabinet and in Congress were deeply involved in the land speculation themselves (Van Buren not among them), Jackson decided to bring it to a halt with characteristic decisiveness. When Congress adjourned for the summer in 1836, he issued the Specie Circular, requiring the Land Office to accept only gold and silver in payment for land, except from those actually intending to settle on the land they bought.

This at once pricked the bubble in land speculation, but its other consequences were severe. The increased need of Western banks for specie drained the Eastern banks of much of their supply, causing them to call in loans. And Western banks began to fail in large numbers as speculators defaulted. Economic contraction began to roll eastward in the fall of 1836, just as Van Buren was winning the presidency.

By the time he was inaugurated on March 4, 1837, depression stalked the land. The price of cotton in New Orleans had fallen by half. The Wall Street stock market crashed that month. By fall every bank that still survived had suspended payment in gold, and most of the country's factories had closed. The number of factories, and the number of people employed in them, had grown by leaps and bounds in the two decades since the end of the War of 1812. For the first time in American economic history there was now a large class of workers dependent on wage income, and many of them were out of work. Food riots broke out in several cities.

Here again timing proved the enemy of Martin Van Buren—this

time on the grander scale of the tides of economic theory. Adam Smith, whose *The Wealth of Nations* was published coincidentally in 1776, argued powerfully for minimal government influence on the economy. He was especially influential in the new United States and by the middle third of the nineteenth century, the doctrine of laissez-faire (a term coined by the French Physiocrats, who had influenced Smith) was at its zenith. Van Buren, as much a Jeffersonian as his predecessor, was a firm believer in the idea that governments had no business trying to influence the economy. He didn't try.

On September 5, 1837, he sent a message to a special session of Congress, calling only for a currency of gold and silver and criticizing state-chartered banks and their issuance of banknotes. He hinted at establishing federal depositories that would be independent of the banking system to replace the Bank of the United States. When this plan finally became law, in 1840, as the Independent Treasury Act, it proved the major financial program of his presidency, but did nothing to alleviate economic distress among the people. What would prove to be the longest depression in American history (recovery did not begin for six years) ground on throughout Van Buren's presidency.

Although they renominated Van Buren, the Democrats could not agree on a vice presidential candidate and the campaign was notable for its personal abuse and misrepresentation. William Henry Harrison, who had been born in one of Virginia's grandest houses and whose father had signed the Declaration of Independence, was depicted by the Whigs as a simple, log-cabin-dwelling frontiersman, while Van Buren, the poor farmer's son, was ridiculed as an aristocrat, eating off gold spoons in "the Palace."

With the economy still sinking after four years of his presidency, Van Buren didn't stand a chance. Instead his presidency, like Lyndon Johnson's 130 years later, proved that it takes more than surpassing political skills to make a successful president.

Mr. Gordon is author, most recently, of An Empire of Wealth: The Epic History of American Economic Power *(HarperCollins, 2004).*

9.

WILLIAM HENRY HARRISON

SURVEY RANKING: None

BORN: February 9, 1773, Berkeley, Virginia

WIFE: Anna Tuthill Symmes

RELIGION: Episcopalian

PARTY: Whig

MILITARY EXPERIENCE: Kentucky militia (major general)

OTHER OFFICES HELD: Secretary of Northwest Territory (1798–99), delegate to U.S. Congress (1799–1800), governor of Indiana Territory (1801–13), U.S. representative from Ohio (1816–19), state senator (1819–21), U.S. senator (1825–28)

TOOK OFFICE: March 4, 1841

VICE PRESIDENT: John Tyler

DIED IN OFFICE: April 4, 1841

BURIED: North Bend, Ohio

by Glenn Harlan Reynolds

"Tippecanoe and Tyler too!" That slogan is the one thing most people know about William Henry Harrison. A few also remember that he died after only one month in office, purportedly from pneumonia contracted while giving a long-winded inauguration speech. These are the high points of Harrison's career, and in fact they outline his greatest impact, which was in the winning and the expiring, rather than the governing.

But his campaign is worth remembering too. Harrison was the first modern presidential candidate. A seeker of political office for much of his life, he planned his presidential run early and can fairly be credited (if that is the word) with inventing the perpetual campaign. After an unsuccessful run in 1836, he spoke wherever he could find an audience, courting Whigs, anti-Masons, and war veterans. Though a descendant of Virginia gentry, he ran as a frontiersman and boasted of his military record (including the famous, if somewhat overrated, defeat of Tecumseh at the Battle of Tippecanoe) and of his statement to Simón Bolívar, which he made while he served as ambassador to Colombia: "The strongest of all government is that which is most free."

His indefatigable pursuit of the presidency paid off. In 1840, his delegates seized control of the Whig Party convention and nominated him. Harrison carefully avoided mentioning the slavery issue (he was thought to support the spread of slavery to the Northwest Territory) and ran with Virginian John Tyler under the slogan "Tippecanoe and Tyler too." Image, not issues, was the strategy.

Slogans and mass rallies (whose attendance was measured by the acre) were the centerpiece of his campaign, and so were other modern characteristics, like spin and personal attacks. When critics suggested that Harrison—at sixty-seven the oldest man ever to seek the presidency—should be pensioned off with a keg of cider, Harrison responded by running a "log cabin and hard cider" campaign that stressed appeal to populist sentiments, while portraying incumbent Martin Van Buren as an effete aristocrat who drank wine from silver coolers. The campaign was regarded as undignified, but it worked: Harrison won an enormous electoral victory, and voter turnout was drastically higher than in the election of 1836. Then, as now, political marketing, however undignified, seemed to appeal to the voters.

Harrison delivered an inaugural address that lasted an hour and forty-five minutes, penned by Daniel Webster, into the teeth of a blizzard. Though long on tributes to constitutional government, the speech contained few memorable lines. Probably the best passage is this one:

> The boasted privilege of a Roman citizen was for him a shield only against a petty provincial ruler, whilst the proud democrat of Athens would console himself under a sentence of death for a supposed violation of the national faith . . . that it was the act not of a single tyrant or hated aristocracy, but of his assembled countrymen. Far different is the power of our sovereignty. It can interfere with no one's faith, prescribe forms of worship for no one's observance, inflict no punishment but after well-ascertained guilt, the result of investigation under rules prescribed by the Constitution itself.

He also warned of the corrupting effect of government subsidies: "We have learned, too, from our own as well as the experience of other countries, that golden shackles, by whomsoever or by whatever pretense imposed, are as fatal to [liberty] as the iron bonds of despotism."

Would Harrison have governed in light of these principles? We'll never know, but he kept another promise made in the address: the promise not to run for a second term. Harrison died one month after taking office and was succeeded by John Tyler.

Harrison was the first president to die in office, and in many (perhaps most) nations of that time, or even of our own, such a death would have prompted a succession crisis. But not here. The succession was smooth, setting a precedent that has endured through seven presidents' deaths in office and one's resignation. That's quite an accomplishment for a one-month presidency.

Mr. Reynolds is Beauchamp Brogan Distinguished Professor of Law at the University of Tennessee. He writes at InstaPundit.com.

10.
JOHN TYLER

SURVEY RANKING: 35

BORN: March 29, 1790, Charles City County, Virginia

WIVES: Letitia Christian (died 1842), Julia Gardiner (married 1844)

RELIGION: Episcopalian

PARTY: Whig

MILITARY EXPERIENCE: Virginia militia (captain)

OTHER OFFICES HELD: Virginia state delegate (1811–16, 1823–25, 1839), U.S. representative (1817–21), governor (1825–27), U.S. senator (1827–36), vice president (1841)

TOOK OFFICE: April 4, 1841

VICE PRESIDENT: None

LEFT OFFICE: March 4, 1845

DIED: January 18, 1862

BURIED: Richmond, Virginia

by John S. Baker, Jr.

John Tyler set plenty of precedents as president. He was the first vice president to become president upon his predecessor's death. The circumstances surrounding that accident of history produced several

other constitutional and political precedents. Some other precedents were personal. Tyler was the first president born after adoption
of the Constitution. Widowed while in office, Tyler was the first president to marry during his term. He fathered fifteen children by his
two wives, more than any other president.

Tyler was the sixth president from Virginia. Like fellow Virginians
Washington, Jefferson, Madison, and Monroe, but unlike his immediate predecessor, William Henry Harrison, Tyler understood the
president's role under the Constitution. His defense of the presidency against Congress and his own party should have earned him a
more appreciated place in history.

Tyler was the second half of the odd couple known as "Tippecanoe
and Tyler too." The Whig Party, which held a majority in Congress,
had nominated Harrison in the expectation of controlling his presidency. For vice president, in order to attract votes from Southern
states' righters, the Whigs chose Tyler, a former Democrat who had
broken politically with Andrew Jackson. When Harrison died after
only one month in office, Senator Henry Clay and other nationalist
Whigs learned that they had placed in the presidency a man who
would oppose their legislative agenda. As a states' rights republican,
Tyler rejected the nationalist Whig program for a national bank, high
tariffs, and federally financed internal improvements.

The Constitution provides that upon the president's death, "the
Powers and Duties" of the office "shall devolve on the Vice
President." When Harrison died, the meaning of this language was in
question. Members of Harrison's cabinet, mostly chosen by Clay,
considered Tyler to be only the vice president, acting as president.
Yet, although a "strict constructionist," Tyler rejected this reading and
insisted that he was the president. He therefore took the oath as
president and moved into the White House. Today it is unquestioned
that upon a president's death, the vice president assumes the office
of president, not merely its "powers and duties." But for Tyler's
precedent, it might have been otherwise.

Although an unelected president, Tyler was more presidential than
his predecessor. Apparently, Harrison had agreed that executive
decisions would be based on a majority vote among members of the
cabinet, with the president having one vote. Although Tyler retained

all of Harrison's cabinet, he rejected this proposal as inconsistent with his responsibilities as president. Had he not resisted power sharing, Tyler would have lacked the unity of decision making that he later exhibited when insisting on the prerogatives of the president in appointments, removals, legislative inquiry into the executive branch, his execution of the laws, and especially his exercise of the veto.

President Tyler made his mark with the veto. He vetoed Clay's attempts to recharter a national bank and to set high tariffs. After the bank vetoes, the Whig Party expelled Tyler, and his cabinet resigned en masse, except Daniel Webster, who did so later. Whigs in the House initiated an impeachment effort. Tyler thus became the first president expelled from his own party, the first president to face an impeachment resolution (it failed), and the president with the most cabinet changes in a single term. As a final, ignominious first, on his last day in office, on a minor piece of legislation, Congress for the first time overrode a presidential veto.

Tyler's opposition to a national bank and higher tariffs reflected classic Jeffersonian republicanism, but his use of the veto did not. Legislative supremacy was an article of faith among Jeffersonian republicans. Jefferson's strong presidency accomplished his "revolution" with the help of a friendly Congress. President Madison's limited use of the veto was constrained by his understanding of congressional supremacy. Jackson, the first Democratic president, was the first to use the veto as a policy-making weapon against Congress.

As a senator, Tyler supported President Jackson's veto of a national bank as a defense of the states. But he eventually broke with Jackson because he concluded that on other matters—especially the Force Bill, which gave Jackson the power to collect the tariff taxes by force if necessary—Jackson had departed from Jeffersonian principles. Still, when Jackson exercised his veto, he justified it in constitutional terms. While Tyler gave constitutional reasons for vetoing the bank, his reasons for vetoing an increased tariff were nonconstitutional. Thus Tyler reverted to the Hamiltonian view of the veto power as an instrument of presidential independence.

Tyler's defensive use of the veto differed from the way Jackson used it. Jackson was not politically dependent on Congress, because he was the first president since Jefferson who was neither elected by the House nor nominated by a caucus of the party's congressional members. In contrast, Tyler, an unelected president without a party, lacked the political support to act other than defensively.

Tyler's strength as president was grounded in a faith in his constitutional principles. His constitutionalism coincided with the politics of his region, but his was not a parochial presidency. Certainly, he represented the planter, slaveholding class of Virginia. He attempted, however, to moderate the threats posed by sectional factionalism. He vetoed high tariffs, which favored the manufacturing interests of the North and West over the agrarian interests of the South. As he had as a senator, he sought a compromise that raised revenue, but not the protectionism that fueled Southern secessionism. He cooperated in the passage of the Log Cabin Bill, which allowed settlers, rather than speculators, to purchase public lands in the Northwest.

Tyler had an aristocratic manner, which enabled him always to deal most courteously with Congress, despite their differences. But he lacked the common touch necessary for popular appeal. For a president seeking reelection, without the support of a party, that posed quite a problem. He attempted to form a reelection campaign around support for annexation of Texas.

Texas had proclaimed itself a republic, independent of Mexico, in 1836, and Tyler tried to annex it through a treaty. But because of the presence of slavery in Texas, the president was unable to win the support of the requisite two thirds of senators. He planned to run in 1844 as an independent against his former friend Henry Clay, the Whig candidate and an opponent of annexing Texas. Tyler thought that Van Buren, who also opposed annexation, would be the Democratic candidate. Instead, Democrats nominated James Polk, who supported annexing Texas. At the urging of Jackson, who wanted to block Clay, Tyler withdrew from the race and supported Polk. When Polk won, Tyler was able to get congressional approval for the annexation of Texas and, three days later, the annexation of Florida.

The admission of Texas as a state set another constitutional precedent. Instead of a treaty, on which only the Senate votes and which requires approval by a two-thirds vote, Tyler brought Texas into the Union as a state via majority votes in both houses of Congress. Tyler and his supporters relied on Congress's power to admit new states under Article IV, Section 3 of the Constitution. This maneuver was based on the constitutional text, but was hardly an example of "strict construction."

Tyler has been controversial among scholars. Some have characterized him as a principled, states' rights constitutionalist. Others have described him as an ineffectual political opportunist. Tyler's construction to the Constitution, which made him president rather than acting president; his exercise of the veto for nonconstitutional reasons; and the incorporation of Texas without a treaty were not examples of "strict construction," in the sense of narrow construction. At least the first two, however, reflected the Framers' view as expressed in the *Federalist Papers*.

Tyler's presidency demonstrated the difficulty of operating as a Jeffersonian republican within a constitutional system derived from different principles. As president, Tyler could not both protect and balance state interests while deferring to a Congress intent on overriding the interests of Southern states. On constitutional and policy grounds, Tyler used the veto to protect state interests in an effort to defuse secessionism. Tyler's respect for the Constitution's doctrine of limited powers required a strong presidency. His presidency confirmed the observation of *Federalist No. 51* that the interests of the man will defend the office.

Even after leaving office, Tyler was caught in the conflict between adherence to the "compact theory" underlying Jeffersonian states' rights republicanism and preservation of the Union. As president, his vetoes were efforts to keep the divisions between North and South from widening, although those divisions did widen during his term. Years after leaving the presidency, Tyler convened a peace conference that attempted to negotiate a compromise to avert a war between the states. When that failed, he joined his state in secession. He died as a member of the Confederate Congress.

Mr. Baker is Dale E. Bennett Professor of Law at Louisiana State University.

11.
JAMES KNOX POLK

SURVEY RANKING: 9

BORN: November 2, 1795, Mecklenburg
County, North Carolina

WIFE: Sarah Childress

RELIGION: Methodist; attended Presbyterian services

PARTY: Democrat

MILITARY EXPERIENCE: Tennessee militia (colonel)

OTHER OFFICES HELD: Tennessee state representative (1823–25),
U.S. representative (1825–39), House speaker (1835–39), governor
(1839–41)

TOOK OFFICE: March 4, 1845

VICE PRESIDENT: George Dallas

LEFT OFFICE: March 4, 1849

DIED: June 15, 1849

BURIED: Nashville, Tennessee

---

by *Douglas G. Brinkley*

The United States was not destined to stretch across the continent—
that is, until James K. Polk was elected president. During his term,

Polk brilliantly oversaw a complex balance of military, diplomatic, and domestic affairs during a period when "the fate of North America was decided," as historian Bernard DeVoto writes in his Pulitzer Prize–winning *The Year of Decision: 1846*.

As a biographical figure, Polk is not that appealing. A straitlaced Methodist who never had children, Polk forbade drinking and dancing in the White House. His advocacy of temperance, in fact, caused Sam Houston to quip that the only thing wrong with Polk was that he drank too much water.

But as anyone who has read the massive *Diaries of James K. Polk* can attest, he was not a man to be taken lightly. Even before reaching the White House, he had distinguished himself first as a lawyer and later as a legislator and governor. Short in stature, Polk early on garnered a political reputation for relentless courage, forthrightness, and toughness, winning the nickname "Napoleon of the Stump" for his slightly arrogant, no-nonsense demeanor. He was also called "Young Hickory" for carrying on principles laid out by "Old Hickory," Andrew Jackson.

As president, Polk outshone even his own impressive résumé, becoming one of our strongest and most independent-minded chief executives ever. Although he won the election of 1844 by a narrow margin, Polk never doubted his roaring mandate to govern. President Polk faced a divided Democratic Party and might therefore have chosen the more pragmatic strategy of political compromise. Instead, however, the eleventh president entered office with a clearly defined agenda that focused on restructuring the country's financial system and expanding the western reaches of the nation.

President Polk used his superb understanding of politics to bridge party gaps. At a time of divisive regionalism and intraparty conflict, Polk was able to push through a reduction in tariffs as well as reestablish an independent Treasury for the United States. The independent Treasury proved crucial in alleviating the domestic financial problems that plagued the young republic.

Where Polk was most effective, however, was in expanding the geographical boundaries of the United States. Naturally, the Louisiana Purchase of 1803 did more than any other single act in bringing about Jefferson's idea of an empire of liberty. As enormous as the Mississippi watershed was, however, its possession did not give the United States a presence on the Pacific. It was not until Polk's presidency that the U.S. firmly established itself on the western coast of the North American continent.

During the campaign of 1844, Polk ran on a nationalistic platform that stressed the procurement of Oregon Territory as far north as latitude 54 degrees 40 minutes. At the time, this was the southern boundary of Russian-owned Alaska. One of Polk's campaign slogans was "Fifty-four Forty or Fight!" By 1846, though, it had become clear that compromise would be necessary. Through skillful negotiation, Polk was able to reach a favorable agreement with the British that established the national boundary at 49 degrees north. This was the precise border that Polk had pushed for in earlier negotiations, only to encounter British refusal. By upping the ante, Polk was able to reach a permanent settlement that favored the United States.

The cornerstone of Polk's 1844 campaign, however, was the annexation of Texas, and it was in dealing with this vast region that Polk was at his executive best. As president-elect, Polk helped outbound President Tyler with the annexation of the Lone Star State. Texas had been independent of Mexico since 1836, but Mexico continued to press its interests there. After the U.S. annexed Texas, Mexico quickly responded with military preparation to bring Texas back under Mexican control. By early 1846 there was a military standoff on the Rio Grande River between the two young nations. When Mexican forces incited violence by ambushing an American patrol, killing sixteen U.S. cavalrymen in the process, President Polk seized upon the opportunity to declare war.

Although the Mexican army was four and a half times the size of the U.S. Army, Polk pursued an aggressive military policy. U.S. forces were dispatched into the heart of Mexico. Simultaneously, smaller American armies invaded the Mexican territories of New Mexico and Upper California.

Polk proved a superb commander in chief through the duration of the Mexican War. As political turmoil on the home front escalated, Polk remained focused on his goal of forcing Mexico to cede New Mexico and Upper California while also dropping its claims to Texas. In the fall of 1847, General Winfield Scott led a victorious American army into Mexico City. President Polk thus had the upper hand in peace negotiations with Mexico. In a wise move to avert future border disputes, Polk offered Mexico $15 million for New Mexico and Upper California. In securing Texas as a U.S. state, acquiring New Mexico and California, and peacefully resolving the Oregon territorial dispute, President Polk secured America's status as a continental power.

Although he left the office of president an unpopular man, James Polk was the most successful one-term president the United States has known. He was a brilliant politician and an outstanding commander in chief whose hallmark was setting goals and accomplishing them. He, more than anyone since Thomas Jefferson, ensured that U.S. interests would be protected from sea to shining sea.

Mr. Brinkley is director of the Eisenhower Center for American Studies at the University of New Orleans.

12.
ZACHARY TAYLOR

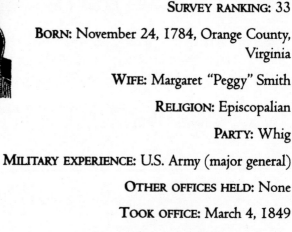

SURVEY RANKING: 33

BORN: November 24, 1784, Orange County, Virginia

WIFE: Margaret "Peggy" Smith

RELIGION: Episcopalian

PARTY: Whig

MILITARY EXPERIENCE: U.S. Army (major general)

OTHER OFFICES HELD: None

TOOK OFFICE: March 4, 1849

VICE PRESIDENT: Millard Fillmore

DIED IN OFFICE: July 9, 1850

BURIED: Louisville, Kentucky

by Brendan Miniter

Today Zachary Taylor's reputation is that of a dim-witted professional soldier who managed to get elected as the twelfth president of the United States. Once in office he proceeded to destroy his political party with a succession of blundering decisions, before suddenly dying sixteen months into his term. He's one of those nineteenth-century presidents most Americans don't know much about.

That's too bad, because a little knowledge of Taylor and his presidency is essential to understanding why, in the 1860s, the nation abandoned political solutions to a fundamentally moral dispute.

The Civil War was still a dozen years off when Taylor won the White House in 1848. The nation had just won the Mexican War and gained undisputed control over territory that would later become Arizona, Nevada, New Mexico, Utah, and part of California and Colorado. The war also firmly established the Rio Grande River as Texas's southern border.

The Mexican War had made Taylor a hero. Born into a socially successful Virginia family in 1784, he was distantly related to both James Madison and Robert E. Lee. His family moved west, to Kentucky, where he grew up. The Mexican War made him famous when he beat General Antonio López de Santa Anna at the Battle of Buena Vista. He was also a disheveled-looking man who rarely combed his hair and was known as "Old Rough and Ready." He was a slave owner and had been, briefly, the father-in-law to Jefferson Davis. (Taylor's daughter died shortly after marrying the man who would later become president of the Confederacy.)

Taylor won the Whig Party's nomination in part through a letter-writing campaign from the front. He had never voted, much less held elective office. Yet despite his Virginia origins, he was palatable to voters in the North because he'd grown up in the West and spent much of his life as an army officer in remote places. Both North and South, voters could read into his candidacy the qualities they wanted.

After the election, however, vague political views became a liability. In the North, Whigs were losing voters in key districts to free-soil politicians who were taking firm stands against expanding slavery in the new territories. Before the Mexican War even ended, Representative David Wilmot, a Pennsylvania Democrat, had proposed a bill to ban slavery in any territory gained in the conflict. His bill passed the House in 1847, but the Senate adjourned before taking it up. By the time Taylor was in the White House, the Wilmot Proviso was a political litmus test.

Taylor wouldn't publicly take a position on the proviso, although he promised during the campaign not to veto it if it passed. He knew that fellow Whigs faced pressure from the South to oppose the Wilmot Proviso. Southerners also wanted a tougher national fugitive slave law. And Texas was another source of tension. The Lone Star

State had come into the union in 1846 as a slave state and now was claiming part of the New Mexican territory. The Texans were threatening force; allowing them to prevail would also allow slavery to spread onto new land.

In response, Taylor hatched a secret plan to bring California and New Mexico into the union as free states before Congress had time to act, thus sidestepping the Wilmot Proviso. His plans came to naught, however. New Mexico applied for status as a territory, not a state. (It didn't become a state until 1912.) California applied for statehood, but as Michael F. Holt writes in *The Rise and Fall of the American Whig Party,* it left out a vast stretch of land that would have included the Mormons in modern-day Utah. That left a lot of territory that had yet to determine whether it would be free or slave when it eventually entered the union. And keeping these plans a secret protected Southern Whigs at the expense of losing congressional seats in Kentucky and Indiana and local elections elsewhere.

The party was splitting apart, and Northern Whigs were learning that compromising with the South over slavery was political suicide. But it was too late for the Whigs. Their president would soon be dead. On July 4, 1850, Taylor tried to stay cool during ceremonies at the Washington Monument (then under construction) by eating cherries and cucumbers and drinking iced milk. Later that evening, he fell ill with stomach pains. He may have contracted cholera from the poorly refrigerated food. His doctors blistered his skin and bled him, treatments that likely worsened his condition. On July 9 he died.

Millard Fillmore assumed the presidency and hammered out the Compromise of 1850. He was the last Whig president; the party soon disappeared.

There was some speculation among historians that Taylor might have been poisoned. So in 1991, 141 years after his death, his body was exhumed. Tests ruled out arsenic. Taylor turned out not to be the first president to be assassinated. He was just a war hero who proved no match for the political battles in Washington.

Mr. Miniter is assistant editor of OpinionJournal.com.

13.

MILLARD FILLMORE

SURVEY RANKING: 36

BORN: January 7, 1800, Cayuga County, New York

WIVES: Abigail Powers (died 1853), Caroline McIntosh (married 1858)

RELIGION: Unitarian

PARTY: Whig

MILITARY EXPERIENCE: Union Continentals (major)

OTHER OFFICES HELD: New York state assemblyman (1829–31), U.S. representative (1833–35, 1837–43), state comptroller (1848–49), vice president (1849–50)

TOOK OFFICE: July 10, 1850

VICE PRESIDENT: None

LEFT OFFICE: March 4, 1853

DIED: March 8, 1874

BURIED: Buffalo, New York

by Melanie Kirkpatrick

It is perhaps a measure of the scope of Millard Fillmore's presidency that his most enduring achievement may have been his bathtub. The thirteenth president is reputed to have installed the first tub with hot running water in the White House, a luxury for which later presidents—not to mention all those who came into close contact with them—must have been exceedingly grateful. The Historical Society of Washington says running hot water was first piped into the first family's second-floor bathroom in 1853.

Beyond plumbing, Fillmore's achievements in office were not large. That is explained in part by the brevity of his tenure—a mere two and a half years. But it also had to do with his leadership style, which was one of accommodation and compromise.

Fillmore was elected vice president in 1848; he reportedly didn't meet his running mate, Zachary Taylor, until after the election. Fillmore, the New York state comptroller and a former three-term congressman from Buffalo, secured the nomination by virtue of his "moderate" stand on slavery—he was against it but thought the South had a legitimate right to it. His name on the ticket helped carry the important New York vote, and the Whigs won a narrow victory.

But then he became president after Taylor's sudden death. His inauguration signaled an abrupt shift in the highly charged politics surrounding the subject of the day: slavery.

For the first six months of 1850, Congress had debated little else—focusing specifically on the issue of whether slavery should be extended to new states joining the union. Many Northerners said no; slavery should be limited to states that already had it. The South said an emphatic yes; if new states were all free, then slaveholding states would be outnumbered in future Congresses. The status of California was particularly urgent, as the discovery of gold there in 1848 had drawn tens of thousands of new settlers, who wished to organize as a state. The slavery question had to be settled before the Golden State could be admitted.

Fillmore's modest personality had served him well when he was vice president. He presided over Senate debates with "such impartiality," his obituary in *The New York Times* noted, "that it was not known which side of the controversy he favored" or how he would vote should he be called upon to break a tie. In fact, he favored the compromise put forward by Senator Henry Clay of Kentucky, and upon becoming president, Fillmore moved quickly to press for its enactment. In September, he signed into law the five pieces of legislation known as the Compromise of 1850. It was the single most important accomplishment of his presidency.

Under the compromise:

* California entered the union as a free state.
* Texas was paid $10 million for its claim to a portion of New Mexico.
* New Mexico and Utah became territories without mention of their "slave" or "free" status, which was to be left to their legislatures.
* The slave trade was made illegal in the District of Columbia. Slaves could still be owned in the nation's capital, but no longer bought or sold there.
* The Fugitive Slave Act required the capture and return of any slave who escaped to a free state.

Fillmore called the compromise "a final settlement" of the slavery question. The South's secession was put aside and war was averted—but only for a decade. In the end, the Compromise of 1850—most especially the Fugitive Slave Act—divided the nation even more sharply. Both sides became increasingly embittered, prodded on in part by the publication in 1852 of Harriet Beecher Stowe's *Uncle Tom's Cabin,* which had been directly inspired by the Fugitive Slave Act.

Fillmore felt it his obligation to enforce the law vigorously, and his administration dispatched federal agents to track down runaway slaves. "I have regarded it as my duty in these cases to give all aid legally in my power to the enforcement of the laws," he explained in his State of the Union address of December 1851, "and I shall continue to do so wherever and whenever their execution may be resisted." This stance contributed in large part to his unpopularity among Northern abolitionists, including those in his hometown of Buffalo, whose location along the Canadian border made it a key stop on the Underground Railroad. The Whigs did not nominate him for president in 1852.

There is not a great deal else to say about Fillmore's presidency. In the foreign policy arena, his most noteworthy achievement was the opening of Japan. In 1852 Fillmore dispatched a naval force to demand that Japan inaugurate trade relations with the U.S. But by the time Commodore Matthew Perry and his "black ships" sailed into Tokyo Bay in July 1853 bearing a letter from the president, Fillmore was no longer the holder of that office.

Fillmore was the last Whig president. At the close of his term, he retired to Buffalo. In 1856 he ran for president as the candidate of the anti-Catholic Know-Nothing Party (officially called the American Party) but lost miserably, carrying only Maryland. He believed the Civil War was unnecessary, and while he supported the Union during that conflict, he was highly critical of President Lincoln and refused to join the Republican Party. In 1864, he supported Democrat George McClellan for president.

Yet if Fillmore was a weak president, personally he exhibited great strength of character. Born in 1800 in a log cabin in western New York in what was then the frontier, he had no formal education. He was apprenticed to a clothier at fourteen, taught himself law, and was admitted to the bar in 1823. He made his way up the political ladder in New York state by dint of hard work. In 1855, while on a European tour, Fillmore was offered an honorary degree from Oxford University. The degree was in Latin. He declined, saying no man should accept a degree in a language he cannot read.

Ms. Kirkpatrick is associate editor of The Wall Street Journal's *editorial page.*

14.

FRANKLIN PIERCE

SURVEY RANKING: 38

BORN: November 23, 1804, Hillsborough, New Hampshire

WIFE: Jane Appleton

RELIGION: Episcopalian

PARTY: Democrat

MILITARY EXPERIENCE: New Hampshire militia (brigadier general)

OTHER OFFICES HELD: New Hampshire state representative (1829–33), U.S. representative (1833–37), U.S. senator (1837–42)

TOOK OFFICE: March 4, 1853

VICE PRESIDENT: William King (1853)

LEFT OFFICE: March 4, 1857

DIED: October 8, 1869

BURIED: Concord, New Hampshire

by Cynthia Crossen

If you think you have a Herculean marketing challenge, consider Jayme Simoes's.

Mr. Simoes, president of a Concord, New Hampshire, public relations agency, is trying to drum up interest in a nineteenth-century president. It's not the revered Abraham Lincoln or the fierce Andrew Jackson. Mr. Simoes's man is the only elected president in American history who ran for renomination and was spurned by his own party: the hapless bungler, Franklin Pierce.

"By the time he left office in 1857, Pierce couldn't have been elected dogcatcher," Mr. Simoes concedes.

Two thousand four is the bicentennial of the fourteenth president's birth, however, and Mr. Simoes says it's time to take a fresh look at this misunderstood man from New Hampshire, whom history has treated with such brutal indifference. Mr. Simoes set about to raise money for a year-long commemoration of Pierce, including lectures, exhibits, and perhaps even an "inaugural ball." He also went looking for a good Franklin Pierce impersonator.

The reaction to his campaign was tepid. "There are three schools of thought about Franklin Pierce," Mr. Simoes said in early 2003. "One, Pierce was great, he gets a bad rap, we should feel sorry for him. Two, he was the worst president in our history, he's best left forgotten. Three, Franklin who?"

Mr. Simoes, a native of Chicago, in 1992 moved to Hillsborough, New Hampshire, where Pierce had a home. "I knew nothing about Franklin Pierce when I arrived," he says. But he quickly got drawn into doing volunteer work for the local historical society and began giving tours of the Pierce house. "I started thinking, 'Something funny is going on here,'" Mr. Simoes says. "There's no presidential library, recent definitive biography, or even a historian who specializes in Pierce."

The Federalist Society–*Wall Street Journal* survey ranks Pierce thirty-eighth of forty presidents, beating out only Warren Harding and James Buchanan. "He was a complete failure as a president," says David Holzel, a presidential trivia buff who, with two partners, created a Web site with a second-by-second countdown to Pierce's bicentennial. "The only important thing that happened during his administration was the first perforated postage stamps were made."

Pierce came to power in one of the most terrifying eras in American history, when the tension between North and South was just starting to turn bloody. Pierce was the only kind of Democratic candidate who had a chance of winning the general election of 1852: a so-called doughface, meaning a Northerner with Southern sympathies. Even so, it took forty-nine ballots before the party nominated him.

The opposing party, the Whigs, countered with Winfield Scott, a hero of the war with Mexico who also supported the right of Southerners to own slaves. Like all presidential campaigns, this one quickly got down in the mud. The Whigs pointed out that while Pierce had served as a brigadier general in Scott's army, his record in battle was unimpressive.

In his first skirmish, Pierce quickly fainted after falling from his horse, "being injured in that portion of a man's anatomy that is least tolerant of suffering," as the historian David K. E. Bruce put it in 1939. The Whigs gleefully distributed a tiny book, one inch tall and half an inch wide, called *The Military Services of Gen. Pierce.* Alluding to Pierce's reputation as a heavy drinker, the Whigs called him "the hero of many a well-fought bottle."

Yet Pierce was, by all accounts, handsome, charming, and charismatic. "After Pierce, the country was made safe for good-looking empty suits," says Todd Leopold, entertainment editor of CNN.com and another contributor to the Pierce bicentennial Web page. Pierce's friend, the writer Nathaniel Hawthorne, who had attended Bowdoin College with him, described him as "a beautiful boy, with blue eyes, light, curling hair and a sweet expression of face."

But for many voters, the most appealing thing about Pierce was that they knew nothing about him. His campaign nickname was "Young Hickory of the Granite Hills," and his party's slogan was "We Polked 'em in '44, we'll Pierce 'em in '52," according to Paul F. Boller, Jr., in his 1984 book, *Presidential Campaigns.* Pierce's handy victory surprised even the citizens of New Hampshire.

In his 1906 *Recollections of 13 Presidents,* John Sergeant Wise, who had met Pierce, tells of the reaction of a lifelong acquaintance of Pierce's when he learned the man had won the presidency. "Now Frank's a good fellow, I admit," the elderly man said, "and I wish him well. He made a good state's attorney, thar's no doubt about that, and he made a far judge, thar's no denying that, and nobody kaint complain of him as a congressman. But when it comes to the whole Yewnited States, I dew say that in my jedgment Frank Pierce is agoin' to spread durned thin."

Indeed, Pierce made one mistake after another, and while it's possible that no president could have averted the Civil War, "Pierce did his best to bring it on," says Larry Gara, author of *The Presidency of Franklin Pierce*. "Not consciously, of course, but he was so indecisive, and he blamed everything on the abolitionists, as if they were just troublemakers."

Pierce kept pandering to the South, supporting, for example, the Kansas-Nebraska Act of 1854, which allowed settlers in those territories to decide whether they wanted to allow slavery. He kept appointing pro-slavery governors to these territories, which so angered the abolitionists that a local civil war ensued. (During his administration, Kansas became known as "Bloody Kansas.") He also used federal troops to help enforce the Fugitive Slave Act, further stirring abolitionist fury.

By the time he finished writing his book, Mr. Gara said, "I felt rather sad for Pierce. He was one unlucky guy." It didn't help that Pierce's best friend and secretary of war was Jefferson Davis, then directing the very army he would later try, unsuccessfully, to defeat.

Pierce and his wife, Jane, lost all three of their children, the last an eleven-year-old boy who was killed in a train crash a few months before Pierce took office. Pierce was subject to depression, and sometimes drowned his sorrows in alcohol. But he was a vigorous defender of the Constitution, and he had a few important foreign policy accomplishments to his credit: He acquired land from Mexico in the Gadsden Purchase, and he supported the nation's first trade agreement with Japan. He was also the first president to appoint a Jewish ambassador, and he supported the rights of immigrants.

To the extent he is remembered, however, it's as a supporter of slavery. "I don't see Pierce as a hero, but I don't see him as a villain, either," says Mr. Simoes. "When we marginalize a U.S. president, condemn him to the attic like a crazy uncle, we lose track of how we got to where we are today."

Ms. Crossen is a senior special writer for The Wall Street Journal. *A version of this article appeared in the* Journal *on February 11, 2003.*

15.

JAMES BUCHANAN

SURVEY RANKING: 40

BORN: April 23, 1791, Mercersburg, Pennsylvania

WIFE: None

RELIGION: Presbyterian

PARTY: Democrat

MILITARY EXPERIENCE: Pennsylvania militia (private)

OTHER OFFICES HELD: Pennsylvania state representative (1814–15), U.S. representative (1821–31), U.S. senator (1834–45), U.S. secretary of state (1845–49)

TOOK OFFICE: March 4, 1857

VICE PRESIDENT: John Breckenridge

LEFT OFFICE: March 4, 1861

DIED: June 1, 1868

BURIED: Lancaster, Pennsylvania

---

by Christopher Buckley

It's probably just as well that James Buchanan was our only bachelor president. There are no descendants bracing every morning on opening the paper to find another headline announcing: "Buchanan Once Again Rated Worst President in History."

Their only consolation is that political scientists occasionally tire of ranking him last and, just for the heck of it, bump him up to next-to-worst president, with Warren Harding (temporarily) assuming the bottom slot on the greasy pole. But then what can one hope for, of an executive whose most famous utterance was to his successor on the day he handed over the reins of the fractured nation: "My dear sir, if you are as happy on entering the White House as I am on leaving, you are a very happy man indeed"? And how would you like to be followed by Abraham Lincoln, number one or two on the top ten list of great presidents?

Considering Buchanan's curriculum vitae leads one to ask, What, oh what, went wrong? His achievements and honors positively shimmer. He was an excellent lawyer pulling down $11,000 a year, no small sum in the 1820s. He was elected to the Pennsylvania legislature, then to the U.S. House. He was elected chairman of the Judiciary Committee, appointed minister to Russia (by President Andrew Jackson, in order to keep him from running for vice president), elected to the U.S. Senate and reelected twice, appointed secretary of state, appointed minister to Britain. James Buchanan was a résumé god, a nineteenth-century George H. W. Bush. If only he'd stopped there. But whom the gods would make worst president in U.S. history, first they convince to run for the White House.

An essay on Buchanan by the historian Jean Harvey Baker in a collection entitled—ironically, in his instance—*To the Best of My Ability* contains the following phrases: "ill suited . . . undermined his pledge . . . advice of cronies . . . inflammatory position . . . improperly intervened . . . infuriating . . . limited himself . . . passed over for renomination . . . schism in the party . . . vacillating . . . rudderless . . . bungled . . . presidential failure . . . erratic trimmer . . . twisted . . . stubbornly . . . deaf ear . . . feckless . . . exculpatory vehemence."

The Greatness That Was the Buchanan Era included *Dred Scott*, the economic panic of 1857, secession, and Fort Sumter. You have to look hard to find four more dismal nodes in American history. Open the Buchanan file to any random page and you'll find such accolades as: "never regarded as a brilliant speaker," "neither a brilliant nor visionary thinker," and even "expelled from college." The one woman about whom he was serious was the daughter of Pennsylvania's leading ironmaster, who, by the way, didn't like Buchanan and tried to break up the courtship. After he fumbled the romance, she committed suicide. Later on, there were rumors that his persistent bachelorhood was owing to an abiding Uranian affection for Alabama senator—and, briefly, vice president under Franklin Pierce—William Rufus King.

On the plus side, Buchanan was known for a sense of humor, though alas this "seldom showed itself in his public statements" (Pennsylvania Historical Museum Commission). Well, let's not pile on. The record shows that he was "distinguished looking." And he was. In photographs, he looks out at us with a becoming, diffident sense of his own handsomeness, head tilted forward and to the left. This was not a pose. He was farsighted in one eye and nearsighted in the other. Historians have remarked on this ophthalmic peculiarity as emblematic of his karma: Some things he saw clearly up close; the big picture was—well, a bit blurry.

Buchanan saw the major issue of his day—slavery—both ways, as (a) evil, but (b) a state issue. Buchanan's 1856 platform was premised on the idea that the Compromise of 1850 ought to stand, and that Congress had no constitutional mandate to intervene in the matter of slavery. It was a principled, lawyerly view. The only problem with it was that it was (a) wrong and (b) ultimately dividing. While Buchanan dithered and finessed and tried to have it both ways, a senatorial candidate named Lincoln was out on the hustings famously declaring that a house divided against itself could not stand. Tempting as it is to blame Buchanan the lawyer for his nearsightedness on the issue, Lincoln was also a member of the bar.

He *was* consistent. As early as 1826, thirty years before becoming president, he was parsing away: "I believe [slavery] to be a great political and great moral evil. I thank God, my lot has been cast in a State where it does not exist. But, while I entertain these opinions, I know it is an evil at present without a remedy . . . one of those moral evils, from which it is impossible for us to escape, without the introduction of evils infinitely greater. There are portions of this Union, in which, if you emancipate our slaves, they will become masters. There can be no middle course." Boldly put, sir!

The Buchanan treasury of quotations, such as it is, is marked by an on-the-one-hand, on-the-other-hand evenhandedness that leaves him with sores from straddling the fence:

- "It is better to bear the ills we have than to fly to others we know not of."
- "What is right and what is practicable are two different things."
- "Liberty must be allowed to work out its natural results; and these will, ere long, astonish the world."
- "All that is necessary to [abolish slavery], and all for which the slave States have ever contended, is to be let alone and permitted to manage their domestic institutions in their own way."

In 1854, two years before assuming the Mantle of Ungreatness, he championed the Ostend Manifesto. (You may remember it as a trick question on your last American History final exam.) In Ostend, Belgium, he declared that the United States had the right to purchase Cuba, or to annex it by force if necessary. Well, that's certainly bold. But this had less to do with Manifest Destiny—which the expansionist Buchanan resolutely favored—than with giving the South another slave state. It's hard not to level the charge of appeasement against Buchanan.

He tried to win by splitting the difference. In the end, it came to naught, as appeasements invariably do. In January 1861, the ship he had dispatched to resupply Fort Sumter was fired on and forced to withdraw. One month later, the Confederacy was officially inaugurated in Montgomery, Alabama.

He was passed over by his own party for renomination. (Four years before, he had carried only 45 percent of the popular vote in a three-way race.) There was, at least, a happy by-product to his failure: The schism he created within his own party ultimately assured the election of the Republican candidate, Abraham Lincoln. Soon Buchanan was on his way to the Capitol in a carriage with his successor, telling Abe how relieved he was to be rid of the job.

He retired to Wheatland, his estate in Lancaster, Pennsylvania, where he died in 1868. Though domestically tranquil, his remaining years could not have been happy. He was blamed for the Civil War. Vandals kept defacing his portrait in the U.S. Capitol, requiring it to be removed for safekeeping. (*That* must have hurt.) Posters calling him "Judas" were plastered on walls.

He finally did what most Democratic ex-presidents do—write a book blaming everything on the Republicans. It was not a best-seller. One of his last pronouncements upon himself has a sad quality to it. "Whatever the result may be," he said, "I shall carry to my grave the consciousness that I at least meant well for my country."

"At least he meant well" isn't quite up there with, say, Edwin Stanton's pronouncement at the deathbed of Lincoln: "Now he belongs to the ages."

Yet let's cut the poor guy some posthumous slack and grant him the benefit of the doubt that he did, at least, mean well. Perhaps historians, the next time they convene to decide who was the absolute worst president ever, will also factor in his good intentions and move him up two notches so that his ghost can experience the giddy feeling of looking down—if only temporarily—on Warren Harding *and* Franklin Pierce.

Mr. Buckley is editor of Forbes FYI *and author, most recently, of* Florence of Arabia: A Novel *(Random House, 2004).*

16.
ABRAHAM LINCOLN

SURVEY RANKING: 2

BORN: February 12, 1809, Hardin County
(now Larue County), Kentucky

WIFE: Mary Todd

RELIGION: Unaffiliated

PARTY: Republican

MILITARY EXPERIENCE: Illinois militia (captain)

OTHER OFFICES HELD: Illinois state representative (1834–41), U.S.
representative (1847–49)

TOOK OFFICE: March 4, 1861

VICE PRESIDENTS: Hannibal Hamlin (1861–65), Andrew Johnson
(1865)

DIED IN OFFICE: April 15, 1865 (assassinated)

BURIED: Springfield, Illinois

by Jay Winik

It was the loneliest of decisions. On his first day on the job, in March
1861, Abraham Lincoln, bags under his eyes, already faced a military
crisis: Fort Sumter was surrounded by rebel batteries, and supplies

were running dangerously low. What to do? Reinforce it? Give diplomacy a chance? Force a showdown?

Lincoln prevailed on the best and the brightest in his cabinet for advice. The legendary General Winfield Scott, hero of the Mexican War and a towering fixture in Washington, counseled surrender of the fort—it was, he said, of inconsequential military value. Gideon Welles, Lincoln's navy secretary, also favored giving it up. So too did Secretary of State William Seward. Echoing the sentiment of much of the country, he emphatically wanted to evacuate: Any aggressive moves, Seward contended, would eviscerate Unionism in South Carolina and ignite a civil war; the best way to end the crisis was to give Sumter up and provide Unionists throughout the South time to consolidate their strength. This way, those who endlessly harangued about Republican coercion would be silenced, a great crisis could be ended, and a ghastly civil war avoided. (In fact, behind Lincoln's back, Seward had already brazenly assured Southerners that Sumter would be evacuated.) And Lincoln's troubles with his advisers were compounded by his public tribulations. One *New York Times* headline blared: "WANTED: A POLICY."

What to do indeed. But Lincoln would soon rip back—no concessions. "The tug has to come," he memorably said, "& better now than any time hereafter." He told his cabinet a supply fleet would be dispatched to Sumter. Soon thereafter, Sumter fell. Lincoln shrewdly announced the rebels had fired the first shot, "forcing" on him a decision of "immediate dissolution, or blood." And thus would commence a chain of events leading to a great war that would drag on for four bloody years and consume some 620,000 lives.

Lincoln's niche in history—and in our affections—is secure. His greatness comes from many things: He ended slavery, saved the Union, stitched the country together toward war's end, and gave a new birth to freedom. He penned eloquent addresses that will forever reside in the nation's memory. He died a martyr. And almost uniquely, he was a leader of such inexhaustible magnanimity and vision that by war's end he could put himself in the position of rescuing not just the North's bloodied young men but, in his own distinct manner, those of the South as well.

Lincoln seems to rise above other presidents onto a different moral plane, becoming a Christ-like figure, or the closest thing that exists in our national consciousness. Yet he was a riddle of quirks and eccentricities. His self-derogation was real: "My poor, lean, lank face." So was his simplicity: His clothes were invariably out of season or fashion; he referred to himself as "A" and greeted visitors with "howdy"; and he stuffed notes in his pockets and stuck bills in a drawer. He abounded with contradictions: a man of great moral fiber who was a shameless politician; a man of vast intellect who scoffed at great works of literature or history because they were "too heavy for an ordinary mind to digest"; a man of humble origins who blazed with ambition and never quit. (Local settlers once gibed that he was a "wild, harum-scarum kind of man who always had his eye open on the main chance.") No wonder *The New York Times* called him "peculiar."

More books have been written about Lincoln—a staggering seven thousand by one estimate—than any other single American figure. Yet one question remains. Its answer is elusive but it is well worth dwelling upon. How, when the country was suddenly confronted by the mightiest challenge since its auspicious birth, did Lincoln manage to rise to the occasion?

Neither history nor our love affair with Lincoln should obscure just how ill-prepared he was for the job, or the many mistakes he made early on. Before he became president everything about his career smacked of the persistent efforts of a political junkie and an average political hack. He had not held office in over a decade and had never been more than an obscure one-term congressman. Unlike George Washington and Andrew Jackson, he had virtually no military experience. Unlike Thomas Jefferson and James Monroe, he had virtually no diplomatic experience. He had never lived or even traveled abroad. He had no executive experience, almost no formal education, no powerful mentors, and had never overseen anything larger than a two-man law office. He was risk-averse to boot. And then there was the matter of his fragile temperament. He was a man so prone to gloom that he once mourned, "I laugh because I cannot weep."

Was this the man to guide the country in its greatest crisis? Where would he find the inner resolve and wisdom to weather the cataclysm he now faced? To be sure, he craved this war like a criminal wants a firing squad. Yet somehow—and this is the source of the Lincoln legend and of Lincoln's greatness as well—in the sobering months and years ahead, this once second-rate politician would find himself. By some combination of design and fate, he would become this nation's greatest war president—and make this country what it is today.

It was never easy. Not in the beginning, not in the middle, not in the end. From the outset Lincoln, inexperienced and disorderly, found he had to address daunting matters for which prescriptions and precedents scarcely existed. Every executive agency, from the White House to the army, was in turmoil. Cabinet members worked at cross-purposes—when they weren't undercutting the president. A military machine had to be built literally from scratch. And there was the "Negro" problem, stalking and haunting Lincoln at every turn. Finally, Washington itself was a whirlwind of disarray and confusion. But Lincoln pressed on.

He made tough, controversial decisions. Concerned about "the enemy in the rear," he was unapologetically zealous in censoring telegraphs and the mail; in suspending habeas corpus and in imprisoning ordinary citizens (so-called disloyalists) and even duly elected legislators; in defying Chief Justice Roger Taney (when Taney rebuked Lincoln's suspension of habeas corpus, Lincoln fired back, "Are all the laws but one to go unexecuted, and the government itself go to pieces lest that one be violated?"); and in even closing down newspapers. He bravely weathered a storm of public opinion arrayed against him, year after year, every bit as fierce as the Vietnam War protests. In 1864, the North was still in a foul mood. As famed journalist Horace Greeley put it, "Our bleeding, bankrupt almost dying country longs for peace." It did indeed. That year, in the presidential election, Lincoln's own former top general, George McClellan, ran against him on a peace plank. Yet Lincoln pressed on.

And he pressed on even though he had generals who wouldn't fight, couldn't fight, or failed to press the advantage when they did fight. In turn, he sacked general after general. But with brooding detachment, Lincoln endured his own mistakes—they were many—and the brittle highs and deepening lows of the war. And he did so with dogged tenacity.

Dogged tenacity. It is a simple explanation for greatness—but in Lincoln's case, probably quite true. One of the great questions in history is, Why didn't Lincoln give up or give in? Why, when the opportunity for ending the killing presented itself, did he not grab the easy way out, or the expedient way, as a lesser man and a lesser president might have been tempted to do (and as Lincoln himself had done in the past)? He would have been no different from a long list of kings, monarchs, emperors, and other heads of state who bowed to the irrepressible pressures for compromise, or to the forces of nationalism sweeping the globe—and who, far from being condemned for it, were praised for their statesmanship.

Consider how tempting it might have been to any other president. At several points during the war, it looked as though the Confederacy could, or even would, win, or at least not lose, which amounted to the same thing. The worst riots in American history, the four-day New York draft riots of 1863, raged *after* Gettysburg, and left anywhere from 105 to 1,000 dead, with black residents lynched and hung from lampposts. And there was no respite; storms of antiwar protests sliced through the Midwest. Once Lincoln had finally appointed Ulysses S. Grant, it was unclear whether the public would persevere with him. The Democrats were demanding an immediate cessation of hostilities ("after fours years of failure . . . by the experiment of war"). As the appalling number of Union casualties rose in 1864—yes, as late as 1864—the North was still far from victory, and nearly 200,000 men had deserted the federal army.

The toll on Lincoln's psyche was brutal. During the Battle of the Wilderness in May 1864, when Grant and Robert E. Lee squared off for the first time, Lincoln barely slept for four days, wandering the White House corridors. ("I must have some relief from this terrible anxiety," he muttered over and over, "or it will kill me.") Even then, as the war dragged on and the carnage mounted, it became clear that the sacred struggle would be neither brief nor easy nor, for that matter, necessarily victorious. While Bill Sherman was stalled in the West, Grant suffered some 52,000 casualties in those six weeks alone—nearly as many as were lost in the entirety of the Vietnam War; at Cold Harbor, he lost a frightful 9,000 men in one hour—three times as many as had died in Pickett's Charge the year before. Lincoln himself declared the "heavens hung in black." But when Congress and even Mary Lincoln called for Grant's head after this terrible carnage, Lincoln snapped back: "I can't spare him. He fights!"

The critics of Lincoln never let up: "There is a cowardly imbecile at the head of the government," warned one newspaper. "Disgust with our government is universal," said another critic. In one of the unkindest cuts of all, the dapper Massachusetts senator Charles Sumner called him "a dictator," while another senator, Benjamin Wade of Ohio, speaking for the elites of Washington society, wrote him off as "poor white trash." Yet into the volatile mix, Lincoln, who deeply hated slavery, would issue the most revolutionary document since the Declaration of Independence, the Emancipation Proclamation—and then later he would lobby vigorously for the Thirteenth Amendment to end slavery for all of time. And into this mix, at war's end, he would, in the last speech of his life, declare his support for some blacks to vote—another first in this nation's history (prompting one John Wilkes Booth to growl: "That means nigger citizenship").

And when the war stalled, we saw another side of Lincoln: a man tough as nails. By the summer of 1864, Lincoln understood that only the strongest measures would save the Union. He embraced the concept of total war, an escalatory measure that would have been unthinkable at the conflict's outset—and that the South itself had rejected—and let loose General Bill Sherman. Sherman's March to the Sea unleashed hundreds of miles of death and destruction. The South got the message: "Since Atlanta I have felt as if all were dead within me forever," Mary Chesnut, the Southern diarist, shuddered. "We are going to be wiped off the face of the earth!"

Yet Lincoln's heart was never hard. Having waged total war, at war's end it was he who spoke of a magnanimous peace to knit a badly divided country back together again ("with malice toward none; with charity for all"); it was he who stood up to the radical Republicans and those voices in his own cabinet who wanted harshness and revenge, instead embracing charity and compassion toward the defeated Confederates; and it was he who sketched the postwar vision to knit the country together in April 1865, thus sparing America the grisly wake of internecine war that has too often been the norm throughout history, as in Northern Ireland or the Balkans or even the Middle East today. As Lee himself put it, "I surrendered as much to Lincoln's goodness as I did to Grant's armies."

There is one more thing worth pondering. As the Civil War entered its waning months, far from being triumphant or cocky, Lincoln was an overwhelmingly melancholy man. Instead of glory, Lincoln once confessed, he had found only "ashes and blood." Like many great generals who have had to send tens of thousands to their deaths, he had a corner of remorse lodged deep in his gut, furiously eating away at him. It is little wonder that the whole experience of the presidency was barren for him; Carl Sandburg once remarked that there were thirty-one rooms in the White House, and Lincoln was not at home in any one of them. But even as a deathly weariness settled over him, Lincoln was never mawkishly self-pitying. Again, he pressed on. It was remarkable, and we are once more forced to ask, how did he do it?

In watching Lincoln evolve as president, one comes away with the sense that he began to feel as if he had somehow been placed on this earth, elected as president, in the eye of this terrible war, as part of some grander design—to save the Union. And then, for perhaps the first time in his life, he felt not the familiar drumbeat of ambition or of political satisfaction, but of destiny. And when that happened, he was a rock.

And if that meant preserving the Union, well, all else be damned. Perhaps this even explains his curious, almost indifferent attitude toward his own death. "I long ago made up my mind that if anybody wants to kill me, he will do it," Lincoln remarked. And this too: "It is important that the people know I come among them without fear."

On April 14, 1865, as Lincoln readied himself to go to Ford's Theatre, he had been told several times that the evening would be a particularly dangerous one; yet he refused to take along an extra guard. To some, these are the convictions of a man without hate or malice, or the signs of a cavalier recklessness or a morbid bit of bravado, or evidence of yet another troubling blind spot. All this might be true. But with hindsight, we can perhaps also see that they are the actions not of a passive man, but of a man hurtling toward his ultimate fate, without fear or hesitation.

Then came the loud muffled sound, like a violent clap of hands, or the crack of wood. It was the bullet, fired by John Wilkes Booth, that bore into Lincoln's brain.

Presidents may do many things, but they do not have the luxury of complaining, or blaming others, or eluding responsibility, no matter how terrifying its dimensions. Why is it that some lose winnable wars, but others win losable wars? Or some evade the issues of the day, while others tackle them head-on? These are the mysteries of leadership. Second-rate presidents may act "great" during routine times, when it is easy to do so, but only the truly great ones rise to the occasion in difficult times. And where second-rate presidents are somehow always shaped, and prodded, and manipulated by the forces of history, great ones find ways to bend those forces of history to their goals. Thus it was for Lincoln.

He instinctively understood the moral burdens he had to shoulder; he appreciated the high seriousness of the crisis; he grasped its tragic dimensions while never losing sight of the good that could somehow be made out of this awful conflict. And he did this with both a human empathy and a steely resolve that, even now, history has trouble fully sorting out or explaining.

Mr. Winik is author of April 1865: The Month That Saved America *(HarperCollins, 2001), which aired as a two-hour History Channel documentary special in April 2003.*

17.
ANDREW JOHNSON

SURVEY RANKING: 37

BORN: December 29, 1808, Raleigh,
North Carolina

WIFE: Eliza McCardle

RELIGION: Unaffiliated

PARTY: National Union (Republican)

MILITARY EXPERIENCE: U.S. Army (brigadier general)

OTHER OFFICES HELD: Mayor of Greeneville, Tennessee (1830–33),
Tennessee state representative (1835–37, 1839–41), state senator
(1841), U.S. representative (1843–53), governor (1853–57), U.S.
senator (1857–62, 1875), military governor of Tennessee (1862–65)

TOOK OFFICE: April 15, 1865

VICE PRESIDENT: None

LEFT OFFICE: March 4, 1869

DIED: July 31, 1875

BURIED: Greeneville, Tennessee

by Jeffrey K. Tulis

Andrew Johnson is generally regarded as one of the worst presidents
in American history. This assessment is not as obvious as one might

think. Since the Second World War, presidential success has been routinely defined as the effective use of power to establish the executive's preferred public policies. The most articulate expression of this idea is Richard Neustadt's book *Presidential Power,* first published in 1960 and still the most influential study of the American presidency. By this standard, Andrew Johnson was a remarkably successful president. His vision of "reconstruction" of the South prevailed. The postbellum nation was refounded on his principles, not those of Congress's Radical Republican majority. And his vision lasted, shaping American politics generally, and Southern politics especially, well into the mid-twentieth century.

To be sure, few of his policies were enacted into law, and his opponents legislated many of their policies over his many vetoes. Johnson was the first American president to be impeached, and he escaped conviction by only one vote. All the more impressive, then, was Andrew Johnson's ability to use executive powers to frustrate the will of his opponents and to advance his vision.

Yet Johnson was an awful president precisely because he was an effectively powerful president. His tenure in office reminds us how cramped and inadequate is a notion of success confined to power and shorn from the ends for which power is deployed, or oblivious to the constitutionality of the means by which power is exercised.

Johnson's "reconstruction" was built upon the premise that black Americans were inherently unfit for full citizenship and that reintegration of Confederate rebels into the Union was more important than the development of a robust civil society for former slaves. To advance his vision, Johnson repeatedly ignored the deliberate will of Congress, and he fashioned policy through a use of unilateral power that was, and still is, unprecedented. Johnson refused to enforce many properly enacted laws; he refused to spend money appropriated for congressionally constructed institutions; he pardoned countless Confederates, arrested by his own military establishment, who would not pledge allegiance to the United States; he seized and returned land to former slave owners that had been legally confiscated and distributed to slaves who had worked the land; he used patronage power to bully politicians throughout the nation to support his version of reconstruction; and in a formal message to

Congress he threatened to use military force against Congress to protect his understanding of the Constitution.

Johnson's was the first and most effective "administrative presidency"—a presidency that made major policy by employing unilateral powers, executive orders, and bureaucratic maneuvers rather than through legislation. Of course, these same devices could be described as the tactics of a statesman were they deployed to thwart the will of an unjust majority or a tyrannical Congress. Reflection on the administration of Andrew Johnson is a useful corrective to the thin, "value-free" notion of success common to most textbooks on the presidency today. The meaning of the power Johnson deployed cannot be adequately described without discussing the purposes of his power, the content of his policies.

But there is a still deeper sense in which Andrew Johnson's presidency reveals problems in our contemporary understanding of American politics. Defects of our constitutional order that we now assume to be defining ideals of presidential politics were invented by Andrew Johnson and were fundamental causes or consequences of his impeachment. Johnson's repudiation of settled nineteenth-century constitutional norms offers a picture of the twentieth-century presidency in bold relief. Examining Johnson's use of executive power is a useful way to reconsider the merit of contemporary understandings of presidential leadership by making our familiar and comfortable practices seem odd and uncomfortable, as they used to be.

Johnson was the first president to attempt to transcend the limits of his office through daily and direct appeals to the people. Today we take it for granted that a president should be a popular leader and that he should develop his political authority through a "personal" relation with the people at large. But this view of leadership was an anathema in nineteenth-century American political culture. Andrew Johnson's was the first plebiscitary presidency or, to use Theodore Lowi's term, the first personal presidency.

Personal presidents see power and authority as attributes of their own democratic skills rather than as derivative from their constitutional station. One might say that the Constitution becomes an instrument of their personal power rather than the principal source and limit of their official power and authority. Even secondary sources of power and authority, political parties, are refashioned as instruments useful to a personal president rather than as an enduring organization producing, teaching, molding, and limiting presidents.

That Andrew Johnson should be the first plebiscitary president is odd given that he ascended to the presidency after Lincoln's assassination, not by democratic election. But Lincoln had chosen Johnson to be his running mate because he had been the only well-known Southern Democrat who opposed secession. Thus Johnson came to office with much of his own Democratic Party opposed to him. After he became president, Johnson repudiated the policies of his new party, the refashioned Republicans, Lincoln's National Union Party. Johnson's base was therefore not in any pre-existing organization but in the coalitions he could cobble together personally through appeals that did not track prevailing party positions or organizations, and through patronage dispersed to build personal support rather than as a reward for service to a political party.

Johnson was a semiliterate man whose wife taught him to write when he was in his twenties. But he had an extraordinary gift for delivering speeches on the stump, impassioned appeals that skewered his opponents as he responded, quickly and effectively, to the reaction of his audience. These were not polished orations, prepared in advance with appropriate literary references or attention to how the speech would be read after it was delivered. Johnson's talent was for the extemporaneous, crowd-pleasing harangue.

When Johnson became president he conducted the office in the only way that he knew—as a demagogue. His main strategy to secure support for his policy toward the South was a "Swing Around the Circle," a speaking tour in which he delivered sixty speeches, all variations on one speech. He carried a rough outline in his head and modified it to respond to each audience. In the typical speech, Johnson would invoke the spirits of Washington and Jackson, claim his own devotion to the principles of Union, deny that he was a traitor as others had alleged, attack some part of the audience (depending on the kinds of heckles he received), defend his use of the veto, attack Congress and single out particular congressmen (sometimes denouncing them as traitors for not supporting his policies), compare himself to Christ and offer himself as a martyr, and conclude by declaring his closeness to the people and appealing for their support.

Nothing could be further from the Founders' intentions than for presidential power to depend upon the interplay of orator and crowd. Whether or not the speaker persuaded his immediate audience, the effect of such activity upon the president's office and upon the deliberative process as a whole was likely to be deleterious. Such was the case with Andrew Johnson. Indeed, the tenth article of impeachment was for his stump rhetoric: "Andrew Johnson has brought the high office of President of the United States into contempt, ridicule and disgrace, to the great scandal of all citizens."

If Johnson's main legacy was to disgrace the office by repudiating forms and formalities of leadership practiced in the nineteenth-century constitutional order, his other lasting legacy seemed to move in the opposite direction. Johnson found it in his political interest to *overlegalize* the political relationship of president and Congress. After repeatedly losing legislative disputes with Congress, he sought scenarios for the Supreme Court to arbitrate the disputes between them. For Johnson, the courts and the people were preferred venues in a process of political forum shopping. In turning to the courts to arbitrate his disputes with Congress over the constitutionality of their respective powers, Johnson ignored then well-settled practice and precedent that such disputes are not properly resolved that way under our Constitution. Johnson opposed the use of military tribunals in the postwar South, claiming that such extraconstitutional institutions are inappropriate in peacetime when ordinary civil institutions could function. While this position sounds reasonable and "constitutional," one must remember that the civil courts Johnson supported in the South were staffed by the very people who were supposed to be tried in the military tribunals.

Johnson's most effective and lasting use of this strategy of legalization was his successful effort to convince a majority of the Senate that for a president to be convicted of "high crimes and misdemeanors" one need to have committed acts that violate criminal law. For this reason, the impeachment charge of "bad rhetoric" was dropped and never brought to a vote. Johnson was acquitted of the other charges that he violated the Tenure of Office Act by firing Secretary of War Edwin M. Stanton partly because, from a strictly legal point of view, his own position that the act was unconstitutional was supported by precedents extending back to the removal debate in the first Congress, in 1789.

Deference to courts and to legal communities and practices gives the appearance of care and fidelity to the Constitution. But the legal processes operate under the Constitution, which embraces other political forms as well. Those political forms wither and decay to the extent that their practices are overlegalized. The Constitution analogizes the impeachment process to ordinary criminal trials in order to make a political process less partisan and more impartial than it would otherwise be. Johnson convinced the nation to take that *analogy* as a *literal* command, and the nation has accepted that understanding ever since.

Even most historians have bought Johnson's misreading and have convinced themselves that his conviction would have compromised the "independence of the executive" and subverted our Constitution over the long run by politicizing the impeachment process. We should at least entertain the possibility that the opposite is the case, that Johnson's acquittal subverted our Constitution over the long run. Johnson's legal literalism has deprived Congress of its core constitutional weapon in separation-of-powers disputes—the power to democratically punish an executive who disgraces his office or who abuses the Constitution by repeatedly undermining laws enacted by a deliberative democracy.

Mr. Tulis is a professor of government at the University of Texas, Austin, and author of The Rhetorical Presidency *(Princeton University Press, 1987).*

18.
ULYSSES SIMPSON GRANT

SURVEY RANKING: 29

BORN: April 27, 1822, Point Pleasant, Ohio

WIFE: Julia Dent

RELIGION: Methodist

PARTY: Republican

MILITARY EXPERIENCE: U.S. Army (general)

OTHER OFFICES HELD: None

TOOK OFFICE: March 4, 1869

VICE PRESIDENTS: Schuyler Colfax (1869–73), Henry Wilson (1873–75)

LEFT OFFICE: March 4, 1877

DIED: July 23, 1885

BURIED: New York City

---

by Michael Barone

In 1878 Ulysses S. Grant visited the flying Bersaglieri regiment in Milan. A horse had been picked for him to ride—a "restless, wicked appearing animal," his military escort said, fearing that the fifty-six-year-old former president would be thrown. But Grant's eye lit up.

He mounted, and "the horse, after a few futile plunges, discovered that he had his master, and started off in a gentle trot." Grant had loved horses from his boyhood in Brown County, Ohio, and, like George Washington, was rated one of the great horsemen in the army. This mostly silent man was exquisitely sensitive to the nature of the beast and able to harness its vast power and direct it to his own ends, as he had done with the Union army and, to an extent not usually appreciated, with the presidency.

Grant loved to travel. In his successful military career and in unsuccessful years in civilian life he saw much of North America in the years before the Civil War—New York, Philadelphia, Cincinnati, St. Louis, New Orleans, South Texas and northern Mexico, Mexico City, the Canadian border at Detroit and upstate New York, Panama, San Francisco, the Oregon Territory, and Galena, Illinois. He did yeoman work as a quartermaster and fought bravely in Mexico. He developed a deep sympathy for Mexicans and for blacks and for Indians. He was hopeless at commerce, too trusting of others and insufficiently assertive of his own interest.

When the Civil War broke out, Grant was determined to fight and wangled a commission as captain in Illinois of troops headed south on the Mississippi River. He rode his men as he rode his horses, sympathetic to their needs and their plight but determined above all to achieve victory. In an age of eloquent oratory and chivalrous circumlocution, he wrote out his orders swiftly in plain and unmistakably clear words. In an era of grand gestures, he was famously imperturbable. Earlier than others, he saw that victory required not the occupation of territory but the destruction of the Confederate armies. Abraham Lincoln found in him the general he wanted and in March 1864 appointed him general in chief.

Lincoln's death a year later left Grant as a central figure in government and in politics. He sent General Philip Sheridan and fifty thousand troops to South Texas to help Benito Juárez oust the Emperor Maximilian. He approved Andrew Johnson's grant of amnesty and he threatened to resign if Johnson did not quash the indictment of Robert E. Lee for treason. He insisted on the continued military occupation of the South. When Johnson tried to send him on a diplomatic mission to Mexico, he refused to go.

All this allowed Congress to exclude the Southern states and pass the Fourteenth and Fifteenth amendments and the Reconstruction Acts placing the South under military government. Grant appointed generals who ousted state governments that refused to recognize black rights and ignored Johnson's attorney general's ruling that made it easier for former Confederates to register to vote. When Johnson fired Secretary of War Edwin Stanton in 1867 and appointed Grant to take his place, Grant worked stubbornly to prevent Johnson from transferring effective generals. This led to Stanton's reinstatement and Johnson's impeachment in 1868. In May Johnson was acquitted by one vote, and four days later the Republican Party unanimously nominated Grant for president. Through all this Grant proceeded deftly but firmly, always with an eye to controlling the facts on the ground.

Inaugurated ten months later, President Grant faced four major problems: the rights of blacks in the South, the place of Indians in the West, the flood of soft greenback currency across the country, and the *Alabama* claims against Britain. On each of them Grant took a bold and venturesome stand, with varying results.

Reconstruction was the most difficult. Grant moved quickly to secure passage of the Fifteenth Amendment, guaranteeing blacks' right to vote. When the night riders of the Ku Klux Klan started terrorizing and murdering blacks and whites who supported their rights, Grant persuaded Congress to pass a law prohibiting such acts and sent in the army and U.S. marshals to enforce it. Grant broke the Klan's back, and Southern blacks voted in 1872 in numbers not seen again until 1968.

In 1874 in Louisiana, White Leaguers murdered Republican officeholders, and the army fought a pitched battle with them in the streets of New Orleans. In the 1874 election, Democrats, running against military occupation of the South and making racist attacks on free blacks, won a majority in the House and made gains in the Senate. Grant persisted in putting down the White League after the election.

But in two decisions in 1876, the Supreme Court gutted enforcement of the Fifteenth Amendment and the Ku Klux Klan Act. Blacks still voted in large numbers in 1876, but Grant's successor, Rutherford Hayes, as part of the deal settling the disputed presidential race, withdrew the remaining federal troops from the South. Grant had acted out of the conviction that blacks should be treated equally with all other Americans; no other president would do more for civil rights until Harry Truman.

Grant also believed that Indians could and should be treated the same as other Americans. He deplored the fighting between settlers and Indians on the frontier and put most of the blame on settlers. He wanted to protect Indians on reservations, provide promised funds, educate them, and provide individuals with title to land, so that they could blend into American society. He enlisted Quakers and churchmen to replace corrupt public officials. For a time violence lessened. It flared up again when settlers streamed in after gold was found on reservation land in the Black Hills of the Dakota Territory. Sheridan persuaded Grant to let him round up Sioux leaders and force them into other territory. That was what George Armstrong Custer was doing when he went to the Little Big Horn in 1876. Grant's policy of treating Indians as individual citizens, not as members of tribes, was a road not taken in Indian policy, except in Oklahoma, where many people of Indian descent lived productively and peaceably and not on reservations.

To finance the Civil War, Abraham Lincoln had flooded the country with $400 million in greenbacks, and during and after the war inflation was raging. Grant was a hard-money man. In 1869, when financiers Jay Gould and Jim Fisk tried to corner the gold market, which would have depreciated the currency even more, Grant ordered Treasury Secretary George Boutwell to sell $4 million in government gold to keep the price down, and the Gold Ring was defeated. Then came the Panic of 1873. The Treasury had reduced the $400 million of greenbacks by $44 million; in 1874 Congress passed a bill providing that $44 million be reissued. Grant was under pressure to sign it. But he decided on a veto and made it stick. And he pressured Congress to pass the Resumption Act, requiring all greenbacks to be withdrawn from circulation by 1879. They were, and the country prospered with hard money for decades.

When Grant came to office, feeling against Britain was strong. The British-built *Alabama* and other Confederate ships had sunk 257 Union merchant ships, and the U.S. demanded compensation from

Britain. The Senate had rejected a treaty signed by Andrew Johnson providing for adjudication of the claims. Grant did not enter office in a conciliatory frame of mind, but in December 1869 he called for negotiations to settle the claims and "to lay the foundation of a broad principle of public laws." Secretary of State Hamilton Fish got the British to agree to binding arbitration of all issues between the two nations by a five-member commission with representatives of the U.S., Britain, Italy, Brazil, and Switzerland. The Senate approved the treaty, and the panel awarded the U.S. $15.5 million. It was the first use of binding arbitration to settle an international dispute.

The traditional verdict on Grant is that he was a failure as president. It is said that his administration was laced with corruption, but the claim is exaggerated, and Grant himself insisted on full probes of his longtime aide Orville Babcock (not guilty) and Secretary of War William Belknap (guilty). Grant received bad press from contemporary intellectuals like Henry Adams, who was disappointed, as Adams confesses in his autobiography, that he and his friends were not offered jobs in the administration, and from most historians from the 1880s to the 1950s, who believed Grant's attempts to protect black suffrage and enforce blacks' rights were an outrage.

But as president he showed the same combination of sensitivity and determination, the same horseman's skills, he had as a general. If he failed to secure the enforcement of black rights and the peaceful assimilation of the Indians, it is probable that, given the state of opinion of the white majority, no president could have done so at the time. The goals commend themselves to us today. And he did give the country a hard currency and the world an example of peaceful settlement of disputes: two major achievements.

Grant was not given to grandiloquent boasting and it was only desperate financial need and fatal illness that prompted him to write his *Personal Memoirs,* which recount in spare, measured prose his life up to April 1865. It is too bad that he was unable to give us his version of his presidency.

Mr. Barone is a senior writer at U.S. News & World Report, *a contributor to the* Fox News Channel, *and co-author of the biennial* Almanac of American Politics *(National Journal).*

19.
RUTHERFORD BIRCHARD HAYES

SURVEY RANKING: 24

BORN: October 4, 1822, Delaware, Ohio

WIFE: Lucy Ware Webb

RELIGION: Unaffiliated; attended Methodist services

PARTY: Republican

MILITARY EXPERIENCE: U.S. Army (major general)

OTHER OFFICES HELD: U.S. representative from Ohio (1865–67), governor (1868–72, 1876–77)

TOOK OFFICE: March 4, 1877

VICE PRESIDENT: William Wheeler

LEFT OFFICE: March 4, 1881

DIED: January 17, 1893

BURIED: Fremont, Ohio

by Ari Hoogenboom

Late in life, Rutherford Birchard Hayes concluded, "I am 'a radical in thought (and principle) and a conservative in method' (and conduct)."

The root of Hayes's radicalism was his commitment to equality, which he perceived to be the foundation of the "level society" in his beloved state of Ohio. Hayes believed that government in a democracy reflected the people and that any lasting radical transformation of the United States could be achieved only gradually. Sweeping legislation without universal education and discussion was as vain, he believed, as "trying to force a stream to flow higher than its source." Hayes, as president, adjusted to political reality, advocated reforms that could be achieved, and nudged the nation toward his ideal society. He was, indeed, a conservative radical.

In 1852, as a young lawyer in Cincinnati, he married Lucy Ware Webb. A Methodist, a teetotaler, and an abolitionist, Mrs. Hayes influenced her husband. Although he did not join her church, he attended services regularly with her, drank temperately before giving up alcohol entirely when in the White House, and after marriage became a strong anti-slavery advocate. To limit the spread of slavery, Hayes joined the Republican Party and in 1858 was elected Cincinnati's city solicitor. When the lower South seceded, Hayes opposed any concessions to slaveholders to lure it back into the Union.

Hayes was willing to let the lower South go, but when South Carolina fired on Fort Sumter on April 12, 1861, he was outraged. Deciding he would rather be killed in action than sit out the war, Hayes was commissioned a major in the 23rd Ohio Volunteers (the same regiment in which William McKinley served). An inspirational leader, Hayes served four years, mostly as a colonel, and was wounded five times (once seriously). He was, McKinley observed, "intense and ferocious" in battle, and he emerged from the war a general and, without campaigning, a member of Congress.

In Congress Hayes supported Radical Republican legislation reconstructing the South, with former slaves enfranchised and voting Republican. But he missed his family and in 1867 was delighted to be nominated for governor of Ohio. He was elected, then reelected in 1869. He retired in 1872, but not for long.

Hard times following the Panic of 1873 and corruption in the Grant administration enabled the resurging Democratic Party to capture the House in the election of 1874. In 1875 Ohio Republicans again turned to Hayes and for the third time narrowly elected him governor. His uphill victory made him a contender for the presidential nomination. When the 1876 Republican National Convention split, Hayes—incorruptible and obnoxious to no one—won the nomination.

The Republicans faced a tough struggle. Many Northerners had tired of Reconstruction issues and were disturbed by corruption, unemployment, and falling farm prices. On election day early unofficial returns appeared to give Samuel Jones Tilden, the Democratic nominee, the presidency with a plurality of about 250,000 votes. He had carried some key Northern states and was running strong in the South. But diehard Republicans claimed that Hayes had carried Florida, Louisiana, and South Carolina (the only Southern states still controlled by Republicans), giving him the presidency by one vote in the Electoral College. The ensuing electoral dispute did not end until March 2, 1877, two days before Hayes's inauguration. (For more on the electoral dispute, see the chapter "Presidential Leadership After Disputed Elections," page 241.)

President Hayes was beset by problems. Farmers howled for currency inflation to increase commodity prices and to help pay their debts, while laborers, suffering from wage cuts and high unemployment, lived in desperation. More immediately, the Democrats in Louisiana and South Carolina set up rival governments controlling all but the areas immediately around the statehouses, where federal troops protected shaky Republican regimes. In confronting these difficulties, Hayes, with the weakest mandate of all presidents, had to deal with a Democratic House and work with a Republican Party divided between inflationists and hard-money men, between reformers and spoilsmen, between those who would keep troops in the South and those who would withdraw them.

Hayes is often blamed for, or credited with, ending the Reconstruction era in the South. In truth, except for beachheads around two statehouses, Reconstruction had already ended when he took office. With a minuscule 25,000-man army, deployed mainly in Western territories, with the House already refusing to appropriate money for that army if it protected Republican governments in South Carolina and Louisiana, and with a majority of Northerners opposed to the continued use of force, the question for Hayes was not whether troops should be removed but when. Before ordering the troops out, Hayes salvaged what he could. He secured promises from the extralegal de facto Democratic governments in both states to protect the civil and voting rights of black and white Republicans. Those promises were soon broken, but, given the political realities, it is difficult to see how Hayes could have done better.

In July 1877, a few months after the Democrats took over in South Carolina and Louisiana, Hayes had to deal with the most severe strike in American history. Following repeated wage cuts on many railroads, the Great Strike broke out on the Baltimore & Ohio and spread to other lines and then to factories. Unemployed men and boys joined the strikers, and uncontrolled violence occurred from coast to coast. Although urged by Thomas Scott of the Pennsylvania Railroad to break the strike, Hayes refused. By dispatching troops when they were properly requested by state or local authorities, he helped prevent further violence, but federal troops neither fired a shot nor quelled the strikers. Without funds the strikers soon gave up.

Despite the desire of farmers to increase the money supply, Hayes opposed inflation, whether achieved by printing fiat money or by the unlimited coinage of silver. When Congress in February 1878 passed the compromise Bland-Allison bill, allowing a limited number of silver dollars to be coined monthly, Hayes, convinced that currency not based on gold was dishonest, vetoed it. Congress overrode his veto, but Hayes and subsequent administrations limited the bill's inflationary effect by backing the new silver dollars with gold. The Hayes administration also returned the United States to the gold standard in January 1879 by redeeming greenbacks (which had been worth less than their face value) in gold. Hayes's consistent hard money policies were accompanied by a stunning revival of business and trade. Knowing exactly where Hayes stood on monetary policy made it easier for businessmen to calculate future moves, and agricultural exports were facilitated with the U.S. on the same standard as Europe.

While Hayes didn't shrink from issuing unpopular pardons or vetoing popular legislation, he cultivated public opinion successfully with short speeches on his frequent travels. He regained the president's appointing power by defeating "senatorial courtesy," which enabled senators to dictate appointments in field offices and feed their political lieutenants at the public trough. At the end of his term, senators and representatives could suggest candidates, but not dictate appointments. Hayes insisted on open competitive examinations for appointees at the New York Customhouse (the largest federal office), and the success of civil service reform there helped pass the 1883 Pendleton Act.

Hayes also won the battle of the riders. In the second half of his term, Congress, controlled by Democrats, attached to necessary appropriations bills clauses to repeal laws enforcing the Fourteenth and Fifteenth amendments. This tactic threatened to shut down the government. Hayes vetoed the appropriations bills with stirring messages accusing the Democrats of trying to deprive the president of the veto power and promoting intimidation and fraud at the polls. Public opinion rallied to Hayes, the Democrats were beaten, and the divided Republican Party was reunited.

By enhancing the power of the presidency, Hayes was a forerunner of strong, modern presidents. He could have been reelected, but he chose to serve only one term, believing presidents would do better if they were not angling for reelection. The Republicans' 1880 presidential nominee, James A. Garfield, triumphed.

In retirement, Hayes was a precursor of the progressive movement. He was a leading advocate of prison reform to rehabilitate convicts, and he opposed the death penalty. Convinced that universal education would lead to a more equal society, Hayes fought hard but unsuccessfully for federal funding for schools in poor sections of the nation. Believing that the increasing disparity between rich and poor in Gilded Age America caused crime and labor unrest, he favored federal regulation of monopolists and confiscatory inheritance taxes. When Hayes died in 1893 some regulatory steps had been taken and the future would bring more. But even today his egalitarianism seems almost as radical as it did in the late nineteenth century.

Mr. Hoogenboom is a professor emeritus of history at Brooklyn College and author of Rutherford B. Hayes: Warrior and President *(University Press of Kansas, 1995).*

20.
JAMES ABRAM GARFIELD

SURVEY RANKING: None

BORN: November 19, 1831, Cuyahoga
County, Ohio

WIFE: Lucretia "Crete" Rudolph

RELIGION: Disciples of Christ

PARTY: Republican

MILITARY EXPERIENCE: U.S. Army (major general)

OTHER OFFICES HELD: Ohio state senator (1859), U.S. representative
(1863–80)

TOOK OFFICE: March 4, 1881

VICE PRESIDENT: Chester Arthur

DIED IN OFFICE: September 19, 1881 (assassinated)

BURIED: Cleveland, Ohio

by Allan Peskin

Does an essay on James A. Garfield really belong in this volume? The bare facts of his brief administration might seem to indicate otherwise. Inaugurated on March 4, 1881, he was shot on July 2 and lingered until his death on September 19—only two hundred days in office, eighty of which were consumed by a drawn-out deathbed vigil. Since the House was not in session during this time, no legislation could be proposed or passed; the administration's major activity consisted of nominating appointees to public office, one of which (to the New York Customhouse) precipitated a bitter struggle that threatened to tear the Republican Party apart.

By the standard of legislation enacted or policies pursued, the Garfield administration seems to have been a cipher, a judgment echoed by many subsequent historians who omitted Garfield and William Henry Harrison from the various polls that rate presidential performance, and by novelist Thomas Wolfe, who mocked that string of post–Civil War presidents whose "gravely vacant and bewhiskered faces mixed, melted, swam together."

The pantheon of presidential "greats" seems reserved for activists, which, in the nature of things, means those who dealt with major national crises. Presidents with the good fortune to preside over quiet times seem doomed to obscurity. In Garfield's day, America was at peace with itself and the world. Neither presidents nor government were expected to make things better, only to keep them running smoothly.

Garfield shared this passive view. The whole duty of government, he once maintained, was "to keep the peace and stand outside the sunshine of the people." Thus it is unlikely, even if he had been spared to complete his term of office, that he would have advocated the bold policy innovations considered so important by those who rank presidents on a scale of greatness.

But before dismissing Garfield as a bearded nonentity, one has to explain two phenomena that marked his brief tenure: first, the massive voter turnout in the election of 1880; and second, the unprecedented wave of public mourning that greeted his untimely death.

In contrast to present-day elections, in which barely half of the eligible voters bother to cast their ballots, in 1880 almost 80 percent of the voters flocked eagerly to the polls. They must have believed that important issues were at stake and that it did make a genuine difference whether Winfield Scott Hancock or James Garfield occupied the White House. Who are we to tell them that they were mistaken?

When, early on in his administration, the president was struck down by two bullets from the pistol of Charles Julius Guiteau, an unhinged religious fanatic, the public reacted with stunned horror.

During the long deathwatch they eagerly scanned the latest tele-graph bulletins and grabbed the special editions of the newspapers that chronicled the distinguished patient's medical ups and downs. When the end came, the nation erupted in a cathartic burst of extrav-agant grief. Thousands waited patiently in the Washington heat to view the body of the lost leader as it lay in state under the Capitol dome. Tens of thousands lined the railroad tracks to pay homage as the funeral train carried him back to Ohio. Hundreds of thousands crowded into Cleveland to witness the last rites, and millions of copies of memorial tributes, biographies, and eulogies flooded an apparently insatiable market.

Clearly, Garfield in death, if not in life, touched some vital chord of American sentiment. The public mourned him more for what he was than for what he did. They remembered an impoverished boy, reared in a log cabin by his widowed mother, who was redeemed from a life of dissipation by a religious experience, who then rose from menial labor to respectability through education, becoming a professor of ancient languages and then president of his small Ohio college. The Republi-can Party brought him into politics, and the Civil War thrust him onto the national stage as the Union's youngest major general. From there it was an easy step to Congress, where he served for seventeen years, becoming a master of financial legislation and his party's floor leader, then to a surprise presidential nomination and a narrow electoral vic-tory—the only sitting House member ever elected president.

In this unbroken ascent "From Log Cabin to White House" (the title of an adulatory campaign biography), Garfield encapsulated the American dream of the self-made man. "My road," Garfield once said, "must be through character to power." It was that character, rather than any specific accomplishments, that Americans mourned in 1881. In so doing, they demonstrated an aspect of the presidency often overlooked by the polls—that of the visible embodiment of what Lincoln called "the civic religion" of the nation, a mirror we hold up to reflect our most cherished values.

Mr. Peskin is a professor emeritus of history at Cleveland State University and author of Garfield: A Biography *(1978) and* Winfield Scott and the Profession of Arms *(2003), both published by Kent State University Press.*

21.
CHESTER ALAN ARTHUR

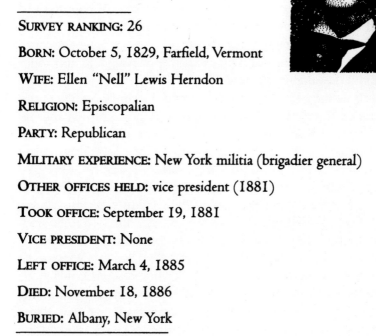

SURVEY RANKING: 26

BORN: October 5, 1829, Farfield, Vermont

WIFE: Ellen "Nell" Lewis Herndon

RELIGION: Episcopalian

PARTY: Republican

MILITARY EXPERIENCE: New York militia (brigadier general)

OTHER OFFICES HELD: vice president (1881)

TOOK OFFICE: September 19, 1881

VICE PRESIDENT: None

LEFT OFFICE: March 4, 1885

DIED: November 18, 1886

BURIED: Albany, New York

by John J. DiIulio, Jr.

Chester A. Arthur is one of our most underrated presidents. As every schoolchild once knew, Arthur is the rotund, whiskered man who became America's twenty-first president in 1881 when President Garfield, after barely four months in office, was assassinated. As depicted by many historians, Arthur is the undistinguished intellect and wealthy onetime Republican Party hack who just happened to be in office in 1883 when Congress passed the Pendleton Act, which laid the foundations for the federal civil service system. According to many presidential studies scholars, he initiated little important legislation and was a weak political leader.

On the contrary, Arthur was the ideal chief executive for an age when the presidency was still regarded primarily as an administrative branch. In addition to the Pendleton Act, he fought many highly consequential legislative battles and put several previously neglected issues on the national political agenda. Throughout his public career, he often demonstrated great moral character, love of country, and personal courage. He himself is partly to blame for how his presidency has been misremembered. Before leaving office, he destroyed his personal papers. But that is no excuse for denying him his proper place in the presidential pantheon.

Arthur's father, a Baptist minister, moved the family from Vermont and founded the New York Anti-Slavery Society. A chip off the old block, Chester became an outspoken abolitionist lawyer and campaigned for Abraham Lincoln in 1860. During the Civil War he served as quartermaster general of New York. After the war, he supported Ulysses S. Grant for president. In 1871 he was rewarded with a post as collector of the Port of New York. While Arthur was campaigning with Garfield in 1880, his wife became ill and died. Though grief-stricken, he pressed on, won election, and became vice president.

Arthur emerged politically from the so-called Stalwart Wing of the Republican Party. Led by New York's U.S. Senator Roscoe Conkling, the Stalwarts were for punishing the South, electing Grant, and preserving patronage. Arthur had been every inch a Conkling-Grant man during his days at the port. He embraced the Jacksonian justification for the spoils system as intrinsic to effective democratic governance. While insisting on honest administration, he continued the practice of using New York's Customhouse as a patronage haven. In 1878, President Rutherford B. Hayes, a Stalwart opponent, had Arthur ousted from the post. In 1880, the Stalwarts fought to have President Grant renominated but failed, accepting Vice President Arthur as their consolation prize. Thus, when Garfield proposed anti-patronage measures, Arthur predictably sided instead with Conkling and the Stalwarts.

This history explains the infamous declaration Garfield's killer, a mentally deranged man named Charles J. Guiteau, made as he fired the fatal shot: "I am a Stalwart, and Arthur is president now." These words might well have assassinated Arthur's reputation. But the "Gentleman Boss," as critics had dubbed him, mourned Garfield's death and reconsidered the case for curtailing federal patronage.

Garfield's murder made at least token patronage-busting reforms politically unavoidable. But Arthur did not simply mouth pro-reform rhetoric. Rather, once he concluded that a federal civil service system was in the public interest, he openly courted the Stalwarts' wrath by appointing only a few of them to plum posts at the Treasury Department and elsewhere, and completing the Garfield-initiated investigation into Post Office corruption. Most to his credit, he put his presidency fully behind the Pendleton Act, including the famous fifth "conditions of good administration" provision declaring flatly "that no person in public service is for that reason under any obligations to contribute to any political fund, or render any political service, and that he will not be removed or otherwise prejudiced for refusing to do so."

Thanks to Arthur's zeal as a convert to the cause, the Pendleton Act institutionalized the appointment of career officials on the basis of merit. It happened not a moment too soon. During the Jackson administration, federal personnel rolls rose to nearly twenty thousand. By the time Arthur signed the Act in 1883, federal workers numbered more than 130,000 and counting. The Pendleton Act was the house that Arthur built, and each subsequent law governing federal public administration—especially the Classification Acts of 1923 and 1949, the 1978 Civil Service Reform Act, and the 1993 Government Performance and Results Act—filled another of its rooms.

Today the federal government has some two million nonmilitary employees, plus more than 10 million people who, though they work for state and local governments, for-profit companies or nonprofit organizations, administer federal programs and depend for their salaries entirely or partly on Washington. This post-1950 government-by-proxy system is no more perfect than the pre-Pendleton government-by-patronage arrangement was. Still, whether we are talking about completing the Interstate Highway System or putting a man on the moon, fighting wars abroad or financing health care at home, delivering the mail or administering college loans—whatever the task—the federal civil service system, warts, waste, and all, has normally succeeded in translating democratically enacted laws into administrative action, and done so in ways that, for all the complaints about "federal bureaucracy," have generally satisfied the public.

We should also salute Arthur as Father of the U.S. Navy. He urged Congress to provide the funding necessary to transform the nation's nineteenth-century wooden ship navy into a twentieth-century steel ship navy. In addition, he championed better treatment for American Indians and opposed virulently anti-Chinese immigration policies. When the U.S. Supreme Court declared the 1875 Civil Rights Act unconstitutional, he called for legislative countermeasures to protect black Americans against discrimination. In foreign affairs, he advocated free ("reciprocal") trade despite diplomatic barriers (courtesy Germany) and divided-party tariff politics (courtesy Southern Democrats).

Shortly after assuming the presidency, Arthur became ill. He suffered from Bright's disease, an incurable kidney disorder. His last official act was to order a pension for a destitute and dying U. S. Grant. In 1884 he made a halfhearted run at renomination, but the Republicans united behind James G. Blaine. Arthur died in 1886. It is time that we remember Arthur and his presidency more kindly.

Mr. DiIulio is Fox Professor of Political Science at the University of Pennsylvania and a senior fellow at the Brookings Institution. In 2001, he served as director of the White House Office of Faith-Based and Community Initiatives. With James Q. Wilson, he is co-author of American Government: Institutions and Policies, ninth edition *(Houghton-Mifflin, 2003).*

22. & 24.
STEPHEN GROVER CLEVELAND

SURVEY RANKING: 12

BORN: March 18, 1837, Caldwell, New Jersey

WIFE: Frances Folsom

RELIGION: Presbyterian

PARTY: Democrat

MILITARY EXPERIENCE: None

OTHER OFFICES HELD: Mayor of Buffalo, New York (1882), New York governor (1883–85)

TOOK OFFICE: March 4, 1885; March 4, 1893

VICE PRESIDENTS: Thomas Hendricks (1885), Adlai Stevenson (1893–97)

LEFT OFFICE: March 4, 1889; March 4, 1897

DIED: June 24, 1908

BURIED: Princeton, New Jersey

---

by Suzanne Garment

The present-day obscurity of Grover Cleveland is instructive. Cleveland's biographers agree that he was a man of exemplary character. His widely acknowledged honesty enabled him to survive a salacious scandal that threatened to engulf him during his first campaign for president. But during Cleveland's two nonconsecutive terms in the White House, spanning the years 1885 to 1897, the country was transforming itself. At the beginning of Cleveland's first term, national politics focused on tariffs, government reform, and the Civil War legacy of sectional bitterness. By the end of his second term, the country was facing depression, agricultural discontent, and labor violence. Cleveland's straightforward virtues did not equip him to ride the historic tides. Indeed, in the wake of the upheavals his type of virtue lost much of its political salience.

Cleveland began practicing law and Democratic Party politics in Buffalo, New York, a rough-edged city that helped shape his style and habits. While working in Buffalo, the unmarried Cleveland frequented saloons, played cards, and developed the eating habits that quickly made him a man of three hundred pounds. During the same years Cleveland displayed his rigorous moral scruples. As sheriff of Erie County, he was so troubled by the murder trial of one of his jail inmates that he personally addressed the jury concerning the defendant's mental instability. When the jury nevertheless convicted the man, Cleveland, breaking with the practice of delegating the unpleasant job of hanging, performed the task himself.

After Cleveland became mayor of Buffalo in 1882, he worked prodigious hours and acquired the nickname "Mayor Veto" for his exercise of the power in behalf of fiscal stringency. Just a year after becoming mayor, Cleveland was elected governor of New York; he continued the long hours and the abundant vetoes. In the governorship Cleveland campaigned for civil service reform, with the help of the young Republican assemblyman Theodore Roosevelt. During these years both Cleveland and Roosevelt acquired an enthusiastic following in the press.

In 1884, continuing his rapid rise, Cleveland ran for president on a platform that favored low tariffs, reform, and attention to the problems of labor but opposed the increased coinage of silver. It was during this campaign, in July 1884, that an anti-Democratic newspaper in Buffalo broke the story of Maria Halpin.

Cleveland had known Halpin in Buffalo. So, evidently, had some of Cleveland's friends. In 1874 Halpin gave birth to a son and named Cleveland as the father. Cleveland agreed to provide financial support for the boy. It has been suggested that he did so because the other possible fathers were married men.

This was not the end of the story. Soon after the boy's birth, Halpin was said to have begun drinking heavily and showing signs of emotional illness. A Buffalo judge—who was a friend of Cleveland's but, we are told, did not consult him—had her temporarily committed to a mental hospital and placed the boy in an orphanage. Cleveland agreed to give Halpin money to start a business in a nearby town, apart from the boy. But she changed her mind, sought to regain custody, and even attempted to kidnap him. In response, the judge permanently revoked her parental rights. The boy was subsequently adopted by a prominent local family, and Cleveland was freed of his support obligations.

The version of the story that erupted in July 1884 did not focus on the postpartum fate of Maria Halpin, who was nowhere to be found. Instead, the story made the out-of-wedlock child into a symbol of Cleveland's general licentiousness, alleging that he had maintained a virtual harem in Buffalo. Cleveland's friends, including Buffalo Republicans, were able to demonstrate the manifest untruth of this picture. As for Cleveland's relationship with Halpin and his support of the boy, the candidate made no attempt to deny the facts.

Winning the presidency despite the scandal, Cleveland became the first Democrat to occupy the White House since the Civil War. He remained as scrupulous as ever: When one of his admirers sent the president-elect a Newfoundland retriever as a gift, Cleveland returned it.

In office, Cleveland continued his habits of hard work and his efforts at civil service reform. He spoke publicly of the "discontent of the unemployed," which he ascribed to the "grasping and heedless exactions of employers," and he proposed federal arbitration of labor disputes. At the same time, he vetoed a bill to subsidize Texas farmers hit by drought, explaining, "Though the people support the Government, the Government should not support the people."

The Democrats lost the presidency in 1888 but regained it in 1892. Cleveland took office and quickly faced a crisis: the widespread apprehension that the United States was about to abandon the gold standard. The administration attempted to allay such fears, but the terms of reassurance were not strong enough. The apprehension turned into full-scale financial panic, then economic depression. Cleveland's party had been split on the question of the gold standard, but increasing numbers of his fellow Democrats now fled from Cleveland's pro-gold position.

In 1892, candidate Cleveland had expressed outrage about the violence with which Henry Clay Frick broke the Homestead strike. But the depression placed President Cleveland in a different position. One product of the depression was Coxey's Army, which marched to Washington to demand paper money and public works. By the time the army arrived in Washington, it numbered fewer than five hundred people. But Secret Service agents trailed the protesters on orders from the attorney general, who in turn had received orders from the president. As the marchers approached the Capitol, police arrested them for the misdemeanor of walking on the grass. In some cases, demonstrators were clubbed. Cleveland was also forced to cope with the riots and mail stoppages in Chicago that accompanied the Pullman strike of 1894. In response to the disruptions, without consulting the governor of Illinois, Cleveland put Chicago under martial law.

In 1894, in the last state and congressional elections before Cleveland left office, his party suffered a large number of electoral defeats, in part because of the successes of the new Populist Party. A few years later President Theodore Roosevelt, whose virtues were considerably more complicated than Cleveland's, would begin to display a correspondingly greater ability to master the new political forces, which mark our own time and which make Cleveland's era and character seem so distant.

Today we remember Cleveland mainly for a scandal that cast aspersions on his character. In truth, however, it is his good character that places him in the upper ranks of presidents. What keeps him from ranking still higher is not any lack of virtues on his part but that he faced an emerging politics to which such virtues did not, for better or worse, seem relevant.

Ms. Garment practices tax law at Weil, Gotshal & Manges in New York.

23.

BENJAMIN HARRISON

SURVEY RANKING: 30

BORN: August 20, 1833, North Bend, Ohio

WIVES: Caroline Scott (died 1892), Mary Scott Lord Dimmick (married 1896)

RELIGION: Presbyterian

PARTY: Republican

MILITARY EXPERIENCE: U.S. Army (brigadier general)

OTHER OFFICES HELD: U.S. senator from Indiana (1881–87)

TOOK OFFICE: March 4, 1889

VICE PRESIDENT: Levi Morton

LEFT OFFICE: March 4, 1893

DIED: March 13, 1901

BURIED: Indianapolis, Indiana

by Jessica King

Representative John Scott Harrison, an Ohio Whig, was the only man in American history to have been both the son of a president (William Henry Harrison) and the father of one. When the congressman wrote his son in the 1850s that "only knaves ever enter the political arena" and that he should steer clear of the newly created Republican Party, Benjamin Harrison might have done well to listen. For while he had gained recognition and some wealth as an Indiana lawyer, he proved to be decidedly second-rate in the White House.

Harrison's disregard of his father's advice is certainly understandable. His pedigree simply propelled him toward service. How could young Ben, namesake of a Virginia governor who signed the Declaration of Independence, grandson of the ninth president, son of a congressman, stay out of the public sphere?

Harrison moved to Indianapolis from Ohio after he was admitted to the bar in 1854. The Indiana capital was a friendly town for Harrison and his wife, Caroline. His name was known, since decades earlier William Henry Harrison had been Indiana's first territorial governor. One year after arriving in Indianapolis, he entered into a partnership with William Wallace, and the two future generals specialized initially in collection cases. His legal career flourished, as did his political one. He successfully ran for city attorney and twice served as reporter of the state Supreme Court.

At the outbreak of the Civil War, Harrison led the 70th Indiana Regiment, and his successes not only brought him home a war hero, but also earned him the rank of brigadier general. Though he poured himself into study of tactics and maneuvers during the war with the same gusto as when he had studied law, he was not a soldier at heart. Returning with fervor to his practice and his politics, he ran unsuccessfully for governor before the legislature chose him as a U.S. senator. His time in battle had helped to shape his views, and as a senator he advocated civil rights for blacks and championed the Grand Army of the Republic, criticizing President Cleveland's veterans' pension bill vetoes.

Harrison lost his Senate reelection by one vote in the legislature, but that left him available to accept the 1888 Republican nomination for president. Continuing the reputation he had built in Congress as a strict protectionist, he resurrected many of his grandfather's famous campaign slogans and ran on the issue of high tariff, delivering his speeches to hundreds of thousands of visitors to his Indiana home. Come election day, Harrison trailed the incumbent, Cleveland, by 100,000 votes, but he carried the Electoral College

233–168. Republican boss Matt Quay and others played a vital role in the electoral turnout, Quay remarking after the election "how close a number of men were compelled to approach . . . the penitentiary to make [Harrison] President."

Harrison was loath to take part in the spoils system of the day, making clear in his inaugural address that his administration would hold its appointees to the highest standards of competence, irrespective of party loyalty. As the "centennial president"—elected almost exactly one hundred years after the official adoption of the Constitution in June 1788—he was compelled to draw attention to the enormous strides the country had made under that powerful document. He promised a "Legal Deal" and followed through with it, appointing six lawyers and two businessmen to his cabinet, and peppering his inaugural address with specific reference to the Constitution and to the rule of law.

During his tenure, six states entered the Union; international relations were strengthened, including the first Pan-American Conference and successful use of arbitration avoiding conflicts with Britain, Germany, Italy, and Chile; and four Supreme Court justices were appointed—conspicuously not among them William Howard Taft, who, at age thirty-two, had asked for the job. (He finally got it in 1921, when he was sixty-three.) Electric lights were installed at the White House; Mrs. Harrison was too frightened of the switches ever to turn them on. One major instance of cooperation between the executive and legislative branches inspired the moniker "Billion Dollar Congress," as Harrison's proposal to increase the power of the navy and support the construction of steamship lines induced the first billion-dollar peacetime appropriation.

Typically, Congress followed its own agenda, especially after Democrats took control of the House after the 1890 election. Among the notable events of the day were the Sherman Antitrust Act, the Sherman Silver Purchase Act, and the McKinley Tariff, which imposed prohibitively high duties on imports. While Harrison favored high protective tariffs and lobbied for the silver purchase, his involvement in these, and indeed in most of Congress's affairs, was limited.

Addressing Congress in 1892, Harrison said, "There never has been a time in our history when work was so abundant or when wages were as high, whether measured by the currency in which they are paid or by their power to supply the necessaries and comforts of life." Less than a year later, the economy fell into the second worst depression in American history, likely due in part to the unexpected negative effects of both the silver purchase and the McKinley Tariff. The country, of course, blamed Harrison. The Republican bosses and Harrison himself devoted little attention to his bid for reelection; Harrison's wife had died shortly before in the White House, and the party leaders were displeased with Harrison generally.

Upon losing reelection to the man he himself had ousted four years earlier, Harrison remarked that he felt as though he had been released from prison. Grover Cleveland reclaimed office, this time winning a wide margin in both the popular vote and the Electoral College. Harrison returned to his forte, practicing law, with more success than ever. He was able to demand a $500 minimum retainer for services and was extremely selective in the cases he chose to grace with an appearance in court. One such case made him one of only three ex-presidents to argue before the Supreme Court.

Except for trivia, there is little to remember about the presidency of Benjamin Harrison. Take away from him the status as only grandson of a president, the only president from Indiana, the last president until the end of the twentieth century to win without a popular vote plurality, and his wife's erecting the first White House Christmas tree, and the presidential file becomes pretty thin. Circumstance afforded him the opportunity to be neither great nor terrible, leaving him, as all surveys say, mired in mediocrity.

At his death, just after the turn of the century, he was known as a better man, and certainly a better lawyer, than president. The *London Standard* noted that while Benjamin Harrison did not "leave a great mark on the history of his country," he was a man of high personal character.

Ms. King is a member of The University of Virginia Law School's Class of 2007.

25.

WILLIAM McKINLEY

SURVEY RANKING: 14

BORN: January 29, 1843, Niles, Ohio

WIFE: Ida Saxton

RELIGION: Methodist

PARTY: Republican

MILITARY EXPERIENCE: U.S. Army (brevet major)

OTHER OFFICES HELD: U.S. representative from Ohio (1877–84, 1885–91), governor (1892–96)

TOOK OFFICE: March 4, 1897

VICE PRESIDENTS: Garret Hobart (1897–99), Theodore Roosevelt (1901)

DIED IN OFFICE: September 14, 1901 (assassinated)

BURIED: Canton, Ohio

by Fred Barnes

William McKinley was a nineteenth-century man but a twentieth-century president. He was stout and unglamorous, a serious Methodist whose idea of a party was to gather with friends and read Bible passages aloud. His only vices were a passion for cigars and, though he once delivered speeches to temperance groups, an occasional taste for a glass of wine. His athletic regimen consisted of a daily half-mile walk. He was a nonreader who believed he learned more from conversation than from books. He was even-tempered, cordial, and patient—in a word, nice. A rare flash of anger by McKinley was provoked by an Ohio politician who told a dirty joke. "I wish that fellow would stay away from here," he said.

Unexciting, old-fashioned, charming in a dignified way, McKinley was nonetheless the dominant political personality of his time. Yet historians have largely neglected him. True, he lacked the exuberance and charisma of Theodore Roosevelt or the driving idealism of Woodrow Wilson. But more than either of them or Franklin Roosevelt, he invented the modern presidency. After more than three decades of congressional supremacy, McKinley changed the balance of power in Washington to favor the White House. He, not Teddy Roosevelt, created the bully pulpit on his frequent speaking tours across the country. He dealt professionally with the press, even providing reporters with prompt transcripts of speeches. Most important, McKinley guided the country into a new role as a major power in the world. He was America's most underrated president.

What's also striking about McKinley is that he avoided the personal and political excesses that have gotten so many presidents and often the country in trouble. He was a partisan Republican with real political enemies, but he never drifted into the paranoia of Richard Nixon or the conspiracy mongering of Bill Clinton. Unlike TR, neither his presidency nor his political career was essentially an ego trip. Presidential power grew under McKinley, for sure, and so did the size of the federal government. But his aggrandizing impulse was nothing like that of FDR or Lyndon Johnson. A conservative in temperament and ideology, he was flexible and deft in his political maneuvering. Thus he succeeded where a brainier but inflexible president like Wilson failed. His private life was mostly devoted to caring for his invalid wife, Ida, who had epilepsy. McKinley had no mistresses.

There are two main raps on McKinley: that he was a tool of Mark Hanna, the Cleveland industrialist and political mastermind, and that he was indecisive during the critical months before and after the Spanish-American War. Both are untrue.

Hanna once commented that while he and McKinley were Scotch-Irish, McKinley got the Scotch, he the Irish. Hanna played a significant role in plotting McKinley's election as president in 1896, particularly as chief fund-raiser and organizer of his campaign for the Republican presidential nomination. As top adviser, he was as important to McKinley's success as Hamilton Jordan was to Jimmy Carter's in 1976 and Karl Rove to George W. Bush's in 2000. And like Jordan and Rove, he was always the subordinate.

Hanna met McKinley in the mid-1870s shortly after McKinley, then a young lawyer in Canton, Ohio, defended coal miners in a strike that turned violent when strikebreakers appeared. Hanna was one of the mine owners. McKinley's performance in court—only a single miner was convicted—left a strong impression on him. The pair became friends and found they agreed on the staples of the Republican agenda—high tariffs and the gold standard. And they shared a vision of an inclusive Republican Party that was attractive to the business class and laborers, and to farmers and every ethnic group but the Irish, who were incorrigible Democrats.

McKinley was elected to the House in 1876 without Hanna's aid and rose to chairman of the Ways and Means Committee. But it was Hanna who managed his successful campaign for governor of Ohio in 1891 and organized the boom that led to McKinley's election as president five years later. Newspaper cartoonists pictured Hanna as a sinister manipulator of McKinley, and the notion caught on. Still, as clever a political operative as Hanna was, McKinley would probably have won both races without his help. What mattered in the end was their intuition that Republicans could be the party of the common man. The Republican sweep of 1894 followed by McKinley's presidency vindicated that view and ushered in three decades of Republican hegemony.

Once McKinley was in the White House, Hanna's influence waned. In fact, influence worked the other way. McKinley had to intercede with the Ohio legislature to get Hanna elected to the U.S. Senate in 1897. The popular notion that Hanna handled patronage for McKinley was false. Together in Washington, they often disagreed. McKinley rebuffed Hanna when he asked for a halt in legal proceedings against a longtime Hanna friend caught up in a postal scandal in

Cuba. And though Hanna bitterly opposed Teddy Roosevelt as McKinley's running mate in 1900, McKinley blithely let TR on the ticket.

McKinley had no experience in foreign relations, concentrating on domestic issues in his presidential drive. But trouble with Spain, unresolved by his predecessor, Grover Cleveland, became the consuming issue of the McKinley presidency. The focus was Cuba, a colony of Spain. Cleveland had been faintly pro-Spanish, but public opinion in America, not just the yellow press of William Randolph Hearst and Joseph Pulitzer, ran strongly in favor of Cubans who rebelled against Spain's oppressive rule. Ignoring the Cuban crisis was not an option.

McKinley, a Civil War veteran, was wary of war. He told a general: "I shall never get into a war until I am sure that God and man approve. I have been through one war. I have seen the dead piled up. And I do not want to see another." He patiently pursued diplomacy to avoid war with Spain, proposing at one point to purchase Cuba. McKinley was deliberate, not indecisive. Spain, like Saddam Hussein in Iraq a century later, procrastinated and refused to follow through on promised concessions. When the American battleship *Maine* blew up in Havana harbor, though probably not on Spanish orders, war was all but unavoidable.

America won quickly, first by destroying the Spanish fleet in the Philippines, then by capturing Cuba. Peace negotiations were tricky. Spain was willing to give up Cuba and Puerto Rico but sought to save face by retaining the Philippines. McKinley played along, appearing to dither on whether to acquire the Pacific archipelago. Actually he had decided from the first naval victory in Manila to acquire the Philippines, but it would have been counterproductive to say so. He let the peace talks progress to the point where American acquisition was the only logical outcome. His view was simple: America was a force for good in the world, and the Philippines would fall into less benign (possibly German) hands should the U.S. fail to step in. All Spain got was a $20 million indemnity.

The war transformed the presidency into the center of power in Washington. McKinley was a hands-on commander in chief; he won congressional approval of two war resolutions that ballooned his authority and ratification of a treaty that confirmed the president's paramount position. The role of Congress was minimized in foreign affairs. McKinley kept in close contact by telegraph with his field commanders. He wired a general who wanted to let the Spaniards retreat with their weapons and without a fight: "What you went to Santiago for was the Spanish army. If you allow it to evacuate with its arms you must meet it somewhere later. This is not war." The commander complied.

Yet while war allowed McKinley to expand presidential power, as it had for Abraham Lincoln, this time there was a difference. Because McKinley enlarged the office in ways besides fighting a war, the result was a permanently broadened role for the president. McKinley traveled more than a president ever had, barnstorming from state to state to promote Republican candidates in the 1898 congressional election. His speaking tours exploited what TR later called the bully pulpit. McKinley lobbied Congress, often using the telephone. He made the White House a "major news center" for the press, according to historian Lewis Gould.

A little-known legacy of McKinley is the so-called special relationship between the United States and Britain. The English were in bad odor after having sympathized with the South in the Civil War. But McKinley saw them as logical allies in the emerging world order and sought to erase old irritants between the two countries. The British supported American power around the world as a counter to Germany, and they were pro-American in the war with Spain. McKinley reciprocated by rejecting aid to the popular Boer cause against Britain. When a Boer delegation visited McKinley, he insisted on talking about the view of Washington from his window. The Boers correctly concluded he was pro-British.

A measure of success in Washington for a political figure— Congress, White House, cabinet—is whether he has "grown" in office. This usually means becoming more liberal, worldly, and cynical. More than most presidents, McKinley grew, but not in that way. He had never traveled outside the U.S. and had little interest in foreign affairs when he arrived at the White House. But he soon realized America should not remain a backwater and he skillfully fostered the transition to world power.

As a congressman, McKinley believed tariffs were the key to prosperity. But as America grew more productive he moved to open overseas markets by promoting "reciprocity"—lower tariffs—with trading
partners. His speech in Buffalo on September 5, 1901, made that
point forcefully. In a receiving line the day after the address, he was
shot by an anarchist; he died eight days later. His final words were a
whispered verse from the hymn "Nearer My God to Thee." In office,
McKinley had grown into the model of a twentieth-century president. But at heart, in character and temperament, he remained a
nineteenth-century man.

Mr. Barnes is executive editor of The Weekly Standard.

26.
THEODORE ROOSEVELT

SURVEY RANKING: 5

BORN: October 27, 1858, New York City

WIVES: Alice Hathaway Lee (died 1884),
Edith Kermit Carow (married 1886)

RELIGION: Dutch Reformed

PARTY: Republican

MILITARY EXPERIENCE: U.S. Army (colonel)

OTHER OFFICES HELD: New York state assemblyman (1882–84),
governor (1899–1901), vice president (1901)

TOOK OFFICE: September 14, 1901

VICE PRESIDENT: Charles Fairbanks (1905–09)

LEFT OFFICE: March 4, 1909

DIED: January 6, 1919

BURIED: Oyster Bay, New York

By John S. McCain

Theodore Roosevelt was only forty-two when an assassin's bullet ended the life and presidency of William McKinley and effected his succession to the office. By the standards of our age, with its longer average life expectancy and extended process of adult maturity, forty-two seems a shockingly young age for an American president. But by the time Theodore Roosevelt became president, he had lived a life so crowded with variety and activity and accomplishment that it would have exhausted most modern-day Americans long before our fortieth birthday.

He had been in turn: a brash, young reformer in the New York State Assembly; a rough-riding frontier rancher; an unsuccessful New York City mayoral candidate; a progressive U.S. Civil Service commissioner; a crusading police commissioner; a whirlwind of a navy assistant secretary who argued, schemed, and prepared for war with Spain; a nationally celebrated military hero of the same war; governor of New York; and vice president of the United States. In his spare time he became a respected amateur natural historian; the author of twelve books covering a wide range of subjects (he would write another twenty-three over the course of his life); a husband, widower, and husband again, and the devoted father of six children. Then he invented the modern presidency.

"Black care," he wrote, using a colorful term for fate, "rarely sits behind the rider whose pace is fast enough." For most of Roosevelt's life, black care never stood a chance. He was an astonishingly industrious man.

He could be impetuous, intemperate, egotistical, and entirely too self-confident. He personalized political differences, attributing all manner of base motives to his opponents. They were all cowards or scoundrels. His public virtues were a little short on compassion, empathy, and patience. He could sentimentalize war to an absurd extent. But he was incorruptible, courageous, resolute, just, and visionary. He believed that the moral obligations that concerned individuals concerned government as well, and nourished the soul of a great nation.

For all his varied interests, national greatness was the dominant concern of his life. "A mere life of ease is not a very satisfactory life" for individuals or for nations, he preached in his famous speech, "The Strenuous Life." It corrupts governments as insidiously as it corrupts men and "ultimately unfits those who follow it for serious work in the world." It was his personal code of conduct and governing philosophy.

Roosevelt's patriotism professed a faith in America's pioneer ethos, the virtues that had won the West and inspired Americans to believe in ourselves as the New Jerusalem, bound by sacred duty to suffer hardship and risk danger to protect the values of our civilization and impart them to humanity. "We cannot sit huddled within our own borders," he warned, "and avow ourselves merely an assemblage of well-to-do hucksters who care nothing for what happens beyond."

His "intense and fervid Americanism" celebrated neither tribal identity nor sentimental attachment to the land. It decried base materialism because it tempted people to indolence and greed and "sapped the hardy virtues of a nation." He denounced both "hyphenated Americanism," and "know-nothingism . . . as utterly un-American as foreignism." He abhorred the multiculturalist's adulation of diversity as more important than national unity. He insisted that every American owed primary allegiance to American political ideals and to the symbols, habits, and consciousness of American citizenship. He believed such patriotism didn't disparage the distinctions of experience in American history, but encompassed and transcended those experiences in a shared and noble endeavor of building a civilization for the ages, in which all people may share in the rights and responsibilities of freedom.

He spoke out against "the spirit of provincial patriotism" that aggrandized the sentimental attachments people feel for their towns and states into something greater than their national pride. He warned that "the overexaltation of the little community at the expense of the great nation" had ruined many nations and had prevented the countries of South America from uniting in one great republic.

Were he alive today he would denounce both liberal and conservative extremes, for the former's emphasis on wants and the latter's emphasis on rights, and for their mutual disregard for the duties inherent in American citizenship. "We have duties to others and duties to ourselves," he avowed, "and we can shirk neither." The Roosevelt code gave equal respect to self-interest and common purpose, to rights and duties.

"When I left college," he wrote, "I had no strong governmental convictions beyond the very strong and vital conviction that we were a nation and must act nationally." It's fair to say he never had another conviction that strong and vital.

His was the most important presidency since Lincoln's. He liberally interpreted the constitutional authority of the office to redress the imbalance of power between the executive and legislative branches that had tilted decisively toward Congress in the half century after the Civil War. He fought party bosses who valued political privileges more than just government. He wrenched reforms from legislators who thought their power to award patronage positions was the purpose of elective office.

He called for the elimination of corporate campaign contributions because he knew they influenced elected officials to favor the wealthy few at the expense of the less advantaged many. He distrusted leading financiers of his day, who put profit before patriotism. He sued to break up railroad trusts, invested the Interstate Commerce Commission with the power to set rates, and mediated disputes between capital and labor. He investigated the notoriously unsanitary meatpacking industry, and with the enactment of the Pure Food and Drug Act, he placed public health before industry profits.

He fought the spirit of "unrestricted individualism" that claimed the right "to injure the future of all of us for his own temporary and immediate profit." Over the course of his presidency, he took 230 million acres of land into public trust, creating scores of national parks, forests, and monuments.

But he was not a radical reformer. He sought not to destroy the great wealth-creating institutions of capitalism, but to save them from their own excesses. He proposed sensible and incremental regulations on commerce. Neither was he a zealot who disdained the compromises essential to lawmaking. That was no better than muckraking in his estimation. He wanted to get things done.

He was a fighting man. But for all his natural belligerence, and aggressive statesmanship, he was always intent on the elevation of his country. He threatened war over the German kaiser's designs on Venezuela and issued a corollary to the Monroe Doctrine that reserved to the United States the right to intervene militarily in Latin American countries where disorder might attract the interest of other great powers. He helped foment insurrection in Panama so that he could acquire the route for his isthmian canal. He built a navy second only to Britain's, the supreme naval power of the era. He sought to preserve peace by confronting potential adversaries with America's resolve and readiness to protect its interests.

But he was also a deft and subtle diplomat. He kept Germany from invading Venezuela, mediated the Russo-Japanese War, and helped resolve a brewing European conflict over Morocco. His accomplished diplomacy contributed as much to America's growing world influence as did his expansion and projection of military power and his unilateral assumption of international rights and responsibilities.

Many politicians, in his age and ours, tend to be preoccupied with extending their own power. Self-aggrandizement is part of human nature, and Roosevelt was not beyond its temptation. He gave up the presidency at the end of his second term, but wanted it back four years later for personal as well as public reasons. Yet the very thought that he would seek high office for purposes more self-serving than patriotic deeply offended both his idea of citizenship and his self-esteem. However much he craved the limelight, however great his personal ambitions, he could not satisfy his ego unless he served the higher purpose of his nation's greatness. And that deeply personal, almost spiritual sense of patriotism made the man as great as his accomplishments.

He understood the central fact of American history: that we are not just an association of disparate interests forced by law and custom to tolerate one another, but a kinship of ideals, worth living and dying for, and that we deserve to have our ideals vigorously represented at home and abroad by our national government. He believed that people who are free to act in their own interests and are served by a government that kindles the pride of every citizen would perceive their interests in an enlightened way. We would live as one nation, at the summit of history, "the mightiest republic on which the sun ever shone."

Mr. McCain, a U.S. senator from Arizona, was a candidate for the Republican presidential nomination in 2000. He is author, with Mark Salter, of Worth the Fighting For: A Memoir *(Random House, 2002), from which portions of this essay are adapted.*

27.
WILLIAM HOWARD TAFT

SURVEY RANKING: 20

BORN: September 15, 1857, Cincinnati,
Ohio

WIFE: Helen Herron

RELIGION: Unitarian

PARTY: Republican

MILITARY EXPERIENCE: None

OTHER OFFICES HELD: U.S. solicitor general (1890–92), federal
appeals judge (1892–1900), governor of the Philippines
(1900–04), U.S. secretary of war (1904–08),
chief justice of the United States (1921–30)

TOOK OFFICE: March 4, 1909

VICE PRESIDENT: James Sherman (1909–12)

LEFT OFFICE: March 4, 1913

DIED: March 8, 1930

BURIED: Arlington, Virginia

by Theodore B. Olson

Few presidents have enjoyed careers as wide-ranging and distinguished as William Howard Taft's. At the time President Benjamin

WILLIAM HOWARD TAFT 131

Harrison made him the sixth solicitor general of the United States in 1890, he was only thirty-two years old. He had already graduated second in his class at Yale in 1878, received his law degree two years later from the University of Cincinnati, and distinguished himself as prosecutor, tax collector, private lawyer, and judge.

After serving as solicitor general for two years (and, according to a leading biographer, winning sixteen of the eighteen cases he argued on behalf of the United States), Taft went on to serve as a judge on the U.S. Court of Appeals for the Sixth Circuit, as the dean of the school where he earned his law degree, as president of the U.S. Philippines Commission, as the first civil governor of the Philippines, and as Theodore Roosevelt's secretary of war. In 1908 he was elected the twenty-seventh president of the United States.

Four years later, when TR's third party candidacy derailed his bid for reelection, he became Kent Professor of Law at Yale. Later he was elected president of the American Bar Association, and he served as joint chairman of the War Labor Board during Woodrow Wilson's presidency. In 1921, President Harding appointed him chief justice of the United States; he left the bench only a few weeks before he succumbed to heart disease in 1930.

Perhaps Taft's most admirable and effective leadership quality, evident throughout his long and fruitful career, was his judicial temperament. He much preferred law to politics, for, his renowned girth notwithstanding, he naturally embodied the restraint and moderation that ideally animate the former. His mindfulness of constitutional constraints was evident in his passionate public disagreement with Roosevelt over the latter's aggressive assertions of executive power. As his subsequent service on the Supreme Court confirmed, Taft certainly believed in a strong presidency. But he was greatly concerned about the prospect of stretching presidential powers beyond constitutional limits. He thus commented that Roosevelt "ought more often to have admitted the legal way of reaching the same ends."

Taft agreed with much of Roosevelt's presidential agenda, especially in the areas of regulation of industry and natural resource conservation, but he questioned the constitutionality of Roosevelt's methods. "The administration of President Roosevelt, like a great crusade, awakened the people of the United States, and accomplished great advances in the . . . powers of the Federal Government," he wrote. He further noted, however, that "we have a government of limited power under the Constitution, and we have got to work out our problems on the basis of law."

Though Roosevelt's presidential ambitions for 1912 and related public criticism of Taft caused Taft great stress and deep personal hurt, he declined to respond by rebuking his former mentor. He broke his silence only when Roosevelt began attacking the Supreme Court in public pronouncements, asserting the right of the public to override its decisions through direct balloting. Taft viewed himself as defending the constitutional balance, and he branded Roosevelt a dangerous, Constitution-flouting extremist. "I have got to win, not for myself, but to prevent this attack on the independence of the judiciary and to prevent the triumph of [a] dangerous demagogue."

Taft's concerns about the proper balance of power among the branches of the national government proved unpersuasive during the progressive political ferment of his time. And his disdain for politics limited his effectiveness in executing his responsibilities as president. "Politics, when I am in it, makes me sick," he had written to his wife in 1906, and he would feel no different with the passage of time. Upon winning the presidency by a landslide, he wrote, "If I were now presiding in the Supreme Court . . . I should feel entirely at home, but [here] I feel just a bit like a fish out of water." Lacking charisma, innovator's impulse, fighter's mentality, concern for his public reputation, and political savvy to function as an effective leader in the greatest of political arenas, he could not prevail in the factional quarrel that ended his presidency after one term.

One telling episode during Taft's presidency revealed where his natural leadership talents lay. It involved what at the time he must have considered to be a pressing issue over the meaning of the term "whiskey." The secretary of agriculture had designated certain products as "whiskey," thereby rendering them subject to federal taxation. The distillers complained so much that President Taft referred the matter to his solicitor general, Lloyd Bowers, for a legal opinion. "After hearing testimony that fills 2,365 pages, '[a] voluminous mass of documentary evidence,' and extensive briefs and argument by multiple counsel, Solicitor General Bowers entered a detailed and lengthy report" defining precisely which products could properly be characterized as "whiskey, and which could not," wrote Solicitor General Seth Waxman in 1998.

The distillers were so displeased that they appealed directly to the president. Taft decided that the meaning of "whiskey" was of sufficient importance that he personally conducted an additional and lengthy hearing at the White House. Much to the distillers' disappointment, he adopted an even broader definition of "whiskey" than had his solicitor general, and he directed that the regulatory agencies use his definition. By today's standards it is remarkable that the chief executive would spend so much of his own time and resources on an obscure legal dispute. Taft's exquisite, conscientious attention to detail in matters of fact finding, legal interpretation, and due process suggests why he proved so effective as an administrator and a judge, but less so as president.

Nevertheless, Taft managed to make significant contributions during his presidency. His administration in one term brought twice as many antitrust suits against large corporations as had Roosevelt's in two, and it did much to advance the cause of conservation. On his watch, the postal savings system and the parcel post were established, as was the Department of Labor. Arizona and New Mexico, the last of the forty-eight contiguous states, were admitted to the Union, and Congress passed the Sixteenth and Seventeenth amendments, providing for a federal income tax and the direct election of senators, and sent them to the states for ratification. Moreover, through the establishment of the first-ever executive budget, Taft significantly strengthened the position of the president vis-à-vis Congress. "[Mine was] a very humdrum, uninteresting administration," he once declared, "but . . . I think that . . . I can look back [with] some pleasure in having done something for the benefit of the public weal."

After losing the 1912 election, Taft found victory in defeat. He entered the most fulfilling period of his illustrious life, first as a law professor and then as chief justice. He remains the only president to have served on the Supreme Court, the position he regarded as his greatest honor. Looking back on his career, he remarked, "I don't remember that I ever was President." As chief justice, Taft was finally in a position where his judicial temperament was unambiguously an asset. He understood that a judge's role is to interpret, apply, and be bound by the law regardless of his personal views. He thus strictly enforced the Eighteenth Amendment and the Volstead Act despite his opposition to Prohibition. He remained faithful to his commitment to constitutional constraints even as he upheld strong executive power by sustaining the president's critical constitutional prerogative to remove executive appointees without the Senate's concurrence.

Just as Taft had exhibited sensitive and sympathetic statesmanship as an administrator years earlier in the Philippines, so he also made significant contributions to judicial administration as chief justice. Having joined a bitterly divided court, he brought harmony and increased efficiency to the justices' collective work. He effectively discouraged his brethren from writing dissenting opinions: 84 percent of the 1,554 full opinions announced by the Taft court during the 1921–28 terms were unanimous.

He persuaded Congress to replace the vast majority of mandatory appeals to the Supreme Court with the modern certiorari system, which provides the court with substantial control over its docket. That reform, more than any other, has resulted in the solicitor general's vital gatekeeping function in Supreme Court litigation. Because he decides whether to seek the Supreme Court's review in a broad range of cases involving the government, the solicitor general has a special responsibility—both to the court and to the executive branch—to seek such review only where appropriate, and to encourage the court to rely, at least to some extent, on his judgment regarding which cases are most deserving of the Supreme Court's consideration.

As solicitor general, president, and chief justice, William Howard Taft left each office stronger than he found it. Through his understated, restrained brand of leadership, he enhanced the authority of each of those important institutions during his service at their helm. And he did so while preserving our "government of limited power under the Constitution." It is for that service, most of all, that we should remember him.

Mr. Olson, a Washington lawyer, was solicitor general of the United States, 2001–04.

28.

THOMAS WOODROW WILSON

SURVEY RANKING: 11

BORN: December 28, 1856, Staunton, Virginia

WIVES: Ellen Axson (died 1914), Edith Bolling Galt (married 1915)

RELIGION: Presbyterian

PARTY: Democrat

MILITARY EXPERIENCE: None

OTHER OFFICES HELD: Governor of New Jersey (1911–13)

TOOK OFFICE: March 4, 1913

VICE PRESIDENT: Thomas Marshall

LEFT OFFICE: March 4, 1921

DIED: February 3, 1924

BURIED: Washington, D.C.

by Max Boot

Woodrow Wilson was a hard man to like. He was smart and some-times charming, but more often he was smug and supercilious. Like

Richard Nixon, he could force himself to be gregarious, but by nature he was a loner who trusted almost no one. He was not puritanical—in fact, he cheated on his first wife—but he was a devout Presbyterian whose pronouncements gave off a strong sniff of sanctimony.

The contrast with his great rival, Theodore Roosevelt, did not work to Wilson's advantage. Wilson himself said of Roosevelt, after their last meeting: "There is a sweetness about him that is very compelling. You can't resist the man." The acidulous Wilson was eminently resistible.

But it would be a mistake to ground historical judgment purely on personality. Some men with charm to burn, such as Bill Clinton, turn out to be poor presidents; whereas some unlovable characters, like Calvin Coolidge, do a surprisingly good job. Wilson's record in office was mixed: spectacular achievements in domestic policy, spectacular failures in foreign policy—and lasting influence in both spheres.

The first Southerner to win the White House since the Civil War, and the only president with a doctorate, Wilson was reared in Virginia as the son, grandson, and nephew of Presbyterian ministers. His family imparted in Wilson a strong faith, but also a relatively liberal one; Wilson would never be mistaken for a fundamentalist yodeler like William Jennings Bryan.

Wilson was a slow learner, leading modern biographers to suspect that he suffered from dyslexia. It may be that he was simply lazy. At the College of New Jersey, not yet known as Princeton University, he proved to be an indifferent student but a leader on campus.

After graduation in 1879, Wilson pursued the legal career his father had mapped out for him. But after a few years of legal drudgery, Wilson rebelled and entered Johns Hopkins graduate school to study politics. At twenty-eight, and in just his second year of graduate study, he published a book called *Congressional Government* that quickly became a classic. It was much praised for its insights into how the government worked, a remarkable feat given that Wilson had never visited the capital. *Congressional Government* was full of disdain for the traditionally limited powers of the presidency. Wilson preferred the English parliamentary model, in which a prime minister exercised greater sway. Few could have imagined that this young scholar eventually would get a chance to put his ideas into practice.

Wilson returned to Princeton, where he taught for twelve years and served as president for eight. In 1910 he was elected governor of New Jersey, running as a progressive advocating stronger government to cure society's ills. Just two years later, after forty-six ballots, the Democratic Party nominated him for president. In years past the prize was not worth having; Republicans had dominated national politics since the Civil War and had won the preceding four presidential elections by lopsided margins. But with the GOP split between William Howard Taft and Teddy Roosevelt, Wilson won the presidency with less than 42 percent of the vote by capturing the core Democratic constituencies: Southern conservatives and Northern and Western liberals.

Despite having only two years experience in government, Wilson grabbed the levers of power effectively. He instituted the first regular White House press conferences and ended the tradition of presidents not addressing Congress in person. His salesmanship won enactment of his New Freedom agenda: reducing tariffs, passing the Clayton Antitrust Act, creating the Federal Reserve to manage the monetary system, and setting up the Federal Trade Commission to check supposed business abuses. He also introduced the first income tax (1 percent on taxable incomes above $3,000), made possible by the ratification of the Sixteenth Amendment in 1913. This was not quite the welfare state, but Wilson did succeed in weaning the Democrats from their Jeffersonian origins—pro–states' rights, anti-Washington—and turning them into the big-government party.

He wrought an equally momentous transformation in foreign policy. Until then, the Democrats had been the isolationist party. Wilson, by contrast, was a liberal imperialist in the Teddy Roosevelt mode. He became the most interventionist president in U.S. history. He was especially active south of the border, where his goal was to "teach the South American republics to elect good men."

In 1914 he sent sailors and marines to occupy Veracruz, largely out of antipathy for General Victoriano Huerta, Mexico's bloodthirsty dictator. The occupation of Mexico's principal seaport did help to topple Huerta, though his successor wasn't much better. In 1915 Wilson occupied Haiti, where U.S. marines would stay for nineteen years. The next year, the marines moved into the Dominican Republic, which they would run for eight years. The motives behind these interventions were a complex mixture of idealism (instilling democracy) and realpolitik (ending disorder that might have served as an excuse for European intervention).

Wilson's next foray abroad had a simpler motive. In 1916, the Mexican rebel leader Pancho Villa raided a small town in New Mexico. Wilson sent General John J. Pershing with more than ten thousand men deep into Mexico in pursuit of the *pistoleros.* They never did catch the famous outlaw, and they almost sparked a war with Mexico.

By early 1917 Wilson was eager to pull U.S. troops out of Mexico. He had a bigger mission for them in Europe. During his first term, Wilson had tried to keep out of the Great War. He had even overlooked the German sinking of the *Lusitania,* which killed 128 Americans, averring that he was "too proud to fight." He sought, and narrowly won, reelection in 1916 on the slogan "He kept us out of war." Like FDR and LBJ, he then turned around and entered a major war—with good reason. The Germans were practicing unrestricted submarine warfare and plotting to give the U.S. Southwest back to Mexico in return for help in a war on America.

Although he committed millions of men to the Allied side, Wilson made clear they were not fighting for the same aims as Britain and France. He wanted a "peace without victory" based on his Fourteen Points speech, in which he championed, among other things, freedom of the seas, reduction of armaments, national self-determination, and a "general association of nations" to ensure "political independence and territorial integrity to great and small states alike."

Once the war was over, Wilson journeyed to the Paris Peace Conference to implement these ideals in person. He was not terribly successful. The British and French were bent on a harsh peace that would prevent a recurrence of German militarism. Wilson went along with their demands for the occupation of the Rhineland, a "war guilt" clause, and large reparations payments. This diktat engendered bitterness in Germany that the Nazis exploited a few years later. Other Wilsonian schemes, such as the creation of Yugoslavia and Czechoslovakia, took until the 1990s to backfire. Iraq may yet join the list of failed states created after World War I.

Wilson hoped that all the flaws of the Versailles Treaty would be fixed by the creation of a League of Nations. But he could not win Senate ratification on his terms. The Republican majority, led by Henry Cabot Lodge, was hardly isolationist, but they wanted reservations to make clear that the U.S. would not be drawn automatically into League of Nations wars to "preserve" all international borders, as Article X suggested. The pigheaded (and badly ailing) president made no concessions, and in fact ordered his Democratic followers to vote against the treaty on two occasions rather than support Lodge's reasonable amendments.

After Wilson left office in 1921, Warren Harding pushed through a peace treaty that did not contain the League of Nations provision. More important, it did not contain any U.S. security guarantees for Britain and France. This, more than the League, could have helped avert another world war by setting up a forerunner of NATO. It was not to be, and the 1919 peace treaty marked only a twenty-year cease-fire in the battle between Germany and its neighbors.

Wilson's other major failure had to do with communism. His attorney general, A. Mitchell Palmer, took strong steps to stamp out "subversive" activities. The Palmer Raids, along with other administration actions (such as imprisoning the socialist leader Eugene Debs), have been much reviled by civil libertarians, often with good cause. But Wilson deserves more opprobrium for his little-known intervention in Russia. In 1918 he sent tens of thousands of U.S. troops to guard war supplies in north Russia and Siberia. If they had marched on Moscow, as Winston Churchill proposed, they could have strangled the Bolshevik baby in its crib. Wilson missed this opportunity with a halfhearted intervention that accomplished nothing.

In spite of his foreign policy disasters, Wilson left a powerful legacy of internationalism and idealism. "Wilsonianism"—putting the promotion of American ideals at the center of American foreign policy—was not exactly invented by Wilson, but it is most closely associated with him. In both of its varieties, "hard" and "soft," it has proved our most durable foreign policy tradition. Soft Wilsonians, ranging from Jimmy Carter to, oddly enough, Calvin Coolidge (he signed the 1928 Kellogg-Briand Pact outlawing war), place their faith in international treaties above all else. Hard Wilsonians, whose ranks include both Roosevelts, Harry Truman, Ronald Reagan, and George W. Bush, believe in fusing power with principle. That is what the U.S. is doing by trying to democratize Iraq. Woodrow Wilson would have approved, though he probably would have bungled this ambitious project.

Mr. Boot is Olin Senior Fellow at the Council on Foreign Relations and author of The Savage Wars of Peace: Small Wars and the Rise of American Power *(Basic Books, 2002).*

29.

WARREN GAMALIEL HARDING

SURVEY RANKING: 39

BORN: November 2, 1865, Blooming Grove, Ohio

WIFE: Florence Mabel Kling

RELIGION: Baptist

PARTY: Republican

MILITARY EXPERIENCE: None

OTHER OFFICES HELD: Ohio state senator (1899–1903), lieutenant governor (1904–05), U.S. senator (1915–21)

TOOK OFFICE: March 4, 1921

VICE PRESIDENT: Calvin Coolidge

DIED IN OFFICE: August 2, 1923

BURIED: Marion, Ohio

By Jeremy Rabkin

No one ranks Warren G. Harding among our greatest presidents. His administration did not face the sorts of challenges that call for heroic leadership. Harding came to office when the Great War had already been won—and President Wilson's peace treaty had already been rejected by the Senate.

Still, Harding must be considered the most successful postwar president in American history. Andrew Johnson faced impeachment after the Civil War. Harry Truman left office with less support, in the opinion polls, than Richard Nixon retained on the day he resigned. Bill Clinton, coming to office after decades of Cold War, also squandered the public's trust and ended up facing impeachment.

Harding remained quite popular when he died in 1923. Unlike other postwar presidents, Harding's policies received the endorsement of the electorate. In two successive presidential elections after his death, voters returned close political associates of Harding to the White House and confirmed large majorities in both houses of Congress for his party.

Harding recruited men of distinction to his administration. His cabinet included a future chief justice (Secretary of State Charles Evans Hughes), a future president (Commerce Secretary Herbert Hoover), and the only treasury secretary in American history to win the confidence of three successive presidents (Andrew Mellon, who served continuously from 1921 to 1932). Harding was not afraid to give prominent positions to men who might outshine him. He appointed a former president, William Howard Taft, as chief justice.

The Harding administration launched the economic boom that continued through the 1920s. A continued series of tax cuts revived investment. The tax cuts were accompanied by disciplined reductions in spending. Harding was the only postwar president to reduce federal expenditures below their prewar levels.

At least some of the administration's success in reducing federal spending should be credited to the efforts of the Bureau of the Budget. This office provided systematic executive oversight of federal spending patterns for the first time. In the previous administration, proposals to establish such an agency had foundered on conflicting claims for control between Congress and the president. The Harding administration fostered the compromise, embodied in legislation of 1921, that remains to this day: a separate General Accounting Office for Congress and a budget bureau (now called the Office of Management and Budget) that answers exclusively to the president.

Tax cuts were offset by an increase in the tariff. But here too the Harding administration laid a foundation for future reform by persuading Congress to establish an independent tariff commission (whose functions have devolved to today's International Trade Commission and U.S. trade representative). The Tariff Commission provided, for the first time, some specialized administrative guidance to congressional tariff setting, historically characterized by open-ended logrolling.

In foreign affairs, the Harding administration faced the central problem of cleaning up the debris from President Wilson's failure in peacemaking. The possibility of renegotiating some form of American participation in the League of Nations was raised even by prominent Republicans, but the Harding administration firmly rejected it. Instead, the U.S. negotiated separate peace agreements with Germany and the successor states of the Habsburg and Ottoman empires. Secretary Hughes declined even to answer formal letters from the League. The administration wanted no doubt regarding American rejection of this first venture in international control of national security policies.

The Harding policy was not one of isolation, however, but of independence. Harding was prepared to consider American participation in the League's Permanent Court of International Justice, as the U.S. had previously participated in other ventures in international arbitration. (The proposal came to naught when the League would not agree to proposed American reservations.)

The administration sponsored an ambitious program of naval disarmament at the Washington Naval Conference of 1921. The ensuing treaty provided, for the first time, a pledge of parity between the U.S. Navy and Britain's Royal Navy, which implicitly confirmed a strategic understanding between the world's greatest naval powers. It also limited the Japanese to a battleship strength pegged at three fifths of the tonnage allowed to Britain and America, while capping French and Italian naval strength at a still lower level. The agreement allowed all naval powers to avoid the expense of a naval arms race during the twelve years of the treaty's operation. Unlike President

Wilson, Harding was shrewd enough to include senators in the negotiation of the treaty, and he reaped the political reward when the
Senate ratified it with a unanimous vote. The Washington Treaty was
the first substantial U.S. commitment to arms control in American
history.

Harding, as a former newspaper editor, was skillful in cultivating
Washington reporters. He set a tone of reconciliation, which defused
much of the rancor of Wilson's last years in office. Almost all social-
ists and labor leaders imprisoned after the 1919 Red Scare, for example, were freed during Harding's first year in office. Women, newly
enfranchised by the Nineteenth Amendment, offered even higher
levels of support to Harding than did men, and Harding passed this
Republican-favoring "gender gap" on to his successors.

Harding's administration received much more sympathetic cover-
age in the newspapers of that era than in subsequent assessments of
historians. In the last months before his death in 1923, Harding's
administration was tainted by scandal. Interior Secretary Albert Fall
turned out to be peddling favors in the scandal known to history as
Teapot Dome (after the site of one improperly granted oil-drilling
lease). Harding himself was not personally implicated. It is notable,
moreover, that here, in contrast to later cabinet scandals, Congress
trusted the Justice Department to pursue necessary prosecutions—
as Harding's appointees did with much success after the resignation
of the tarnished attorney general.

More than these scandals, however, Harding's reputation has
been shadowed by the collapse of the economy at the end of the
1920s. Historians who admire the New Deal tend to fault Harding
and his successors for not anticipating the policy initiatives of the
1930s—forgetting that FDR's policies still left the country struggling
in economic depression after eight years, while the economic expansion of the Harding era was more sustained and broad-based than in
any previous period. Those who fault Harding for boycotting the
League of Nations imagine that the League would have been more
successful if only the United States had added its prestige to it—forgetting that even with American participation, the United Nations
has not been much help to the world or much of an asset to
American policy.

Some historians have sneered at Harding for his lack of polish and eloquence. Harding did not speak in the high-flown rhetoric of his predecessor. He did not even have a university degree, while Woodrow Wilson had been a university president. Harding's most memorable line, emphasizing the country needed "not nostrums but normalcy," relied, as critics have sniffed, on a made-up word. But the dictionary's version, "normality," does not quite capture what Harding meant. Harding himself referred to political rhetoric as "bloviation"—another neologism that is a lasting contribution to American English. Unlike some other presidents, before and since, Harding did recognize the difference between bloviation and good sense.

Mr. Rabkin is a professor of government at Cornell University.

30.

JOHN CALVIN COOLIDGE

SURVEY RANKING: 23

BORN: July 4, 1872, Plymouth, Vermont

WIFE: Grace Goodhue

RELIGION: Congregationalist

PARTY: Republican

MILITARY EXPERIENCE: None

OTHER OFFICES HELD: Massachusetts state representative (1907–08), mayor of Northampton, Massachusetts (1910–11), state senator (1912–15), lieutenant governor (1916–18), governor (1919–20), vice president (1921–23)

TOOK OFFICE: August 3, 1923

VICE PRESIDENT: Charles Dawes (1925–29)

LEFT OFFICE: March 4, 1929

DIED: January 5, 1933

BURIED: Plymouth, Vermont

by John O. McGinnis

Historical evaluations of presidents consistently underrate Calvin Coolidge. What other president cleaned up scandals in Washington, presided over a period of unprecedented prosperity, and commanded a laconic eloquence, only to be ranked average or below average? The reason for such slights is wholly ideological: Coolidge provided (at least until Ronald Reagan) the most effective presidential defense of limited government in the twentieth century. In an era when intellectuals almost unanimously favored Leviathan, his stance against excessive state power alone was enough to discredit him. As it becomes clearer that big government has been responsible for more social failures than successes, Coolidge's reputation has nowhere to go but up.

The harsh ideological judgment of Coolidge has also relied on a false stereotype of his political views and ignored his many virtues that transcend partisan politics. Coolidge was no reactionary. While he opposed the radical progressive agenda to transform the nature of American society, he favored woman's suffrage and shorter work hours for both women and children. Indeed, his skillful melding of the views of traditional Republicans and Republicans of the Teddy Roosevelt variety enabled him to unite a party that had been badly divided. Coolidge was a compassionate conservative before compassionate conservatism was cool.

His compassion did not prevent him from becoming a scourge of government waste. He announced to Congress that "the collection of any taxes which are not absolutely required, which do not beyond reasonable doubt contribute to the public welfare, is only a species of legislative larceny." And unlike some politicians, his actions were as good as his words. During the 1920s, as in the late 1990s, the federal government was running a large surplus, and as now a Republican Congress seemed determined to dissipate it on pork barrel projects and untested programs. Coolidge wielded the veto and the threat of veto to protect the public fisc. In particular, he vetoed the McNary-Haugen bill, which attempted to support farm prices through government subsidies.

Because of this frugality Coolidge was able to cut taxes, especially for those earning under $10,000 a year. This was in keeping with Coolidge's ultimate defense of economy in government: "I favor the policy of economy not because I wish to save money, but because I wish to save people. . . . Every dollar we carelessly spend means that the life of those toiling will be so much the more meager. Every dollar we prudently save will mean that their life will be so much more abundant. Economy is idealism in its most practical form."

Some political historians blame Coolidge's economic policies for the Depression. But this is a convenient ideological myth rather than hard historical fact. Economists and historians of the economy almost universally locate the roots of the Depression in mistakes in monetary policy and the passage of the crushing Smoot-Hawley Tariffs—misguided government interventions that occurred after Coolidge left office. And for all the talk of FDR's greatness, economists agree that many of his policies made the Depression endure.

President Coolidge also raised the ethical standards of Washington more effectively than any president before him. After the Teapot Dome scandal, Coolidge ordered special prosecutors appointed and former Interior Secretary Albert Fall was convicted of taking bribes. When Attorney General Harry Daugherty interfered with an investigation into other malfeasance of the Harding administration, Coolidge forced him to resign. Coolidge's actions show that when the president is a man of vigilant integrity, no independent counsel law is necessary.

But Coolidge was no naïf about the strategies necessary to manage the modern administrative state. Like Ronald Reagan, the modern president whose policies his most resembled, he recognized the need for delegation: "There are many things you . . . must not tell me. If you blunder you can leave or I can invite you to leave. But, if you draw me into all your department decisions and something goes wrong, I must stay here. And by involving me you have lowered the faith of the people in their government." Whether sound or not, this is the administrative creed of a very sophisticated politician.

Coolidge conducted himself in the presidency with a modesty becoming of the chief executive of a democracy. When his son died while Coolidge was in office, he mourned in private. Nor did he alternately hector the public and condescend to it, like many recent contenders for the White House. When Coolidge did speak, it was with an almost epigrammatic power. His best known quote, "The business of America is business," actually is part of a larger statement: "The chief business of America is business, the chief idealism of America is idealism." In context, Coolidge's remarks provide a nice gloss on what we now know as Hayekian principles: When government is limited, both good economic and good social norms bubble up from below.

Beyond his specific accomplishments, Coolidge is to be admired for his defense of traditional American celebration of the individual against the transformation toward collectivism that the liberals attempted in the Progressive Era. His unusually lengthy inaugural address of 1925 went back to first principles of political philosophy. He took direct aim at the progressive notion that property rights were an obstacle to social betterment. To the contrary, property rights were essential to the "very stability of society," and the rights and duties that were connected with property "had been revealed through the constitution of society, to have divine sanction."

To the progressive notions that government could be used to reorder human relations, Coolidge responded: "We must realize that human nature is about the most constant thing in the universe and that essentials of human nature do not change." For Coolidge, unlike the progressives, the conservation of American traditions was the key to the success of present government policy: "It is necessary to keep the former experience of our country continually before us if we are to have science of government."

Perhaps most important, he countered the progressive notion that more government programs would lead to a more prosperous society. In addressing the Massachusetts Senate, he observed: "The people cannot look to legislation generally for success. Industry, thrift, and character are not conferred by act or resolve. Government cannot relieve from toil. It can, of course provide for the defective . . . but the normal must care for themselves. Self-government means self-support." It is hard to think of a sentence spoken by an American president that encapsulates the relation between democratic government and limited government better than that last one.

To be sure, Coolidge was not a truly great president, like Washington or Lincoln. While he successfully handled small foreign policy crises in China, Mexico, and Nicaragua without saddling the United States with permanent and expensive commitments, he was never tested by a substantial foreign war. We will never know how he would have handled the economic crises that bedeviled his successor. He also had some flaws. Although he sought an anti-lynching law, he did not always vigorously protect the civil rights of black Americans. (His position on civil rights, however, was far better than that of Woodrow Wilson and many progressive Democrats, who were openly racist.) He did not contest the protectionist tendencies of the Republican Party, nor its restrictive policy on Japanese immigration, although he recognized that this would be a future source of trouble in America's relations with Japan.

Nevertheless, Calvin Coolidge's many excellences are worth recalling anew. They look all the better when compared with the defects of many of the presidents who succeeded him. Coolidge provides a model for the kind of leader needed in a republic: honest, modest, and shrewd. We too require a president who effectively administers government in the limited areas where it is necessary but otherwise releases the genius of the American people from the chains of excessive regulation and taxes.

Mr. McGinnis is a professor of law at Northwestern University.

31.

HERBERT CLARK HOOVER

SURVEY RANKING: 31

BORN: August 10, 1874, West Branch, Iowa

WIFE: Lou Henry

RELIGION: Quaker

PARTY: Republican

MILITARY EXPERIENCE: None

OTHER OFFICES HELD: U.S. commerce secretary (1921–28)

TOOK OFFICE: March 4, 1929

VICE PRESIDENT: Charles Curtis

LEFT OFFICE: March 4, 1933

DIED: October 20, 1964

BURIED: West Branch, Iowa

by Robert H. Ferrell

We should expect Herbert Hoover to get a heavy amount of criticism. After all, the Great Depression started on his watch. But pinning a "below average" label on the thirty-first president is unfair.

Let's consider the situation Hoover was in after being elected in 1928. During his administration and long afterward he put up with a

great deal of criticism. He wryly referred to the naysayers as haber-
dashers, desirous of dressing him in hairshirts. Some of the gibes
came, of course, from his fellow Republicans. Many GOP senators
hated the very notion of a Wilsonian like Hoover winning their
party's nomination. Hoover had worked for President Wilson's war
effort in Europe, primarily organizing a large-scale effort to feed people dislodged during World War I.

Some of the gibes were outright mean-spirited. Senator James E.
Watson of Indiana, a Republican who never had a constructive idea
about government, remarked that Hoover knew less about politics
than a child. During the second half of his administration, his program to deal with the increasingly desperate Depression didn't seem
to solve anything, so his opposition was galvanized. Democrats abandoned the bipartisan spirit, and looked toward winning the presidential election in 1932. One naysayer even wrote a lyric about the
president:

Hoover is our shepherd
We are in want
He maketh us to lie
Down on the park benches
He leadeth us beside the still factories . . .

Leaving office didn't help Hoover escape criticism. In 1933 a fictitious rumor spread that former President Hoover and his secretary
of the treasury, Andrew W. Mellon, had been arrested in New York in
an attempt to flee to Europe with suitcases of gold bullion stolen
from Fort Knox. For years Democratic candidates flailed Hoover with
this story. Even President Truman in 1948 joked about it.

President Hoover deserves better. Consider his philosophy of government, which is largely accepted today. That view was clearly laid
out in *American Individualism,* a small book published in 1922 after
he became commerce secretary under Warren Harding. It was printed
with Hoover's name on it, but it was written by Mark Sullivan, a reporter and friend of Hoover's.

Individualism is the best expression of democracy, the book
explains, because it is the duty of every person to stand up to the
emery wheel of competition. The role of the government is to

ensure access to the wheel. Public funds could be spent on scientific research, highways, or anything with "some great major purpose." Federal funds might subsidize enterprise if they benefited the public good. However, the government shouldn't provide a subsidized service, which would create interest groups that would destroy democracy. Hoover looked forward to a prosperous America "where men and women may walk in ordered freedom in the independent conduct of their occupations." Hoover had hope, but he was no philosopher. He was a man of action, of solutions.

At the outset of his presidency Hoover sought to increase the efficiency of government, as he had done for the economy as secretary of commerce. But midway through his term, he was forced to put his fears of an activist government aside and offer more government solutions. By midsummer of 1931 he realized the stock market, which had been up and down (mostly down) since October 1929, had a profound impact on confidence in the economy. A low stock market meant fewer jobs. There followed a markedly successful program of virtual intervention.

Hoover always believed that the Depression originated in Europe, so in the early summer of 1931 he arranged a moratorium on war debts owed to the U.S. and reparations owed by Germany to the Allies. He personally won support for this by writing individual letters to congressmen, so that when Congress met in December 1931, it gave immediate assent to the plan. He followed this with the Reconstruction Finance Corporation and the Glass-Steagall Act, to enlarge credit domestically; he was not the author of either of these, but he readily sponsored them. For a president whose critics later announced his incessant inaction, this program, supported by both Republicans and Democrats, was a remarkable achievement. His activism manifested itself in little ways too. Unlike Calvin Coolidge, who took phone calls in the hall, Hoover had a phone brought into the Oval Office.

The wave of bipartisanship ended when Hoover tried to enact a federal 2.5 percent sales tax. It was April 1932, and over the next few months the fury gathered because of congressional and presidential disagreement over how to deal with the appalling decline in the economy. Public works, long advocated by Senator Robert F. Wagner of New York, vied with congressional pleas for outright relief. Hoover agreed with Wagner to undertake construction programs, if they held lasting value—a precursor to FDR's massive Civilian Conservation Corps projects. Relief, Hoover believed, was best provided by the states, localities, and private benefaction.

The summer of 1932 saw the political discourse turn toward nonsense. Democratic candidate Franklin D. Roosevelt made a great speech in Pittsburgh. He said that if elected he would slash federal expenditures 25 percent and balance the budget. Roosevelt won the presidency, but he increased expenditures and didn't balance the budget. Four years later he asked a speechwriter to develop a speech to explain everything. The speechwriter thought about it and came back with the solution: deny he ever made the 1932 speech.

Hoover in 1932 was caught in the worst economic cataclysm ever to confront Western civilization. Seventy years later, economists are still trying to explain why the economy crashed. Hoover clearly did his best. No one really knew what to do; neither Hoover nor Congress nor even FDR was willing to take massive measures in 1932, whatever the damage to the federal budget. The willingness for such expenditures grew after 1933, and even then only the buildup to World War II primed the economic pump.

Oddly, Hoover's image was slightly rehabilitated by Harry Truman in 1945. Learning that Hoover was in Washington, staying in a hotel, Truman telephoned and asked if he would come and see his "old home." Hoover accepted, so Truman sent a car. Hoover walked into the White House and broke into tears when he was asked to survey world food supplies. "Mr. President," he said, "since 1932 no one has asked me to do anything for my country. You are the first one." In 1947, Truman put Hoover on a commission to reorganize executive departments; the panel elected him chairman. Eisenhower appointed him to a similar commission in 1953.

Alas, most scholars of the presidency have chosen to remember the gibes about Hoover, who was in fact a great public servant whose service spanned five decades. He deserves better from history.

Mr. Ferrell is Distinguished Professor Emeritus in History at Indiana University.

32.

FRANKLIN DELANO ROOSEVELT

SURVEY RANKING: 3

BORN: January 30, 1882, Hyde Park, New York

WIFE: Anna Eleanor Roosevelt

RELIGION: Episcopalian

PARTY: Democrat

MILITARY EXPERIENCE: None

OTHER OFFICES HELD: New York state senator (1911–13), governor (1929–33)

TOOK OFFICE: March 4, 1933

VICE PRESIDENTS: John Nance Garner (1933–41), Henry Wallace (1941–45), Harry Truman (1945)

DIED IN OFFICE: April 12, 1945

BURIED: Hyde Park, New York

by Robert H. Bork

It is difficult to say which of our presidents deserve to be called great. Without doubt, Washington and Lincoln are worthy of the accolade, but who, if anyone, comes after that? A frequent third choice is Franklin Delano Roosevelt, who, like Washington and Lincoln, dealt with major national emergencies and profoundly affected the nature of the republic.

Wartime leadership is probably not necessary to greatness, and it is also apparently not sufficient. Woodrow Wilson, for example, led the nation into the First World War and probably destroyed his health fighting to lead America into the League of Nations. Roosevelt in his extraordinary tenure dealt with both the Great Depression and the Second World War, but that alone does not explain why he is widely revered today while Wilson appears, so far as public appreciation is concerned, to be a figure of the second rank.

The difference, one is tempted to say, is a matter of temperament, personal charm, and luck. Roosevelt had all three; Wilson lacked all three. Oliver Wendell Holmes, Jr., is reported to have said that Roosevelt was a man with "a second-class intellect, but a first-class temperament." There has been speculation that Holmes was actually referring to the first Roosevelt, Teddy, but the description certainly fitted Franklin, and that may be the extra something that qualifies the second Roosevelt for the list of great presidents. If so, charisma and popularity are more important than more objective measurements. Roosevelt exuded confidence and displayed a jaunty optimism that lifted the morale of Americans during the bleakness of the Depression and the sacrifices of war.

Viewed objectively, Roosevelt's performance during the Depression was not impressive. His economic measures have been compared to the economic policies of fascism—leaving ownership of businesses in private hands but controlling business activity by heavy regulation and codes of conduct established by associations in the main sectors of industry, trade, and finance. The inevitable result was restriction of output, higher prices, and less employment—precisely the wrong policies to combat the depression that he inherited.

Roosevelt, it is frequently said, saved capitalism by his economic reforms, but that seems a considerable overstatement. In truth, he denounced business leaders as "economic royalists" who had created a "new despotism" and "economic slavery," rhetoric hardly likely to make capitalism popular. More important, his regulations of economic affairs unnecessarily introduced government into many areas of life. Lyndon Johnson's Great Society programs, by and large failures, can be seen as a logical progression from the New Deal.

Roosevelt's enthusiasm for his programs led him to the one great defeat of his peacetime presidency. Immediately after his landslide victory in 1936 over Republican Alf Landon, Roosevelt attacked the Supreme Court, which had regularly struck down New Deal measures as unconstitutional. He sent to Congress a bill, which soon became known as the "court packing" plan, to add six new justices, who, because Roosevelt would appoint them, would be more friendly to the New Deal. He bet the enormous political capital he had gained in his smashing electoral triumph, and he lost. Congress's and the public's reaction was due in large measure to his characteristic deviousness in presenting the plan initially as one to improve the court's efficiency rather than admitting his real motive: to add six New Deal justices.

In 1937 the slow recovery from the Depression was reversed by a new recession, but as James MacGregor Burns put it: "Roosevelt's fumbling and indecisiveness during the recession showed his failings as an economist and a thinker." Luck came to his rescue. The approach and then the actuality of war in Europe gave American business new markets, making the United States, as Roosevelt put it, the "great arsenal of democracy," and the recession ended. He increasingly understood the stakes for America in the prospect of Nazi Germany's victory, and gave as much aid as he could to Britain, but important segments of the public and Congress were isolationist. On December 7, 1941, the Japanese solved that problem.

By most accounts, Roosevelt took seriously his role as commander in chief, involving himself in military planning and occasionally overriding the advice of the joint chiefs. Unlike Lincoln, he kept the same men at the top of the command structure from the beginning of the war to its end. His performance, on the whole, aided the war effort, while his political acuity kept up the morale of the American people.

In planning for the postwar world, his major mistake was in believing that he could handle Stalin through face-to-face meetings. Though their conference with Churchill at Yalta seemed in some respects hopeful, it was soon apparent that the Soviets would not relinquish control of the Eastern European nations they had occupied. Roosevelt generally underestimated the aggressive intentions of Stalin as he had the degree of Soviet espionage in the United States itself. He was also intent on the formation of the United Nations, which, to say the least, has not been an unambiguous blessing for the United States.

Having won his fourth presidential election in 1944, although already a very sick man, the president went to Hot Springs, Georgia. He died there on April 12, 1945, less than three months after his inauguration. The heartbroken reaction of the public was evidence of the degree to which the debonair Roosevelt's unwavering public optimism had sustained America through its trials. In the final accounting, that, along with his conduct as commander in chief, must be placed against some of his failures in the Depression, his expansion of dominating bureaucracies, and his overconfidence in the international political maneuvering toward the end of the war.

Mr. Bork, a senior fellow at the Hudson Institute, has served as solicitor general of the United States and a federal appellate judge.

33.

HARRY S. TRUMAN

SURVEY RANKING: 7

BORN: May 8, 1884, Lamar, Missouri

WIFE: Elizabeth "Bess" Wallace

RELIGION: Baptist

PARTY: Democrat

MILITARY EXPERIENCE: Army Reserves (colonel)

OTHER OFFICES HELD: U.S. senator from Missouri (1933–45), vice president (1945)

TOOK OFFICE: April 12, 1945

VICE PRESIDENT: Alben Barkley (1949–53)

LEFT OFFICE: January 20, 1953

DIED: December 26, 1972

BURIED: Independence, Missouri

by Terry Eastland

In assessing Harry Truman, a good place to begin is by recalling that the authors of *The Federalist* understood the presidency as the unique source of "energy" in government. They identified as "ingredients of energy" the structure and the powers of the office. But they also wanted presidents who would behave energetically—who would use their authority. They envisioned presidents who would act with "dispatch," "vigor," "expedition," and "firmness"; who could make a "decision," with "promptitude," no less. Significantly, they understood "energy in the executive" in terms of leadership, for they anticipated presidents who would undertake "extensive and arduous enterprises" in the public's behalf.

The authors of *The Federalist* would have been pleased with Truman. Of course, he had his shortcomings. But his presidency is a study in "energy in the executive"—energy that often benefited the nation.

Consider the momentous question before Truman as to whether he should use the atomic bomb against Japan. He became president upon FDR's death in April 1945 and hadn't known about the bomb until then. Concluding that the bomb would end the war quickly and save lives, he didn't hesitate to authorize its use. In late July he issued the ultimatum Japan swiftly rejected—surrender unconditionally or face "utter and prompt destruction." In early August the two bombs were dropped, first on Hiroshima and then, a few days later, on Nagasaki. Both cities were vaporized, and more than 150,000 people were killed. The Japanese surrendered.

Truman's decision has long been second-guessed. Maybe the Japanese would have given up if we had demonstrated the bomb out in the ocean somewhere, or if the emperor's personal safety had been guaranteed. There is also the argument that the entry of the Soviets into the Pacific war (as a 1946 U.S. intelligence study concluded) probably would have forced the Japanese to surrender in any case.

Such criticisms assume that something other than the bomb would have persuaded the Japanese to give up. Yet it was hardly obvious at the time that any of the alternatives would have achieved that goal. What was obvious in the summer of 1945 was the Japanese military's determination to resist. Even before Hiroshima and Nagasaki, conventional bombs had killed 260,000 Japanese and wounded another 410,000—and yet the Japanese were not about to yield. Had Truman held back the bomb, there would have been more fire-bombing of Japanese cities and likely huge numbers of casualties.

And there would have been a ground invasion of the main Japanese islands. If the fighting in Okinawa was any guide, fighting in the main islands would have killed tens of thousands of Americans and probably millions of Japanese. Truman's decision, made with "promptitude," indeed, achieved what he intended—an early end to the war and the saving of life.

Truman also displayed energy in a context that required his sustained attention. After World War II, the biggest problem facing not just the United States but the world was the expansionist Soviet Union. The Soviets had pushed into Eastern Europe, but Truman determined that they should go no further. "Containment" was a policy of many parts, all of them initiated by Truman. It included aid to Greece and Turkey and promises of aid to other nations threatened "by armed minorities or by outside pressures"; provision of economic resources to stimulate the postwar recovery of European countries; the Berlin Airlift, the purpose of which was to sustain the Western position in that city; the North Atlantic Treaty Organization, whose member states (initially, the U.S. and eleven other Western nations) agreed to maintain a military force to defend against a Soviet invasion; and the Point Four Program, which provided economic help to underdeveloped countries.

Containment plainly qualifies as one of those "extensive and arduous enterprises" mentioned in *The Federalist*. It required firmness in responding to a threat to freedom itself and then multiple decisions as to how to counter that threat. It also required the skilled use of various executive powers—including the powers to negotiate treaties, command the troops, and recommend legislation.

Strikingly, America wasn't the only beneficiary of containment, since it also helped people in other countries. In a post-presidency speech on presidential power, Truman recognized the impact of America's executive power worldwide: "Today the tasks of leadership falling upon the president spring not only from our national problems but from those of the whole world. Today that leadership will determine whether our government will function effectively, and upon its functioning depends the survival of each of us and also on that depends the survival of the free world."

Containment was a policy that rejected a pacific or isolationist stance, on the one hand, and an especially aggressive effort to roll the Soviets back, on the other. The former would have encouraged the spread of communism, at freedom's further expense. The latter, Truman believed, would have risked a huge hot war. Containment wasn't binding on Truman's successors, but they more or less continued the policy. Its ultimate vindication lay in the demise of the Soviet Union and the end of the Cold War.

Truman was also the energetic executive when it came to civil rights and attacking racial discrimination. In late 1946 Truman created by executive order a special committee on civil rights, many of whose recommendations eventually were acted upon. They included ending the poll tax (accomplished through the Twenty-fourth Amendment, ratified in 1964), requiring federal grantees not to discriminate on the basis of race (achieved by the Civil Rights Act of 1964), and outlawing racial discrimination in private employment (also done through the Civil Rights Act). As well, Truman used his executive authority to broaden equal opportunity in the federal civil service and then to end racial discrimination in the armed forces. Meanwhile, in friend-of-the-court filings in the Supreme Court, his Justice Department sided with parties challenging segregation.

Truman managed to make a difference on civil rights while still in office even as he framed much of the agenda that the nation would address over the next twenty years. He did so through a commission he appointed, executive orders he issued, and legal briefs he authorized. He had no help from Congress. Truman's motives in behalf of civil rights may well have been mixed, but his actions constitute his legacy. And today the actions he took draw no important dissents, for the obvious reason that Truman was right. America was founded on the notion that "all men are created equal," and Truman used the powers of office to help the nation live up to that principle.

In the 1948 campaign, Truman famously ran against the "do-nothing Congress," a label that couldn't be applied to his presidency. It made a difference at home and abroad, confirming the Framers' expectation of presidential leadership.

Mr. Eastland is publisher of The Weekly Standard.

34.

DWIGHT DAVID EISENHOWER

SURVEY RANKING: 8

BORN: October 14, 1890, Denison, Texas

WIFE: Marie "Mamie" Geneva Doud

RELIGION: Presbyterian

PARTY: Republican

MILITARY EXPERIENCE: U.S. Army (five-star general)

OTHER OFFICES HELD: None

TOOK OFFICE: January 20, 1953

VICE PRESIDENT: Richard Nixon

LEFT OFFICE: January 20, 1961

DIED: March 28, 1969

BURIED: Abilene, Kansas

by Edwin Meese III

Dwight Eisenhower was the quintessential president for the era in which he served in the White House. It was a time of peace and prosperity. The economic expansion and the new opportunities that emerged after World War II, though partially interrupted by the Korean War, flowered during the 1950s. Educational opportunity, technological advancement, and industrial progress contributed to the view that America was the most powerful nation in the world, capable of achieving almost anything.

Eisenhower demonstrated the quality of leadership that fit this attitude of the American people. As Stephen Ambrose has written in *Eisenhower: Soldier and President,* "He was so comforting, so grandfatherly, so calm, so sure of himself, so skillful in managing the economy, so experienced in insuring America's defenses, so expert in his control of the intelligence community, so knowledgeable about the world's affairs, so nonpartisan and objective in his above-the-battle posture, so insistent on holding to the middle of the road, that he inspired a trust that was as broad and deep as that of any President since George Washington."

The decade was not without problems, both at home and abroad. Ike, as he had become known to the American people, first had to deal with the war in Korea. The Soviet Union was a continuing threat to world peace and stability. Maintaining European unity was often a vexing problem. There were the perennial challenges of military spending and budget deficits. Race relations were a potential flashpoint for domestic conflict. And McCarthyism was a divisive force that provoked heated controversy even within the administration.

Few men have been as well prepared for the presidency as Eisenhower. Most of our chief executives have come to that position with extensive political experience and have previously held public office. Some have been military leaders. Eisenhower's unique military experience more than compensated for his lack of partisan political activity or prior office.

Eisenhower graduated from West Point in 1915 and faced the slow pace of promotion during the first twenty-five years of army life between the world wars. He had reached the rank of lieutenant colonel just prior to World War II. Over the next five years he advanced to general of the army, one of only nine men ever to hold five-star rank in the U.S. armed forces.

During his early army career, he served as a staff officer to several outstanding generals, including John J. Pershing, Douglas MacArthur, and George C. Marshall. In these assignments, Ike distinguished himself by his hard work, his organizational skills, and his excellent writing ability—traits that he exhibited in the White House and demanded from his staff.

But it was his World War II experience, as the supreme commander of Allied forces in Europe, that gave him constant interaction with top leaders of foreign nations, the challenge of coping with complex international affairs, and the detailed knowledge and strategic insight that prepared him to lead the nation. It also provided the public recognition and hero status that made him a formidable candidate.

Eisenhower's qualifying experience did not end with World War II. Shortly after the war he was appointed army chief of staff and then went on to be president of Columbia University. In 1950, taking a leave from the university, he returned to active duty as supreme commander of the military forces of the North Atlantic Treaty Organization. It was from this position that a delegation of political leaders persuaded him to run for the Republican presidential nomination in 1952.

Both during his postwar activities and during his presidency, Eisenhower made clear his position as a successful warrior who was wholeheartedly committed to peace. During the 1952 campaign, while U.S. military forces were bogged down in the Korean War, Ike promised that he would "go to Korea." His trip there, just a few weeks after the election, and his subsequent actions as president brought about an armistice that ended the fighting that had been producing U.S. casualties without any progress toward victory. The result was not a perfect solution—the Korea problem is still with us today—but it stopped the killing and avoided an unlimited war with China.

Eisenhower considered his primary duty to be preserving peace, stopping aggression, and maintaining stability in the affairs of nations. As a soldier he knew the horror and futility of war. He also knew that the increased destructive power of nuclear weapons made unlimited war virtually unthinkable. At the same time, he was keenly aware that Soviet imperialism had to be contained and that freedom had to be protected throughout the world. This is why he strongly supported the United Nations, encouraged a stronger alliance of European countries, and sought a stable relationship with the Soviet Union.

Eisenhower epitomized effective leadership by the way he ran the White House. He understood the value of competence and teamwork and worked hard to select the right people for the right jobs, without

regard to personal friendship. For the cabinet he chose proven business executives and successful professionals, some of whom he had
never met, but whose records indicated their capability. For his White
House staff he recruited men and women who had demonstrated administrative and management skills, including some of his former army
staff officers. Eisenhower reorganized the National Security Council,
increasing its staff capabilities and initiating a planning committee, for
long-range strategy development, and an operations board, to monitor
the implementation of policy decisions. This enhanced NSC provided
a valuable resource as Ike excelled in managing numerous crises: Korea, Chinese threats against Taiwan, the Soviet crackdown in Hungary,
the Berlin crisis of 1959, the downing by the Soviets of a U.S. spy plane,
and other difficult situations.

Two prominent domestic problems confronted Eisenhower during
his presidency: McCarthyism and race relations. Some critics felt that
Ike did not do enough to visibly oppose Senator Joseph McCarthy and
his bullying tactics, which hurt the cause of anti-communism. But
Eisenhower had his own strategy. As he wrote to his brother, Milton,
"Only a short-sighted or completely inexperienced individual would
urge the use of the Office of the Presidency to give an opponent the
publicity he so avidly desires." The strategy worked, at least in the opinion of historian Paul Johnson, who wrote in his book *Modern Times*
that "in the last resort, McCarthy's weapon was publicity; and in a free
society publicity is a two-edged sword. McCarthy was destroyed by
publicity; and the man who orchestrated this destruction from behind
the scenes was the new President, Dwight Eisenhower."

This ability to orchestrate successful results without becoming
publicly visible has been explored in great detail by presidential
scholar Fred Greenstein in his book *The Hidden-Hand Presidency*.
It led to Eisenhower being downrated by many pundits and acade-
micians, but as additional scholarship and the passage of time have
provided new perspectives, Ike is increasingly regarded as a successful leader who governed well, with honesty, wisdom, and a genuine
concern over doing what was right.

This was reflected in his strong sense of justice and his acceptance
of the responsibility of major powers to protect the interest of
weaker nations. Ike exhibited these values in 1956, when Britain,

France, and Israel sought to take over the Suez Canal, an act of aggression that was in violation of the 1950 Tripartite Declaration. Eisenhower thought he had an obligation to support Egypt, as the victim of aggression, even against nations that were close friends of the United States. Ambrose points out that this action of good faith surprised and delighted the small nations of the world and that "Eisenhower's insistence on the primacy of the U.N., of the treaty obligations, and of the rights of all nations gave the United States a standing in world opinion it had never before achieved."

In the matter of race relations, Eisenhower was often criticized for going too slow in seeing that *Brown v. Board of Education,* the Supreme Court's 1954 school desegregation decision, was implemented throughout the land. Ike felt that this process had to move slowly and carefully, to avoid a violent uprising or the closing of public schools in the South. But when his intervention became necessary, as in Little Rock, Arkansas, where the governor defied the courts in 1957, Eisenhower acted decisively by ordering federal troops to restore law and order and to integrate the schools.

One permanent illustration of Eisenhower's greatness as a president is his establishment of the Interstate Highway System. In his early army days he had deplored the deficiencies of America's roads and later contrasted them with the spectacular autobahn of Germany. Ike combined military and economic purposes to build a comprehensive national highway system on a gigantic scale, which has benefited the country ever since.

As one of the few two-term presidents of the twentieth century, Eisenhower left a legacy of peace, fiscal integrity, sound though not spectacular government, prosperity, and honesty in both domestic and foreign affairs. Perhaps his successful leadership and personal popularity are best expressed by the feeling of affection in which he was held as he left office. "The nation liked Ike," it was said, "because Ike liked everybody."

Mr. Meese is Ronald Reagan Distinguished Fellow and chairman of the Center for Legal and Judicial Studies at the Heritage Foundation. He served as attorney general of the United States, 1985–88.

35.
JOHN FITZGERALD KENNEDY

SURVEY RANKING: 15

BORN: May 29, 1917, Brookline, Massachusetts

WIFE: Jacqueline Bouvier

RELIGION: Roman Catholic

PARTY: Democrat

MILITARY EXPERIENCE: U.S. Naval Reserve (lieutenant)

OTHER OFFICES HELD: U.S. representative from Massachusetts (1947–53), U.S. senator (1953–60)

TOOK OFFICE: January 20, 1961

VICE PRESIDENT: Lyndon Johnson

DIED IN OFFICE: November 22, 1963 (assassinated)

BURIED: Arlington, Virginia

---

by Peggy Noonan

History will take a cool-eyed look at John F. Kennedy and his accomplishments and failures only when all who were alive when he was alive are gone. Until then his reputation will be dominated by twi-light remembrances and "Where were you when you found out?"

The numerically biggest generation in all American history was at its most impressionable when he was at his most lionized, in the years after his death. Boomers now run the world. It doesn't matter what they know of JFK now, as adults, or what they've learned. They're not going to shake their sense that he was King Arthur lost upon the field. They're not going to let you shake it, either.

But let's try anyway. Let's try not to be partisan or swayed by glamour, or reflexively hostile, or reflexively anything. Let's try to look at him apart from all the hype and hagiography of the forty years after his death.

Start with what we know of his personality. I wish I had known him because I feel certain I would have liked him. By all accounts he was witty and humorous, teasing and bright. He was not an intellectual but he was quick, and one can see from his writings and the testi-mony of his friends about his conversation that he had a talent for focus: He could see the point and get to it. There is no evidence that he ever read or gave any thought to political philosophy. Having fun and enjoying life were important to him. His friends attribute this to his ill health; he wasn't sure he'd be here long. Maybe they are right, and maybe it is also true he just liked having a good time.

He was an attractive and athletic man; he cared how he looked. He was the first big league politician to use ManTan, the sunless tan-ner of the 1950s; he thought it made him look vigorous and wind-blown. He was well tailored and cared about the cut of his suits and the style of his collars. He loved gossip; Gore Vidal said that when he died, the history of everyone's private life went with him.

He knew great and persistent physical suffering, the kind that wears you down and strips the good nature from you. But he was capable of detachment even from this; he had fantastic self-discipline.

He served his country in the navy. He didn't pull strings to get out of the war, he pulled strings to get *into* the war. He fought World War II as the skipper of a PT boat, a glamour posting at the time. One night his ship was chugging along in the darkness in the Blackett Strait when a Japanese destroyer came along and smashed it in two. He rallied his men and saved one of them by clenching a strap from his lifejacket in his teeth, swimming for five hours in the cold, tugging them both to safety.

He had guts. He had guts in terms of the world of electoral poli-tics, rolling the dice to run for the presidency when he was only forty-three, when others were ahead of him in line (Senators Stuart Symington, Lyndon Johnson, Hubert Humphrey). He worked, planned, strategized, and spent. He faced down anti-Catholic feeling with style and shrewdness; read his speech to the Baptist ministers in Houston and you realize his argument was essentially this: I'm Catholic but I'm not *that* Catholic. He won.

And he remained glamorous.

Here we get to the nub. John F. Kennedy didn't know what he was about in terms of his leadership. He didn't know what he stood for, except winning. He had no particular reason for being in politics beyond the sense that it was the family business—Honey Fitz, his father, Joe, his older brother's political destiny thwarted by death—and his father wanted him to do it. Young JFK was very frank about this in his letters to friends and comments. He could feel his father's eyes "burning into the back of my head."

Kennedy's father was a charming monster who was an isolationist in foreign affairs and a constant interventionist in all other spheres, especially that of his family. In Clark Clifford's memoirs, the old Democratic Party warhorse-in-lawyer's-pinstripes wrote of his first meeting with JFK, in the 1950s. Senator Kennedy was pliant, pleas-ing, in need of legal assistance. During the meeting old Joe Kennedy called Clifford's office to bark instructions and yell at the senator and at the attorney. Clifford found it chilling. JFK handled his father coolly. To read the scene is to wonder what toll the facts of his life took on JFK, and to ponder a paradox. Old Joe's blind ambition probably made his son president. Old Joe probably made his son sick too, and less capable of performing the job.

Kennedy had a beautiful sense of rhetoric, and made the White House, when he inhabited it, seem a very exciting place—youthful and full of "vigor," his great word. But again, toward what end? Look-ing back forty years later it appears Kennedy was largely driven by fear, not hope. He *was* the age of anxiety. He feared the world would think him weak if he didn't move on Castro; he feared the world would think him belligerent after he moved on Castro. He feared the joint chiefs would be a little too enthusiastic in their anti-communism. He feared the Republicans would call him soft on communism if he didn't cleave to the chiefs. He feared Khrushchev would move on Berlin; he feared Khrushchev would put up a wall; he feared that if he responded to the wall it would heighten tensions.

It is there in the lines and between the lines of all of the histories. He constantly feared looking weak. He feared the nascent civil rights movement would force him to take actions that would be politically unpopular; he feared Democrats who favored civil rights would abandon him if he didn't stand up for blacks; he feared that if he were energetically liberal on civil rights the old Southern mandarins of the party would kill his programs on Capitol Hill; he feared inviting Martin Luther King for a meeting; he feared and feared. For a supposedly sunny man he could see the downside of everything.

But the larger point is that Kennedy never seemed to *believe* in anything. This would seem an odd thing to say. After all, his rhetoric believed in something: It was pro-democracy, anti-communist; it celebrated liberty. But what did he *think* of communism? We don't know, really. When he first met Khrushchev, in Vienna in 1961, he proved, according to the State Department notes, incapable— literally *not capable*—of asserting the moral and practical superiority of free markets over totalitarian economics. What did he think of capitalism? In all the memoirs of his thousand days, in all the biographies, he does not speak of this. One senses that on capitalism he felt the ambivalence of the son of a rapacious millionaire who'd seen dad up close. Hard to be romantic when Pop was such a pirate, and the system allowed such swashbuckling.

He seemed to have believed he could manage better than others, and he seems to have believed in himself. Which gets us to what are called "the latest revelations." There have been many. Most recently, in 2003, the historian Robert Dallek published a Kennedy biography in which he details JFK's illnesses, which were varied and potentially debilitating—including Addison's disease, chronic pain due to the collapse of bones in his spinal column, and intestinal problems including colitis and ulcers—and which should have been fully divulged to the American people both before they voted in the 1960 presidential election and as they observed and judged his presidency. Dallek then recounts the medications President Kennedy took, including corticosteroids, procaine, antispasmodics including Lomotil, testosterone, amphetamines, Nembutal, and, for a few days, an antipsychotic drug.

All of which makes JFK unusual as a president but not necessarily as a man of his time. He was in fact very much of his time—of the Sinatra generation. They got through the Depression, fought the war, and came home too hip for the room. People think the boomers discovered sex, drugs, and rock 'n' roll, but it was their parents, really—children of immigrants, home from Anzio and the South Pacific, beginning to leave the safety and social embarrassment of their parents' religion, informed by what they'd been taught as children about World War I and what happened at Versailles, influenced by Scott and Ernest and the lost generation.

Add some Marx and *The Man in the Gray Flannel Suit,* throw in some Vat 69 and Freud, add some pills—put that all together, shake it, and pour it out: what you get is *partay.* The greatest generation on Saturday night. They were a great generation, and they were more than that, and less. They created the boomers, the welfare state, the world we live in. They were one rocking group, and JFK was very much of them.

Dallek is perhaps too quick to assert that none of JFK's medications or the drugs he took seems to have impaired his leadership. He notes that Kennedy had three doctors treating him, one of whom, the famous "Dr. Feelgood," Max Jacobson, was apparently giving him amphetamine shots during that first summit with Khrushchev in Vienna. After the meeting Khrushchev operated with a new belligerence, sundering Berlin with a wall and placing missiles in Cuba.

President Kennedy did not mean to, but he ushered in the age of political weirdness, the age when it became a cliché that to be a president you had to be media-savvy, compelling, stylish. You had to be first an image, then a man. This has not served us well. Since his time we have seen a fairly odd assortment of individuals as president.

But in part for just that reason, history is not going to stop being fascinated by him. He was the beginning of the modern age.

Ms. Noonan is a contributing editor of The Wall Street Journal *and a columnist for OpinionJournal.com. She is author of* When Character Was King: A Story of Ronald Reagan *(Viking Penguin, 2001) and* A Heart, a Cross, and a Flag: America Today *(Wall Street Journal Books, 2003), a collection of her post–September 11 columns.*

36.
LYNDON BAINES JOHNSON

SURVEY RANKING: 18

BORN: August 27, 1908, Stonewall, Texas

WIFE: Claudia Alta "Lady Bird" Taylor

RELIGION: Disciples of Christ

PARTY: Democrat

MILITARY EXPERIENCE: U.S. Naval Reserve (commander)

OTHER OFFICES HELD: U.S. representative from Texas (1937–49), U.S. senator (1949–61), Senate Democratic leader (1953–61), vice president (1961–63)

TOOK OFFICE: November 22, 1963

VICE PRESIDENT: Hubert Humphrey (1965–69)

LEFT OFFICE: January 20, 1969

DIED: January 22, 1973

BURIED: Stonewall, Texas

By Robert Dallek

Lyndon B. Johnson is a case study in success and failure—a leader whose five-plus years in office between 1963 and 1969 had great positive and negative consequences and changed America forever.

Anyone who knows anything about LBJ would not be surprised at his outsized achievements for good and ill. He was a grandiose character who, as head of the New Deal's Texas National Youth Administration from 1935 to 1937, then as a representative, a senator, and vice president, outdid almost everyone who had served in each of these offices. Mindful of his ambition to be top dog, he liked to recount how after he became the first U.S. senator in the 1950s to get a car telephone, his Republican rival Everett Dirksen called to say that he was speaking from his new car phone. "Could you hold on a second, Ev?" Johnson asked. "My other phone is ringing."

Johnson's pre-presidential strivings were not without impact. The FDR White House saw him at the age of twenty-seven as the best state NYA administrator in the country; his service to his Texas 10th Congressional District constituents rivaled anything provided by other contemporary members of the House; a record as the greatest majority leader before or since marked his twelve years in the Senate; and his thousand days as vice president were remarkable for his abortive efforts to transform the office from a relatively inconsequential position to one carrying considerable influence over both domestic and foreign affairs.

Johnson's greatest achievements and failures came as president. Most everything on the plus side occurred in domestic affairs. John F. Kennedy's assassination in November 1963 demoralized the country, raising fresh doubts about its capacity to manage problems at home and compete with Soviet communism abroad. In what may have been as important an action as any he took in his administration, Johnson rallied the country to use JFK's death as a reason not to despair but to act constructively. In the eight months between November 1963 and July 1964, Johnson won congressional approval of Kennedy's $11 billion tax cut and the Civil Rights Act, which outlawed segregation in places of public accommodation. He announced a War on Poverty and made a commitment to building a Great Society.

The campaign against poverty had mixed results. Though it reduced the number of Americans living below the poverty line from some 22 percent to 11 percent of the population, many of those improved their standard of living not by developing marketable skills but by becoming welfare recipients dependent on government largesse.

The Great Society included more constructive measures that continue to serve the national well-being to this day: Medicare and Medicaid; federal aid to elementary, secondary, and higher education; environmental, safety, and consumer protection laws; the Voting Rights Act; the National Endowments for the Arts and the Humanities, National Public Radio and television's PBS; and the Departments of Transportation and Housing and Urban Development are only some of the most prominent of Johnson's accomplishments.

It was the civil rights laws, however, that had the greatest impact on American society and will be remembered as Johnson's most important actions. As a senator, Johnson understood that as long as the Southern states maintained a de jure and de facto system of apartheid, they would never regain their pre–Civil War position of economic and political power in the nation. Southern segregation not only separated the races from each other in the old Confederacy but also segregated the South from the rest of the nation. As JFK had put it when LBJ challenged him for the Democratic Party nomination in 1960, it is still too soon after the Civil War for a Southerner to win the White House.

Johnson had begun dismantling Southern segregation in 1957 when he led Congress into passing the first civil rights bill since Reconstruction in 1875. The Civil Rights Act of 1964, the Voting Rights Act of 1965, and a fair housing measure in 1968 worked a fundamental transformation in Southern economic, political, and social life and opened the way to a series of Southern presidents between 1964 and 2004 by making the South a more integral part of the nation than it had been since 1860. After Johnson won a landslide victory over Barry Goldwater in 1964, four of the country's next seven presidents were from the South—Jimmy Carter of Georgia, the two George Bushes from Texas, and Bill Clinton from Arkansas.

There is a considerable irony to Johnson's achievement. After the 1964 act passed, Johnson told press secretary Bill Moyers that he had just given away the South to the Republican Party for the foreseeable future. His prediction was prescient. By forcing integration on his native region, Johnson and liberal Democrats alienated great numbers of white Southerners who, shifting to the more conservative Republicans, ended Democratic dominance of Southern politics.

Johnson's greatest stumbles came in foreign affairs, and over Vietnam in particular. Johnson was much less comfortable with overseas challenges than he was with domestic ones. As Mrs. Johnson said early in Lyndon's presidency, "I just hope that foreign problems do not keep mounting. They do not represent Lyndon's kind of presidency." Johnson himself said half jokingly, "Foreigners are not like the folks I am used to."

Nothing plagued his presidency and did more to undermine his historical reputation than Vietnam. In part, Johnson inherited commitments from Eisenhower and Kennedy that he believed could not be jettisoned. Although there are good reasons to believe that JFK never would have Americanized the fighting in Vietnam to the extent Johnson did, LBJ did not have the standing as a foreign policy leader that Kennedy had earned with the successful resolution of the 1962 Cuban Missile Crisis and the 1963 Limited Test Ban Treaty. Without such stature, it was far more difficult to withdraw from or sharply limit U.S. commitments to Saigon than it would have been for JFK.

Besides, Johnson held a set of beliefs that convinced him of the need to preserve South Vietnam from a communist takeover, even at a heavy cost in American blood and treasure. Johnson subscribed to Eisenhower's domino theory: If South Vietnam fell, it would trigger communist victories in other Southeast Asian countries. Worse, it would be like Munich in 1938, encouraging an aggressor nation to take bolder actions. Losing Vietnam might lead to a larger war with the Soviet Union and communist China. Johnson also feared that losing South Vietnam would touch off another round of McCarthyism in the United States, allowing right-wing critics of his administration to block his Great Society bills and defeating him and the Democrats at the polls in 1968.

As a consequence, in March 1965, Johnson began an air campaign against North Vietnam called Rolling Thunder and followed it with the introduction of 100,000 combat troops in July. By the close of his presidency in 1969, Johnson had increased the number of ground forces to 535,000. But the Viet Cong and North Vietnam did not give up. Early in 1968, after the communists had launched a country-wide offensive that belied predictions of their inability to keep up the war against superior U.S. power, Johnson felt compelled to reduce the bombing and open peace talks in Paris.

Vietnam ended LBJ's chances of winning another term, and he withdrew from the race in early 1968. The war had destroyed his popularity in the United States, and after Richard Nixon, his successor, had withdrawn American troops and Hanoi seized Saigon in 1975, Johnson became tarred with the historical legacy of being the only president in American history to have lost a war.

It is always difficult to predict what a relatively recent president's historical reputation will ultimately be. Twenty-five years after Harry Truman left office, not many historians would have predicted that he would now be seen as a near-great president. Johnson will probably never shake off the defeat in Vietnam, while his domestic advances seem likely to assure him a permanent place in the front rank of chief executives. Only one thing seems reasonably sure: Johnson will not fade into obscurity the way so many of our other presidents have. If he will not be quite as large a figure as he was in his own lifetime, he will continue to radiate interest and controversy for as long as there is a United States.

Mr. Dallek is author of Flawed Giant: Lyndon B. Johnson, 1960–1973 *(1988) and* Lone Star Rising: Lyndon Johnson and His Times *(1991), both published by Oxford University Press, and, most recently,* An Unfinished Life: John F. Kennedy, 1917–1963 *(Little, Brown, 2003).*

37.

RICHARD MILHOUS NIXON

SURVEY RANKING: 32

BORN: January 9, 1913, Yorba Linda, California

WIFE: Thelma Catherine "Pat" Ryan

RELIGION: Quaker

PARTY: Republican

MILITARY EXPERIENCE: U.S. Naval Reserve (commander)

OTHER OFFICES HELD: U.S. representative from California (1947–50), U.S. senator (1951–53), vice president (1953–61)

TOOK OFFICE: January 20, 1969

VICE PRESIDENTS: Spiro Agnew (1969–73), Gerald Ford (1973–74)

LEFT OFFICE: August 9, 1974 (resigned)

DIED: April 22, 1994

BURIED: Yorba Linda, California

---

by *Kenneth W. Starr*

Any account of the presidency of Richard M. Nixon must reckon first of all with Watergate. In the three decades since Nixon resigned the presidency, the scandal has receded in the national consciousness.

Yet the shadow of that affair still hangs over the presidency. Our campaign finance laws bear its imprint. The independent counsel law that grew directly out of Watergate provided the legal framework for investigations of executive branch officials for almost three decades, until it was allowed to lapse in 1999. Since Watergate, scandals have come and gone—including that which led to the impeachment of President Clinton—but the touchstone for presidential scandal remains Watergate.

Watergate has long been seen as a failure of the rule of law. President Nixon broke the law by covering up the White House's role in the break-in at the Watergate Hotel. He hindered the Justice Department's investigation of the matter by ordering the firing of Special Prosecutor Archibald Cox. The Watergate affair was a sign that the Nixon presidency was, in the words of historian Arthur Schlesinger, an "imperial Presidency"—an aberration in American constitutionalism. Future presidents had to be prevented from acting as Nixon did, and the solution—according to this view—was to pass new laws constraining the power of the presidency.

But this account misses something important about Watergate: the extent to which the resolution of the scandal was really a triumph for the rule of law. Amid the search for the facts—for the answer to Senator Howard Baker's question, "What did the president know and when did he know it?"—Watergate was a struggle involving legal and constitutional issues of the first order.

The main focus of that struggle was whether Nixon was required to hand over tape recordings of White House conversations related to Watergate. The recordings were thought to be able to shed light on the White House's role in the affair. Both Cox and the Senate committee investigating Watergate subpoenaed the tapes shortly after the public learned of their existence in the summer of 1973. When President Nixon refused to hand them over, the Senate could do little to force him to comply. The special prosecutor, however, could. He went to court and got a legal ruling requiring the president to hand over the tapes. The president appealed. It was becoming clear to the nation that Watergate would eventually be resolved by the Supreme Court.

The case made its way haltingly through the judiciary. The Court of Appeals for the District of Columbia affirmed the ruling that the president had to produce the tapes. On October 20, 1973, Nixon struck back at Cox and ordered him fired. Both Attorney General Elliott Richardson and Deputy Attorney General William Ruckelshaus resigned rather than obey the president's order in what came to be known as the "Saturday Night Massacre." The next April, with the trials of former Nixon aides approaching, the tapes were subpoenaed once more. Again Nixon resisted on the ground of executive privilege, and again a federal court ordered the tapes produced.

The issue finally came before the Supreme Court. There, the president's lawyers advanced three arguments. First, they contended that the dispute over the tapes was entirely within the executive branch and that the court therefore had no power to intervene. The president, not the special prosecutor, had the authority to decide what material should be made available to the grand jury. Second, Nixon's lawyers argued that the tapes were protected by an absolute executive privilege. Discretion to invoke executive privilege belonged to the president alone and could not be reviewed by any court. Finally, they argued that even if executive privilege was not absolute, the tapes were nevertheless "presumptively privileged." The tapes were not to be turned over to the grand jury without a strong showing that they were needed.

Resolution of these issues would help shape the future role of the presidency in our constitutional system. There was little doubt that the president was entitled to some kind of executive privilege; only the scope and basis of that privilege was in question. Nixon argued that the privilege was a constitutional one, and his legal position was strongly supported by history. In their brief to the court, his lawyers cited dozens of instances in which presidents had refused congressional requests for information. One precedent was President Jefferson's refusal to comply with a subpoena in the trial of Aaron Burr.

Executive privilege, Nixon's lawyers argued, belonged to the presidency as an institution. "If a President abuses the privileges and powers of his office," they wrote, "the proper remedy is not to reduce the office, but to deal with the offense, and to do so in accordance with the Constitution."

It was a bold constitutional position. However correct Nixon might have been about the constitutional question, to some his assertion of the privilege looked craven and self-interested. But his position was, in its way, an act of leadership, for it sought to preserve the power of the office for future presidents. If his argument won out, Nixon himself would still be in peril, but the constitutional foundation of the presidency would remain strong and secure.

The Supreme Court ultimately vindicated Nixon's claim of a constitutional privilege: "The privilege is fundamental to the operation of Government and inextricably rooted in the separation of powers under the Constitution," wrote Chief Justice Warren Burger. The public interest demanded that discussions within the executive branch be frank and honest, which was possible only if the president and his advisers could trust that their conversations would remain confidential.

The principle was thus firmly established, but Nixon still lost. The court rejected his claim that the privilege was absolute and established its own authority to determine its limits. The court's duty "to say what the law is"—first invoked long ago in *Marbury v. Madison* and affirmed many times since—was too important. And in the end, the court, not the president, got the final say on constitutional matters. The scope of executive privilege also turned out to be much narrower than that of privileges based in the common law, such as the attorney-client privilege. A general assertion of executive privilege did not outweigh the need for evidence in a specific criminal case. The Supreme Court ordered President Nixon to turn over the tapes.

Before the high court heard the case, speculation had floated that Nixon would not comply if he lost his appeal. His deputy press secretary had on one occasion said that Nixon would abide by a "definitive" decision from the court. Some questioned what precisely he meant by "definitive." In addition, Nixon's assertion that executive privilege could not be reviewed by the court, if taken seriously, appeared to signal resistance to an adverse ruling. But when the decision came down, Nixon dutifully released the tapes. The conversations contained on the recordings were damning, revealing what Nixon knew and when he knew it. Within weeks, the president of the United States resigned.

Whether Richard Nixon's last acts as president—his compliance with the court's decision and his resignation—are to be counted as acts of leadership will remain a subject of debate. Nixon undoubtedly prevented more harm to the country than if he had refused to produce the tapes. But by then Watergate had already dragged on, and what had come to light reflected very badly on Nixon's role in the entire affair. True leadership might have spared the nation the whole mess. What Nixon's compliance does represent, however, is a final act of obeisance to the rule of law and the Supreme Court's authority to define the law. In that, it preserved an important principle for the nation to carry forward.

Mr. Starr is dean of Pepperdine University Law School and author of First Among Equals: The Supreme Court in American Life *(Warner, 2002). He has served as a federal appellate judge, solicitor general, and Whitewater independent counsel.*

38.

GERALD RUDOLPH FORD, JR.

SURVEY RANKING: 28

BORN: July 14, 1913, Omaha, Nebraska

WIFE: Elizabeth Anne "Betty" Bloomer

RELIGION: Episcopalian

PARTY: Republican

MILITARY EXPERIENCE: U.S. Naval Reserve (lieutenant commander)

OTHER OFFICES HELD: U.S. representative from Michigan (1949–73), House Republican leader (1965–73), vice president (1973–74)

TOOK OFFICE: August 9, 1974

VICE PRESIDENT: Nelson Rockefeller

LEFT OFFICE: January 20, 1977

by Thomas J. Bray

Few presidents have ever come into office holding a weaker hand than Gerald R. Ford. The Watergate scandal had left a bitter residue of mistrust and anger. The demoralizing American retreat from Vietnam hung heavy over the land. The economy was headed into the worst downturn since the late 1950s. Inflation stood at 12 percent.

Ford himself had no political base outside the 5th Congressional District of Michigan. He had been appointed vice president by the widely detested Nixon a scant eight months earlier, succeeding the disgraced Spiro T. Agnew, making him the only chief executive never to have been elected either president or vice president.

Jerry Ford was sworn in at a hasty midday ceremony the day after Nixon announced his resignation. That night he addressed the nation from the East Room. He promised openness and candor, and he uttered the line that is perhaps best remembered from his 895 days in office: "My fellow Americans, our long national nightmare is over." A touch melodramatic, perhaps, and not entirely accurate, for there was far more to the nightmare than Watergate. But the line spoke deftly to the feelings of most Americans, even those who had supported Nixon to the end.

It wasn't long, however, before the new president hit the jagged shoals of politics. After barely more than a week in office, Ford picked New York's liberal Republican governor, Nelson Rockefeller, as his vice president, deeply offending the conservative wing of his party. And a few weeks after that came Ford's pardon of Nixon.

Suspicion was rampant that Ford had made a deal with Nixon. Ford tried to tamp down the anger with a rare presidential appearance before a congressional committee to answer questions about the pardon. He argued persuasively that continued focus on the Nixon scandals would consume the country in vituperative debate and detract from Washington's—and Ford's—ability to get on with things. But his rationale might have been more persuasive had Ford swept the White House clean of other vestiges of the Nixon era. Instead, he initially retained the entire Nixon apparatus, from Chief of Staff Alexander Haig to Secretary of State and National Security Adviser Henry Kissinger.

And he seemed to have a hard time placing his own stamp on the issues. "If you don't look too closely," opined a *Wall Street Journal* editorial in late September, "all you will see is a Tower of Babel." After a series of economic "mini-summits" around the country, Ford went to Congress in October, just weeks before the midterm congressional elections, to outline his thinking. He demanded a combination of spending cuts and a 5 percent temporary surtax on incomes to combat the deficit. As for inflation, he pointed to a large WIN button on his lapel and asked "every American to join in this massive mobilization" to "whip inflation now."

Democrats could scarcely believe their good luck. The WIN buttons became an instant laughingstock. And the proposed tax increase yielded the high economic ground to the liberals on the eve of an election. Just to make sure everybody got the point, Democrats promptly proposed a tax cut (which they would just as quickly forget after the election). Ford's approval ratings collapsed, and Democrats increased their majorities in both houses of Congress to nearly veto-proof levels. The economy ended the year down 0.5 percent.

On foreign affairs, it was a time of outright retreat. American combat troops already had been withdrawn from Vietnam, but now the heavily Democratic Congress refused even to provide funds to South Vietnam. In April 1975, Saigon fell. Thousands of terrified South Vietnamese officials were photographed being airlifted from a U.S. facility, one of the most ignominious moments in American history. (The ladder leading to the rooftop helipad is on display in the Ford Museum in Grand Rapids, Michigan, a curious if honest choice of mementos.) Two weeks later, thirty-eight Marines and airmen died in a controversial rescue attempt after the communist government of Cambodia seized an American merchant ship, the SS *Mayaguez*, in international waters.

Ford embraced the Nixon-Kissinger strategy of détente. In July 1975 he outraged conservatives by refusing to meet with exiled Soviet author Alexander Solzhenitsyn in the Oval Office. Just a month later, Ford journeyed to Europe to meet with Soviet boss Leonid Brezhnev and sign the so-called Helsinki Accords. Again conservatives were upset, for the accords seemed to ratify Soviet domination of Eastern Europe in return for vague promises by Moscow to adhere to human rights conventions.

In fairness, Ford did manage to wangle an increase in defense spending, the first in years. And the Helsinki Accords may have helped undermine the moral authority of the Soviet Union by turning the focus on its human rights record. Too, by early 1975 much of the Nixon staff was on its way out. The new president's men included some who are among today's most distinguished public servants: Donald Rumsfeld (Ford's White House chief of staff and later defense secretary), Richard Cheney (Rumsfeld's deputy), and Alan Greenspan (chairman of Ford's Council of Economic Advisers).

And by 1975 Ford had reversed field on taxes, in part because his staff was absorbing some of the thinking about economic incentives that came to be known as supply side economics. Dropping the surtax idea, Ford proposed a $28 billion tax cut, though he insisted on linking it to equal spending cuts—a prescription for gridlock. Yet Ford did show that he had the courage of his convictions on spending, issuing a record sixty-six vetoes in eighteen months, fifty-four of which were upheld. The economy began to surge.

Politically, however, it proved to be too little too late. By the beginning of 1976, Ford's image—as a well-meaning but somewhat clumsy man—had been set. Worse, Ford was about to pay a heavy price for the disaffection on his right. The challenge came from California's popular ex-governor, Ronald Reagan. As Steven Hayward notes in his biography, *The Age of Reagan,* the major media in late 1975 "unsurprisingly greeted Reagan's announcement with a great harrumph." And indeed Ford swept the first five primaries.

But as Reagan honed his message, stirring the Republican faithful with laments about the size of government and bemoaning the "giveaway" of the Panama Canal, Ford found himself in a fight to the death. Reagan, though his campaign was flat broke, won North Carolina, then Texas and California, among others. Ford emerged the victor, but he had been badly wounded. Immediate post-convention polls showed him trailing the Democratic nominee, Jimmy Carter, by as much as 56 percent to 33 percent.

Carter cleverly appealed to moderates with talk of zero-based budgeting, rhetoric about never telling a lie, and vague promises to reform the tax code. Worse for Ford, the economy suddenly leveled off early in the fall, prompting worries of a new downturn. And in the second presidential debate, Ford weirdly asserted that "there is no Soviet domination of Eastern Europe, and there never will be under a Ford administration," a gaffe that dominated headlines for days late in the campaign.

Still, Ford came close, carrying twenty-seven states with 241 electoral votes. Carter barely managed a popular vote majority, 50.06 percent against Ford's 48 percent.

Ford's longtime friend and aide Robert Hartmann would later assess his weakness this way: "Ford was simply too nice a guy; he boasted that he had adversaries but no enemies." But Ford's fundamental decency made him the right man to lead the country after the trauma of Watergate. In 1977, as President Carter delivered his inaugural address, he turned to Ford and said to heartfelt applause: "For myself and my country, I want to thank my predecessor for all he has done to heal our land."

Mr. Bray is a columnist and former editorial page editor at The Detroit News.

39.

JAMES EARL CARTER, JR.

SURVEY RANKING: 34

BORN: October 1, 1924, Plains, Georgia

WIFE: Eleanor Rosalynn Smith

RELIGION: Baptist

PARTY: Democrat

MILITARY EXPERIENCE: U.S. Navy (lieutenant commander)

OTHER OFFICES HELD: Georgia state senator (1963–67), governor (1971–75)

TOOK OFFICE: January 20, 1977

VICE PRESIDENT: Walter Mondale

LEFT OFFICE: January 20, 1981

by Joshua Muravchik

Jimmy Carter's most enduring legacy—though one he stumbled on quite by accident—is the establishment of human rights as a central objective of American diplomacy. The importance of the issue is now taken for granted, but this was not so before Carter. One term before Carter's, Henry Kissinger had declared, in his confirmation hearings for the post of secretary of state, that "it is dangerous for us to make the domestic policy of countries around the world a direct objective of American foreign policy." This ruffled no senatorial feathers. Today, no nominee for that position would dream of uttering such a statement.

Ironically, Carter had apparently thought little about the subject of human rights. The book he published in 1975 to launch his quest for the Democratic nomination, *Why Not the Best?*, spoke of the need for a foreign policy based on "ethics, honesty and morality," whatever that might mean. But nowhere in the volume did the words "human rights" appear.

Indeed, Carter's initial attitude to human rights was negative. One of the chief human rights issues of the day was the right of emigration from the Soviet Union. Congress had passed the Jackson-Vanik amendment linking Soviet trade privileges to the right of emigration. Carter distinguished himself from most other Democratic aspirants by staking out a position of staunch opposition to Jackson-Vanik. He explained his view in terms that were redolent of Kissinger's position. Calling Jackson-Vanik "ill-advised," Carter declared: "Russia is a proud nation like we are, and if Russian communist leaders had passed a resolution saying that they were not going to do this or that if we didn't do something domestically, we would have reacted adversely to it. That's exactly what's happened."

What changed Carter's thinking about human rights was the exercise of writing the Democratic platform. Assured of the nomination by the time of the Democratic convention in 1976, Carter's biggest concern was to unite behind him a party still ravaged by the Vietnam debate. At the platform committee, hawkish Democrats, led by Daniel Patrick Moynihan (who would win a New York Senate seat the same year), plumped for tough language on communist regimes while dovish Democrats advocated penalties against rightist dictatorships. Finally, Moynihan turned to the doves with this proposal: "We'll be against the dictators you don't like the most if you'll be against the dictators we don't like the most."

A ringing denunciation of all human rights violators was thus written into the platform. Soon, Carter gave a speech about human rights, and when his pollsters told him that it went over very well, more such speeches followed. This success was reinforced by President Ford's debate gaffe of saying "there is no Soviet domination of Eastern Europe." Human rights became "a beautiful campaign issue," one Carter aide told *The New Yorker*'s Elizabeth Drew.

Carter spoke about human rights in his inaugural address, and his administration made some dramatic symbolic gestures during the early days of his presidency, so that within a few months, as he recalled in his memoirs, "human rights had become the central theme of our foreign policy in the minds of the press and the public." This last phrase implied that in his own mind, there were higher priorities—and there were.

Popular though it was, Carter's human rights advocacy soon led to diplomatic troubles. Soviet spokesmen denounced it as an "unsavory ploy," while five rightist regimes in Latin America announced they would no longer accept American aid. When the Kremlin angrily protested a State Department release criticizing the persecution of Soviet dissident Andrei Sakharov, Carter flinched. He told reporters that the statement had not been cleared with him and that he wished to avoid "aggravating" relations with Moscow.

Subsequently, in his personal meetings with foreign dictators, Carter behaved obsequiously. Just months before the start of the Iranian revolution, he told the shah that Iran was an "island of stability," because of the "love which your people give to you." And he explained: "The shah is very deeply concerned about human rights."

Nor was this the only autocrat in whom Carter detected such humane beliefs. He hailed Yugoslavia's Josip Broz Tito as "a man who believes in human rights" and who "as much as any other person . . . exemplifies . . . the eagerness for freedom, independence and liberty that exists throughout . . . the world." In Warsaw, Carter offered a toast to "the freedom of the Polish people and to your enlightened leaders—particularly First Secretary [Edward] Gierek and his wife," also commenting that "our concept of human rights is preserved in Poland . . . much better than other European nations with which I'm familiar." Welcoming Romania's Nicolae Ceausescu, Carter proclaimed: "Our goals are the same, to have a just system of economics and politics. . . . We believe in enhancing human rights . . . [and] the freedom of our own people."

As Carter and his team labored to turn the human rights theme into a policy, they found they had to wrestle with several issues. A key one was the issue of consistency. The U.S. was reluctant to criticize, say, China or Saudi Arabia as forcefully as, say, Mozambique or Guatemala. A heavy diplomatic price might be paid for targeting powerful countries, but to focus on weak countries would seem hypocritical.

The toughest issue, however, was the conflict between human rights goals and what was perhaps the paramount aim of Carter's presidency, reconciliation with America's adversaries. Early on, he declared: "We are now free of . . . inordinate fear of communism. . . . For too many years, we . . . fought fire with fire, never thinking that fire is better quenched with water." Later at a summit meeting, Carter hugged and kissed a visibly startled Leonid Brezhnev. This followed the declaration by Secretary of State Cyrus Vance that Brezhnev and Carter "have similar dreams and aspirations about the most fundamental issues."

As with the Soviet Union, so with other adversaries. Carter normalized relations with communist China at a higher price, at Taiwan's expense, than his predecessors had been willing to pay. And he made friendly gestures toward Vietnam, Cuba, and various Third World revolutionaries. But since these adversaries also were among the world's most repressive regimes, the quest for warmer relations with them could not readily be reconciled with the strong espousal of human rights.

In any event, most of these gestures went unrequited, as a string of radical regimes rose to power spewing anti-American invective. Above all, Carter's Soviet policy—a version of détente still more conciliatory than Kissinger had pursued—was torn to shreds by the Soviet invasion of Afghanistan.

The results were ironic. Seeing that Carter's accommodationism only seemed to whet the appetites of our foes, Americans turned instead to Ronald Reagan, who promised to prosecute the Cold War more aggressively than ever. On the other hand, the human rights policy that Carter had been willing to sacrifice in favor of a self-defeating détente ended in triumph. For all of Carter's equivocations and inconsistencies, the mere fact that an American president had used his bully pulpit to raise a cry about human rights had profoundly affected the rest of the world and the American public.

Stung by his electoral defeat in 1980, Carter labored to resurrect his reputation by inserting himself in international affairs more aggressively than any other former president in memory. He wrote to foreign leaders during the 1990–91 Persian Gulf crisis urging them to oppose U.S. military action to liberate Kuwait. He flew to North Korea in 1994 to negotiate what proved to be an illusory nuclear weapons deal, lubricated by Carter's fawning praise for Kim Il Sung reminiscent of his earlier hosannas to Tito, Gierek, and Ceausescu. He then rushed to Bosnia at the behest of Bosnian Serb strongman Radovan Karadzic to forge a short-lived cease-fire that served mainly to stem the momentum for Western intervention to protect the Muslims.

Most inexplicable was the book he published in 1985 about the Middle East conflict, *The Blood of Abraham*. Since the Israel-Egypt peace that he brokered was one of the few achievements of an unsuccessful presidency, it was natural that he should want to underscore his authority on this subject. But this volume was woven of twisted facts and virulent hostility toward Israel. It claimed for example that Israel attacked Jordan in the Six Day War, although the reverse was true, and that the Palestine Liberation Organization was founded in 1964 in response to "increasing Israeli encroachment on lands and rights of the Arabs," whereas the PLO itself explained that the reason for its founding was that "the partitioning of Palestine and the establishment of Israel are illegal." The book served only to stain Carter's reputation as a peacemaker. Once again, he had demonstrated his uncanny instinct for self-defeat.

Mr. Muravchik is a resident scholar at the American Enterprise Institute and author of Heaven on Earth: The Rise and Fall of Socialism *(Encounter, 2002).*

40.

RONALD WILSON REAGAN

SURVEY RANKING: 6

BORN: February 6, 1911, Tampico, Illinois

WIVES: Jane Wyman (divorced 1948), Nancy Davis (married 1952)

RELIGION: Presbyterian

PARTY: Republican

MILITARY EXPERIENCE: U.S. Army (captain)

OTHER OFFICES HELD: Governor of California (1967–75)

TOOK OFFICE: January 20, 1981

VICE PRESIDENT: George Bush

LEFT OFFICE: January 20, 1989

DIED: June 5, 2004

BURIED: Simi Valley, California

By Harvey C. Mansfield

Ronald Reagan was a partisan president and remains one. Our greatest presidents, George Washington and Abraham Lincoln, were America's founder and its savior, and they are held in esteem, or revered, by all. But to like Reagan without reservations, you have to be of his party. Otherwise, you can admire certain of his qualities, but much of what he did you will not approve of. In this Reagan resembles Franklin D. Roosevelt, another partisan president who remains a hero to his party and is grudgingly admired by the party opposite (while being openly admired by Reagan himself).

Reagan was not as successful a partisan as Roosevelt. Reagan did not found a durable majority for his party as Roosevelt did for his. His elections in 1980 and particularly in 1984 were not "critical elections" like Roosevelt's in 1932 but personal victories with modest advantage, or even losses, for his party in Congress. Although Reagan's vice president did succeed him for one term, the Democrats regained the presidency with Bill Clinton's election in 1992. No doubt new circumstances reducing the strength of party organization and loyalty made it harder for Reagan to achieve a lasting party majority; and he did succeed in pushing the Clinton administration to the right. But he had an ambition comparable to Roosevelt's, promising at his first inaugural in 1981 to undertake an "era of national renewal."

The nation to be renewed was the one Roosevelt and his successors had corrupted by rendering the American people too dependent on government. The people's self-rule was the element to be renewed. Asked Reagan: "If no one among us is capable of governing himself, then who among us is capable of governing someone else?" Reagan hit this theme much earlier, in 1964, when giving an address on behalf of Barry Goldwater's campaign, known to Reaganites as "The Speech," the one that first gained him national attention and that prepared his run for governor of California in 1966.

His presidential majority in 1980 was composed of Goldwater's following of "conservatives" and of Richard Nixon's "silent majority," which included Democrats disgusted with the takeover of their party by the New Left, the contingent that made George McGovern the Democratic candidate in 1972. These "Reagan Democrats" from ethnic minorities drew closer to conservatism than they had been when voting for Nixon. Reagan was as eager to win as Nixon but more persuasive than he and more confident that his ideas could prevail without the cover of disguise.

Reagan, however, was always more Republican than conservative.

Because he thought he could win Democrats to his ideas, he did not need the coherence of a doctrine—or wish for its inflexibility. What came to be known as the "Reagan Revolution" comprised major departures not only from the status quo but also from conservative orthodoxy.

A self-made man educated at a small college in Illinois and then employed as an actor in Hollywood, he did not hobnob with intellectuals but worked out his own ideas. His lack of breeding earned him the contempt of liberal intellectuals who typecast him as (in Clark Clifford's words) an "amiable dunce." In fact he was a reflective man who chose among the ideas of his time without regard to convention or fashion.

Having an actor's career did not prevent Reagan from thinking on his own but rather let him learn how to communicate. It takes thought to convey a thought. An actor communicates a general idea through the representation of a particular character such as "the Gipper." And President Reagan became the "Great Communicator" with just this device in his speeches: He kept them simple, kept repeating the same ideas, and always illustrated them with a joke or a story.

He was the best jokester in the presidency since Lincoln, and not all his lines were given to him. Wheeled into a hospital emergency room wounded after the assassination attempt in 1981, he looked at the surgeons and said: "I hope you're all Republicans." His speeches usually featured stories of individuals like the ones he was addressing, only somehow distinctive and illustrative. Presidents since Reagan have tried to imitate his skilled rhetorical instinct for the exemplary.

What were Reagan's ideas? Senator Daniel Patrick Moynihan said with nonpartisan insight in 1980 that the Republicans were the party of ideas even though not the party of the intellectuals. Yet in foreign policy Reagan challenged the thinking of the leading Republican intellectual, Henry Kissinger, in a way that Kissinger himself explained: "Reagan was the first postwar president to take the offensive." He was dissatisfied with the policy of détente because it depended on the mutual vulnerability of the Soviet Union and the United States. It equalized the two powers not only militarily but also morally, thus freezing the status quo. This meant, Reagan saw, that the United States was accepting the legitimacy of its adversary and could not assert the moral superiority of its own freedom. Reagan, in a famous speech of March 1983 that shocked the sophisticates of realism and relativism, did not hesitate to call America good and the Soviet Union an "evil empire."

From the first, Reagan began a deliberate campaign to raise the "costs of empire" for the Soviet Union, especially (but not only) by supplying the Afghans defending themselves against the Soviet invasion of December 1979. In Europe he got an intermediate nuclear force installed over strenuous opposition from the left. Discerning (contrary to most experts) that the Soviet Union was weaker than it appeared and ripe for overthrow, Reagan determined to run an arms race that he thought it would lose.

His key measure was the Strategic Defense Initiative, or SDI, a program for missile defense dubbed Star Wars by critics ridiculing it as science fiction. Fiction or not (SDI is yet unfinished and unproven in 2003), it convinced Soviet generals and leaders that they could not compete, and the evil empire began to disintegrate. Reagan, having originally rejected "summitry" but now turning diplomat, joined with the Soviet leader Mikhail Gorbachev in a deal for arms reduction that proved to be the prelude for communist collapse in the beginning of the first Bush administration. When Reagan at Berlin in 1987 memorably called on Gorbachev to "tear down this wall!" it was not the vain hope it seemed to many.

By taking the offensive Reagan brought final success to the largely defensive policy of containing communism that America had begun in 1945. He saw that America could "stay the course" (a favorite phrase) by departing from the course, and looking back now, one can see that this was his great achievement.

During his administration foreign affairs took second place in the eyes of the public to his efforts on behalf of the "opportunity society," his domestic policy. Like Theodore Roosevelt, he proposed that government should open opportunity to Americans, and thus reengage their capacity for self-rule. To do this Reagan departed again from Republican fiscal orthodoxy to support supply side economics, called Reaganomics by his Democratic critics. Although he began by accusing the Democrats of piling deficit upon deficit, he soon declared that he would not balance the budget on the backs of the American taxpayer. He cut taxes, spent on defense, and let the deficit grow—thinking thereby to inhibit the domestic spending of the Democrats in control of Congress.

In everything he was optimistic and radiated optimism: "America's best days are ahead of her." He was averse to gloom, malaise (in contrast to President Carter), and sacrifice, yet he demanded greatness from his country. He gave the impression that from the industry and generosity of Americans and from the spontaneous freedom of human nature, greatness would come easy.

A stain on his presidency was the scandal in Reagan's foreign policy, the Iran-contra affair, in which Reagan's lieutenants sought to evade a law forbidding U.S. aid to the contras, anti-communist fighters in Nicaragua. It showed the risks he would take and the perils of his system of delegation. It also showed how far the Democrats in Congress would go in taking the part of a communist government against counterrevolutionaries.

Reagan's claim to presidential greatness is that by deliberate but energetic policy and with peaceful means, and against the advice of the experts and the obstruction of partisan opponents, he won the Cold War that America waged for forty-five years against one of the three worst regimes known in human history.

Reagan's domestic legacy has been lasting but controversial: In the declining era of big government he rallied the conservatives, gave them the taste of victory, and left them a hero to cheer. He resolved nothing, but his was an important episode in America's back-and-forth political history between the party that promotes and the party that restrains the people (this is Alexis de Tocqueville's distinction). Blurring the distinction, Reagan was a Republican whose gifts and policies brought his party from one that restrains the people closer to one that sets them free.

Mr. Mansfield is a professor of government at Harvard.

41.
GEORGE HERBERT WALKER BUSH

SURVEY RANKING: 21

BORN: June 12, 1924, Milton, Massachusetts

WIFE: Barbara Pierce

RELIGION: Episcopalian

PARTY: Republican

MILITARY EXPERIENCE: U.S. Navy (lieutenant junior grade)

OTHER OFFICES HELD: U.S. representative from Texas (1967–71), ambassador to United Nations (1971–73), director of central intelligence (1976–77), vice president (1981–89)

TOOK OFFICE: January 20, 1989

VICE PRESIDENT: J. Danforth Quayle

LEFT OFFICE: January 20, 1993

By Pete du Pont

George Bush's presidency was defined by the core values he brought to the White House: honesty, decency, and a commitment to do the right thing, be a team player, and work with the establishment to accomplish his objectives.

Author Michael Beschloss believes it was Bush's father, the establishment Republican senator from Connecticut, who was the primary influence on the young George Bush. Prescott Bush sought to work with other nonideological "responsible Republicans," like Nelson Rockefeller, Henry Cabot Lodge, and William Scranton, men whose political priority was to sit down with the other party's leaders to achieve consensus. In George Bush's formative years that was the establishment's view of proper politics: Principles and policies were less important than bipartisan agreement.

Thus when Bush assumed office he was not a visionary like Ronald Reagan, a political triangulator like Bill Clinton, or a suspicious conspirator like Richard Nixon. He was a moderate of the Eisenhower school, a believer in bringing everyone together around the table to accomplish mutual goals. He sought "a kinder, gentler nation," as he put it in his 1988 Republican convention speech, meaning we should paint our vision in bipartisan pastels rather than the bold primary colors of his predecessor.

These beliefs had been reflected in his campaign for the 1980 Republican presidential nomination, as Bush set himself apart from the ultimate victor, Ronald Reagan, by seeking a middle way on most policy matters, criticizing Reagan's economic programs as "voodoo economics" and admitting that he had little interest in "the vision thing."

Nor in 1988 did Bush, Reagan's vice president, endorse any of the major domestic reform ideas debated in that presidential campaign. He was not for school choice, which the education establishment derided. Nor was he in favor of replacing welfare with work or for giving working people the option of individually owned market Social Security accounts, an idea he characterized as "nutty and dumb." Such ideas were then the antithesis of establishment thinking, but President Clinton would accomplish welfare reform, and Bush's own son would work toward school choice and Social Security reform.

Bush's personal experiences and beliefs—his fifty-eight missions as a navy pilot in the Pacific in World War II, his service as ambassador to the United Nations, chief diplomat in Beijing, and director of the CIA, and his inherited belief that he had a responsibility to do good—led him to focus his presidential energies on foreign policy.

Immediately upon becoming president, Bush sought "a total reevaluation as to where we stood" relative to the Soviet Union, intending to work with Mikhail Gorbachev rather than calling the USSR an "evil empire." When the Berlin Wall fell in 1989, Bush said, "We tried hard to understand the pressures on Gorbachev," because "the stupidest thing any president could have done then would have been to go over there, dance on the Berlin Wall, and stick his fingers right into the eyes of the Soviet military and Gorbachev."

But John F. Kennedy had sharply criticized the Soviet Union while the wall was up in his "Ich bin ein Berliner!" speech, and President Reagan had demanded in 1987: "Mr. Gorbachev, tear down this wall!" It would have been consistent for the new president to visit Berlin when the wall came down and explain to the world the enormous victory freedom finally had won over the totalitarian USSR. But that would have continued confrontation, so President Bush thought it inappropriate even to cheer. When CBS's Lesley Stahl asked how elated he felt, he recorded his answer in his diary: " 'I'm very pleased,' I replied evenly."

After the Iraqi invasion and occupation of Kuwait in the summer of 1990, the president was at his very best. He used his consensus-building skills and considerable international goodwill to persuade the United Nations and Congress to authorize the use of force against Saddam Hussein. With U.S. forces leading the charge, the international coalition he had assembled liberated Kuwait in six weeks. It was superb and successful leadership.

But at the crucial moment Saddam was allowed to remain in power. Continuing the war and occupying Iraq, National Security Adviser Brent Scowcroft explained, would have "unilaterally exceeded the United Nations mandate and would have destroyed the precedent on international response to aggression we hoped to establish." The administration thus placed in the hands of an unwilling international establishment the task of containing a cunning and determined dictator. The ultimate consequence was Saddam's continued enslavement of Iraqis and the murder of thousands of Iraqi Shiites and Kurds, and leaving the task of removing Saddam from power to the next President Bush.

The most consequential domestic policy decision of the Bush presidency was his decision to break his 1988 campaign pledge of "no new taxes" just as a recession began to affect the economy in the summer of 1990. President Bush had successfully dealt with a range of domestic issues, from the war on drugs to the Americans with Disabilities Act (which he says was the domestic act of which he was most proud), but it always seemed that he never much liked dealing with them.

Richard Darman, director of the Office of Management and Budget, and John Sununu, the White House chief of staff, often get the blame for abandoning the no-new-taxes pledge and agreeing to a flawed tax-and-spend budget agreement with the Democrats who controlled Congress. But the negotiation was vintage Bush. He wanted to work with the bipartisan establishment to do the right thing, offering to "sit down in good faith and talk with no conditions."

As vice president, Bush had been loyal to President Reagan's tax reduction policies, which had produced six consecutive years of economic growth (and five of declining deficits as well). But reducing the deficit—occasionally by spending reductions, but most often by tax increases—was the holy grail of the Republican establishment's economic thinking. Consistent with this view, Bush declared the tax increases and spending reallocations of the 1990 bipartisan budget compromise to be "good medicine for the economy."

Thus Washington's economic focus shifted from economic growth to deficit reduction, which turned out to be politically fatal for the president as the voters decided to change leaders in midstream.

President Bush was an ethical and honest chief executive, never ideological and rarely partisan. What was substantively costly and frustrating about the Bush presidency was the kinder and gentler team player approach to everything from economic policy to dealing with the world's most corrupt dictatorship.

Daniel Ostrander, Bush's enthusiastic political biographer, summed up the president's leadership as "good governance through pragmatism." Pragmatism is certainly important to successful executive leadership, but painting one's vision in bold primary colors often helps a president more than the good-government pastels that were the signature philosophy of Bush's leadership.

Mr. du Pont, a former governor of Delaware, was a candidate for the Republican presidential nomination in 1988. He is chairman of the Dallas-based National Center for Policy Analysis and a columnist for OpinionJournal.com.

42

WILLIAM JEFFERSON CLINTON

SURVEY RANKING: 22

BORN: August 19, 1946, Hope, Arkansas

WIFE: Hillary Rodham

RELIGION: Baptist

PARTY: Democrat

MILITARY EXPERIENCE: None

OTHER OFFICES HELD: Attorney General of Arkansas (1977–79), governor (1979–81, 1983–92)

TOOK OFFICE: January 20, 1993

VICE PRESIDENT: Albert Gore

LEFT OFFICE: January 20, 2001

by Paul Johnson

Presenting a just estimate of the Clinton presidency will pose perhaps insoluble problems to historians. The printed record of his doings, misdoings, and omissions is unarguably deplorable from start to finish. Yet he was reelected without difficulty, and some would argue that, had it been constitutionally possible for him to run for a third term, he would have been elected again. It is a fact that historians will have to take into account, for it is central to the success he enjoyed that William Jefferson Clinton was a formidable personality, at least in one sense: Face-to-face, it was almost impossible to dislike him. Indeed it was difficult not to like him very much. As Tony Blair put it to me: "I found I had to like him, despite all the evidence."

Yet who, or what, was one liking? Other men who have gotten into trouble in the White House—one thinks of Andrew Johnson, Warren Harding, Richard Nixon—were distinctive personalities, to be made the subject of deeply etched portraits. They could be grasped. Clinton was, is, elusive. Like Ronald Reagan he was a consummate actor. But whereas Reagan devised his own part, wrote his own lines, and passionately believed in both, Clinton ad-libbed. He believed in nothing, or perhaps one should say in anything, since most positions received his fleeting endorsements at one time or another.

He certainly believed in himself, that is, in his capacity to occupy high office, and this self-justification by faith carried him through all the embarrassments and humiliations to which he was subjected during his eight vertiginous years of power. One minute he would (as in 1994) be answering questions on TV from a silly teenager about his under-pants; the next he would pick up the phone and speak to the Russian president, seemingly unaware of any incongruity.

This confidence in his star and his survival was not attended by arrogance. There was nothing subjectively arrogant about Clinton; had there been, he would have been much easier to destroy. His power, rather, lay in his capacity to edit unwelcome reality out of his life. This may have been hereditary. Clinton's family background was unfortunate, to put it mildly, and there is no more to be said about it other than to applaud his strength in rising above it. His mother, Virginia Kelley, provided a clue in explaining how she survived her rackety life: "I construct an airtight box. I keep inside it what I want to think about, and everything else stays beyond the walls. Inside is white, outside is black. . . . Inside is love and friends and optimism. Outside is negativity, can't-doism, and any criticism of me and mine." Bill Clinton would not have been able to describe his defensive tech-nique so clearly. But that is what he did, with great success. As a result, while never arrogant, he was always secure.

He was clever, quick, and capable of huge efforts over short time spans. He has been compared to a geyser. From a marshy launching pad in Arkansas he got himself to Georgetown, to Oxford as a Rhodes scholar, to Yale Law School, and to a law professorship at the

University of Arkansas. This quickly propelled him into the attorney general's chair in Little Rock, then to the governorship. He was barely thirty-two when first elected governor in 1978 and, though he lost his reelection bid in 1980—his only defeat at the hands of the voters—he thereafter served another ten years, 1983–92, relinquishing power only to take up the presidency.

This performance can be taken either way. When he ran for the presidency, one commentator noted: "Anyone who has been elected governor of Arkansas five times cannot be an entirely honest man." On the other hand, his record in winning and holding voters was there for all to see. In particular he learned exactly how to nurse the local opinion-formers—"the car salesman if white, the funeral parlor owners if black."

He was affable, easygoing, uncontentious, friendly to all. It is true that as governor he accomplished little or nothing. But there were advantages in inactivity: Clinton got to Washington with few enemies and virtually no intellectual baggage, other than a bland support for all progressive causes, veneering over the innate conservatism of a man who knows he can always persuade voters to give him good jobs.

Such baggage as he did possess was the property of the clever woman he met at Yale and married for better or for worse. Hillary Rodham, a year younger, came from Chicago and quickly became a fierce Democratic courtroom fighter, her first significant job being as counsel on the staff formed to impeach President Nixon in 1974.

Hillary gave an ideological edge to Clinton's general fuzziness when he got to the White House. She also stuck a feminist finger in appointment pies, especially of women, sometimes with embarrassing, indeed hilarious, results. Thus Tara O'Toole, nominated assistant secretary of energy, turned out to be a member of a Marxist women's reading circle. Roberta Achtenberg, assistant secretary for fair housing, revealed herself as a militant lesbian who persecuted the Boy Scouts for not allowing homosexuals as scoutmasters. Joycelyn Elders, made surgeon general, after many public rows, had to go when she advocated masturbation.

It has to be said that, from start to finish, there was always a comic aspect to the Clinton presidency. Funny things happened to him on his way to the White House, and in it, and wherever he went. The scandals began early in his first term and never let up, some trivial, even surreal. You had to laugh. Clinton was accused of holding up traffic for an entire hour at Los Angeles International Airport, one of the world's busiest, while a barber came on board *Air Force One* to give him a haircut. When he stayed on the supercarrier *George Washington,* members of his staff were accused of carrying off embroidered bathrobes and fancy towels as souvenirs. Clinton said it was an outrageous lie and blamed the media for the thefts, but a White House payment of $562 told a different story.

Also comic, but to many Americans shocking, was the news that Clinton had agreed to let celebrity seekers sleep in the Lincoln Bedroom at the White House in return for hefty donations to Democratic Party campaign funds. More serious, indeed deeply serious, was the allegation that campaign contributions had been accepted from communist China.

There were also, as the Clinton presidency progressed, endless stories of business corruption involving Clinton and his wife in their Arkansas days, senior staffers in conflict-of-interest accusations, and White House people who went off to become lobbyists. But most of these stories were complex and dreary to follow, hopelessly enmeshed in contradictory evidence. And there were too many of them. One clear, deadly bullet is more likely to finish off a president than a scattering of shrapnel coming from all directions.

Moreover, scandals about money had to compete with sex—a topic that eventually came to dominate the Clinton presidency. Indeed, it could be said to have been Clinton's salvation. His womanizing cropped up early in the presidency when it was revealed that, as governor, he had used state troopers to round him up partners. This was nothing, especially to Democrats hardened by covering up for John F. Kennedy. Presidential illicit sex in the White House, which gradually emerged, albeit of an uncomfortable, hurried, and furtive kind, might have been another matter if Hillary had taken offense and begun divorce proceedings. But she kept her eye on the real ball: Each presidential peccadillo led her to demand and get more political say, with her own future political career in mind. So long as Hillary was forgiving, the nation could be too.

That Clinton covered up his womanizing by lying on oath was dangerous, of course, because perjury and obstruction of justice might be construed as "high crimes and misdemeanors." Indeed they became the engine of the eventual impeachment proceedings. The trouble, however, was that the independent counsel made them the sole engine—China, for instance, was left out.

Clinton clearly lied, glibly and easily, unselfconsciously and gaily—even unnecessarily—all his political life, often justifying his deception by legal quibbles on words, a skill he honed to perfection; his admission that he "smoked" marijuana but "never inhaled" was a characteristic distinction. Clinton, then, was a liar. But to try to nail him for lying about sex was a tactical, indeed a strategic, error. Most men, including most members of the Senate, have lied about sex at some time. Of all the different kinds of lies it is the one that carries the least opprobrium, either among colleagues or with the public. This was probably the real or main reason why the impeachment proceedings, though serious enough to clear the House, could not succeed in the Senate.

But in the meantime, the Clinton presidency had come and gone. It is most improbable that it could ever have been a success story, even on Clinton's own terms. He was indeed a fountain of energy, a geyser, but a spasmodic and uncontrolled one, propelled by galvanic appetites and generating chaos. Aides testified: "He reads half a dozen books at a time." "He relaxes not by watching a basketball game on TV or reading or picking up the telephone or doing crossword puzzles, but doing all simultaneously, while worrying an unlit cigar." "When he would eat an apple, he would eat the whole thing, core, stem, and seeds. He would pick up a baked potato in his hands and eat it in two bites."

The womanizing fitted in well with this galvanic, incoherent approach, but careful, systematic policy planning did not. Indeed to the question "Did Clinton have a strategy in the White House?" the answer must be no. His foreign policy was a long list of failed, aborted, or abandoned initiatives, punctuated by bouts of somnambulation, which, in the case of international terrorism, was to have serious consequences. However, most of Clinton's time and energy as president were spent not on policy or executive activity but in defending himself against accusations. The theme of his presidency might be described as "The Inconvenience of Sexual Appetites." Clinton in fact did nothing. It was not so much masterly inactivity as mistressly inactivity.

That had one outstanding virtue. It turned the Clinton years into one of the longest periods of laissez-faire in U.S. history. If Clinton had been a continent man, and so with time to be an activist president, the consequences would almost certainly have been disastrous for the American economy. As it was, with the president busy elsewhere, the nation thrived mightily, as always when the White House does nothing. The stage had already been set by the Reagan years, but under Clinton all surged forward. During the last quarter of the twentieth century, more than $5 trillion in real terms was added to America's gross domestic product. This was the central paradox of the Clinton presidency, and of course one reason why he remained popular.

Not even Clinton's notorious end-of-term list of pardons for notorious gangsters and former pals could quite extinguish popular support for the man. The charm continued to work, not only in America but abroad. I last saw Clinton near my own house in the celebrated Notting Hill district of London in 2002. He decided to do a walkabout, and plunged into the crowd, an activity he enormously and palpably enjoyed, and which delighted everybody. No one ever matched him as a simple campaigner. It was the thing he did best—perhaps the only thing he did well. It might be said, indeed, that he never did anything else.

In Notting Hill he was not running for office. The locals were not his voters. But he behaved as if they were and they loved it. The old con master was in his element. He found himself in a pub and ordered drinks all round. All cheered. The news spread to the vast crowd outside, and it cheered too. Adrenaline racing, fists thumping chests, hugging and handshaking, wisecracking and slogan swapping, Clinton worked that crowd for twenty minutes, leaving it hoarse and exhausted, delighted and deeply impressed when he swept off in his limo. The only unhappy man was the bartender, who was never paid for ol' Bill's round.

Mr. Johnson is author, most recently, of Art: A New History *(HarperCollins, 2003).*

43.
GEORGE WALKER BUSH

SURVEY RANKING: 19

BORN: July 6, 1946, New Haven, Connecticut

WIFE: Laura Welch

RELIGION: Methodist

PARTY: Republican

MILITARY EXPERIENCE: Texas Air National Guard (first lieutenant)

OTHER OFFICES HELD: Governor of Texas (1995–2000)

TOOK OFFICE: January 20, 2001

VICE PRESIDENT: Richard Cheney

---

by Paul A. Gigot

In November 1999, then-presidential candidate George W. Bush invited some *Wall Street Journal* writers for lunch at the Texas governor's mansion. A natural question was what lesson he had learned from his father's years in office, especially from his failure to win re-election. Governor Bush's answer would foretell much about his own presidency: He said he had learned that if you have political capital you should spend it, and that you should never go into an election campaign without an agenda you want to spend that capital to achieve.

Just over halfway through George W. Bush's presidency, it is far too early for sweeping judgments. But we already know a few things: His is neither an "in-box presidency" like his father's, one essentially responding to events, nor the policy McNugget presidency designed by Dick Morris for Bill Clinton. George W. Bush is a political risk-taker whose goals are ambitious enough that the conventional wisdom by 2003 was that he was "over-reaching."

This Bush trait has surprised many, in particular his critics. When he was running for the job, they described him as an amiable but uncurious and dimwitted scion. A few years later those same critics were describing him as a Machiavelli bent on a "radical" agenda at home and abroad. Clearly they missed something about Bush's political character.

One trait they missed is his profound self-confidence, which can border on the cocksure. Bush is someone who is comfortable both in his own skin and around other people. I first saw this trait covering a day trip through Texas while Bush was governor that included a stop to dedicate a new site at Stephen F. Austin University in Nacogdoches. He was obliged to put his hands in cement, as if at the Hollywood Walk of Fame, and after he had done so he snuck up behind his wife, grabbed her arms, and faked as if he were going to plunge her hands in cement too. Laura was clearly horrified, but Bush roared as only someone at ease in his public role could.

Perhaps this confidence flows from the convictions that attach to his strong religious faith. Perhaps it springs from his pedigree and his early exposure to so many prominent men. Bush attributes much of it to his mother, Barbara, who cultivated the sense of tribal destiny. But whatever the reasons, his personal confidence and certitude are central to his behavior in office.

On the negative side, it can lead him to such glib one-liners as his "bring 'em on" to Iraq's anti-American insurgency. This is not the thing presidents should say when American lives are on the line. He also believes himself to be such an astute judge of character that he sometimes overestimates the value of personal rapport in statecraft. He declared Vladimir Putin a great friend only months before the Russian president jilted him on Iraq.

On the other hand, his confidence is one reason he felt comfortable hiring strong national security deputies. His inspired selection of Donald Rumsfeld, surely his most important cabinet choice, was a deliberate decision to pick a defense secretary with the stature and experience to counter the formidable Secretary of State Colin Powell. He chose Rumsfeld, moreover, even though his father and Rumsfeld had been rivals as young Republican politicians.

Bush is also decisive, refreshingly so after the Clinton years of tortured delay and compromise. And once he makes a decision, Bush rarely looks back in angst, but instead plows ahead on execution. *Bush at War,* Bob Woodward's book about the aftermath of September 11, reveals a president setting the country on an aggressive anti-terror path from the very first days. He decided to invade Afghanistan with only the barest military plan in place and while there was much doubt about the dependability of the Northern Alliance. We also now know that he had decided to topple Saddam Hussein as early as August 2002, long before the U.S. invasion ever began. The months before the first bombs fell were essentially about political and diplomatic maneuvering. His surprise visit to Baghdad on Thanksgiving 2003 further linked his own future with postwar progress in Iraq, notwithstanding advice in some circles to distance himself from the messy insurgency. These are the decisions of a leader willing to take risks.

Bush also loves politics, even its electoral nitty-gritty. In this he is closer to Clinton than to his father, who hated campaigning and legislative horse-trading. The son thrives on both. He also is a much more hands-on manager than the media have portrayed. Amid the haggling over the various U.N. resolutions on Iraq, for example, Bush was his own main negotiator. He could explain to visitors, in great detail, the motives and calculations of each European leader. The play-by-play reminded me of hearing Bush speak in 1999 about the politics of tort reform in Texas.

The difference from his father is also illustrated by the prominence of chief political strategist Karl Rove in this Bush White House. The elder Bush put Lee Atwater at the Republican National Committee and never replaced him after Atwater's death from cancer. George W. Bush, as much as Rove, wants to build a new Republican majority. In his first midterm election in 2002, he gambled political capital to campaign for Republican candidates and retake the Senate. He told his political advisers that he didn't want a "lonely" victory in 2004, and indeed his party picked up four Senate seats.

This politician's calculus has sometimes led him astray on domestic issues. The farm bill was a capitulation to Midwest clout in the Senate, and he accepted far too easily a Medicare bill that traded the certainty of huge new entitlement spending for the promise of future reform. Worse than that, his steel tariffs were a purely political play to pass trade-promotion authority and win a few more House seats in the 2002 election. I believe Bush could have won both without the tariffs, which hurt U.S. manufacturing and the American ability to move the world toward freer trade. The steel issue also illustrates how Bush has controlled all economic decisions from the White House and therefore encouraged a weak Treasury Department. This is dangerous in the long run, especially if there is a currency or financial crisis, when Treasury credibility and expertise would be essential.

Yet Bush is also willing to ignore the polls and take risks based on his own personal political instincts. Bush himself insisted on making Social Security reform a core part of his platform in 2000, and Bush himself kept the cause alive despite staff and Republican congressional pressure to drop it. Bush believes, rightly in my view, that the issue was critical to his 2000 success because it showed him to be a leader willing to tackle something thought to be politically untouchable.

The same can be said about Bush's economic policy. As a Republican of the post-Reagan generation as well as a former businessman, he is an instinctive tax cutter. He compromised too early in 2001 on his original tax cut proposal, letting the cuts phase in over too long a period. But faced with a still-slow economy in 2002 and a new GOP majority in Congress, he doubled his tax cut bet and won a genuinely supply-side victory in 2003. With the bursting of the 1990s bubble, the corporate scandals, and of course September 11, the economy easily could have doomed Bush's presidency, as it ruined his father's. But his gamble on tax cuts, which ignored the Beltway consensus about the dangers of deficits, put the economy on a strong growth path going into his reelection year.

As Bush began his second term, his domestic agenda was more
ambitious than it had been in 2001. He made Social Security reform
his first priority, despite resistance on both sides of the political aisle
on Capitol Hill, and even though the program's finances wouldn't go
into the red until long after he left office. Few presidents are willing
to spend their capital to solve such future problems, and by mid-
2005 the odds on his success were long. But his persistence despite
low public approval was another sign of his political tenacity and risk-
taking character. In this sense he is the anti-Clinton.

Bush's largest presidential bet has, of course, been his response to
September 11. Probably any American president would have toppled
the Taliban after 9/11 and declared war on al Qaeda. This also would
have been the politically safest play for Bush, assuring him of international support and easy domestic consensus.

Instead, Bush has put his own stamp on foreign policy in two risk-
taking ways. The first was to define a policy of prevention, sometimes called "preemption," that shattered the conventions of the
inviolable nation-state that had held since Westphalia in the seventeenth century. Related to this was his decision to target not just the
terrorists, but also their state sponsors. This Bush Doctrine was so
outside the Washington consensus that the speech in which he first
announced preemption was all but ignored. Soon enough, however,
his critics figured out what was going on, especially as Bush moved
relentlessly toward toppling Saddam Hussein in Iraq.

Here, too, the easier decision was to stick with and attempt to
tighten containment. Bush chose instead not merely to depose Saddam but to attempt to make Iraq a pro-American outpost for moderate Islam in the Middle East. In the process, he has broken
foreign-policy orthodoxy that his father, Brent Scowcroft, and other
"realists" on the right would never have dared to challenge. Bush refused to deal with Yasser Arafat, has prodded the status-quo dictatorships in the Arab world (including the Saudis) to reform, and has
proved willing to act without the approval of the U.N. or even of many
traditional allies. In pursuing these goals, Bush is constructing a new
foreign policy vision every bit as ambitious as the one Truman and
Churchill built at the onset of the Cold War. The "ultimate goal," he
said in his second inaugural address, is "ending tyranny in the world."

This is, as Bush said, "the concentrated work of generations," so history's final judgment is a long way off. But by winning reelection during difficult times, Bush proved himself a formidable politician. Whatever their doubts about any single Bush policy, the public likes the president personally and, more important, considers him to be a leader they can trust. Especially in the wake of 9/11, this is an invaluable political asset. A public that suddenly feels vulnerable on the homefront wants a leader who is aggressive in defending American security. It seems clear that Bush's boldness is what won him a second term.

Mr. Gigot is editor of The Wall Street Journal's *editorial page.*

Issues in Presidential Leadership

PRESIDENTIAL LEADERSHIP IN ECONOMIC POLICY

by Robert L. Bartley

Panic spread through financial institutions, and more importantly their depositors. Savvy financiers understood, correctly as it turned out, that within days lines would form outside banks and trust companies, with depositors summarily withdrawing money while it lasted. The situation clearly called for leadership, and a private railroad car sped from the Episcopal Convention in Richmond, Virginia, to bring J. Pierpont Morgan back to Wall Street.

Morgan squelched the Panic of 1907, deciding which banks were beyond salvage and which could be defended, and convening other bankers to raise a loan fund of $25 million in sixteen minutes. Summoned to New York, Treasury Secretary George B. Cortelyou put another $25 million in government funds at Morgan's disposal. Morgan's final step was to liquidate a shaky brokerage by selling its large position in Tennessee Coal and Iron to U.S. Steel, a Morgan creation.

This, finally, had to involve the president of the United States. As Ron Chernow relates in *The House of Morgan*, some thought Theodore Roosevelt had triggered the panic with a Gridiron Club speech castigating "malefactors of great wealth," and of course he'd fashioned himself the great "trustbuster." So another private Pullman headed to Washington carrying emissaries to test his attitude toward this acquisition of further steel properties by the mother of all trusts. Interrupted at breakfast, the president allowed that it was "no public duty of his to interpose any objections."

The anecdote bears repeating, for modern readers may have trouble grasping that throughout most of our history, economic management was not considered a governmental responsibility, let alone a presidential one. The Panic of 1907, indeed, marks the dividing point. The public and politicians concluded Morgan had too much power, and the bankers and brokers worried that there might not be a Morgan for the next crisis. The result was the creation in 1913 of the Federal Reserve System, with its not all that implicit assumption of government responsibility for economic health.

It's scarcely surprising, then, that few if any of our earlier presidents made their names through leadership on economic policy. Most intervened in the economy only gingerly and indirectly; and the most notable intervention was for the worst, though in destroying the second Bank of the United States Andrew Jackson clearly did exercise leadership. More surprising is the record of twentieth-century presidents. While the public and the electorate increasingly hold them responsible for economic health, their record is much the same as earlier presidents—few examples of real leadership and more than a few disastrous interventions.

In the earlier period, of course, you can point to actions that were economically helpful. George Washington hired thirty-four-year-old Alexander Hamilton as his treasury secretary, and Hamilton consolidated the war debts and established the credit of the United States. Abraham Lincoln hired Jay Cooke to sell war bonds, a decision second in importance to the war effort only to his hiring U. S. Grant. The Philadelphia banker financed the war by selling government securities directly to the public—inventing the bond drive familiar in the world wars of the next century.

Presidential decisions, starting with Jefferson's Louisiana Purchase, also led to the development of the continent. The Homestead Act and Morrill Act passed under Lincoln also helped, though perhaps not as much as intended. Yet no presidential name is associated with the grandest infrastructure accomplishment, the construction of five transcontinental railroads between 1869 and 1893. The first of these was constructed thanks to Crédit Mobilier, the holding company that lent its name to one of our great political scandals. The last, Jim Hill's Great Northern, was built without public subsidy and proved itself the most efficient. The presidents of the time—Grant, Hayes, Garfield, Arthur, Cleveland, Harrison, and McKinley—were onlookers.

Jackson's malign economic leadership deserves attention, for it was the first grand example of a continuing pattern—political leaders advancing their fortunes by demonizing economic success. Elected on populist themes, Jackson quite naturally feuded with Nicholas Biddle, head of the Bank of the United States and the nation's de facto central banker. Biddle lobbied for an early renewal of the bank's charter, but Jackson vetoed the bill in 1832. After resoundingly winning reelection, the following year he withdrew government deposits from "the hydra-headed monster of Chestnut Street."

Hamilton had started the first Bank of the United States in 1791, to act as the government's fiscal agent and discharge some of the functions of a central bank, including exercising influence over the issue of currency and economic conditions. Its charter was allowed to expire in 1811. After difficulties in financing the War of 1812 and its aftermath, the second Bank of the United States was founded in 1817. Especially after Biddle became president of the bank in 1823, it developed the interregional lending needed to build a national economy, managed foreign exchange, and engaged in countercyclical monetary policies.

Jackson's veto message complained that profits from the bank went to its shareholders, comprised of "foreigners" and "a few hundred of our own citizens, chiefly of the richest class." In his response, Senator Daniel Webster pointed out that the nation needed foreign investment, and that the shareholders paid for the charter, at a price set by Congress. "Congress passed the bill, not as a bounty or favor to the present stockholders," Webster continued, "but to promote great public interests, for great public objects." He complained that Jackson's message "manifestly seeks to inflame the poor against the rich; it wantonly attacks whole classes of the people, for the purpose of turning against them the prejudices and the resentments of other classes."

These themes did help Jackson in the 1832 elections. But the economy struggled with central banking issues through the Civil War and into the Greenback Era. In the Panic of 1893–96, the Treasury

sought to protect its gold reserve by contracts that withdrew currency from circulation and imposed deflationary pressures deepening the downturn. The need for stabilizing leadership ultimately gave
Morgan more power than Biddle had ever envisioned. But in the
modern era, the themes sounded by Jackson became politically
more prominent. And presidents have more often than not exercised leadership not to advance prosperity but to reduce private sec-
tor rewards for doing so.

The Sixteenth Amendment, sanctioning the progressive income
tax, was ratified in 1913, the same year the Federal Reserve was created. President Taft proposed the amendment; the Supreme Court
had struck down the previous income tax law in 1895. Upon ratification, the tax was levied with a top rate of 7 percent on incomes of
more than $500,000 (equivalent to $9.3 million in 2003 dollars).
Under President Wilson and with entry into World War I, the top rate
quickly soared to 77 percent. Ever since, it's been a point of con-
tention and a rough barometer of presidential leadership.

Three of our twentieth-century presidents were tax cutters—
Coolidge, Kennedy, and Reagan. Not coincidentally, in my view, these
three presidents presided over times of prosperity. This is not to say
that tax policy is the only relevant issue; the fourth period of general
prosperity came under Bill Clinton, a tax raiser. But the tax issue is a
sign of other policies and more general attitudes, perhaps most generally whether an administration is content to let markets work, or
intent on second-guessing the outcomes they produce in pursuit of
noneconomic values and goals.

The pattern was set in the 1920s, when, as the wags had it, "three
presidents served under Andrew Mellon." President Coolidge and
Treasury Secretary Mellon set out a program of systematic yearly tax
cuts, and succeeded in paring the top rate to 24 percent by 1929. The
economy boomed, government revenues increased, and the stock
market soared. The conventional wisdom, codified by sages such as
John Kenneth Galbraith, is that by promoting prosperity in the
1920s, Coolidge and Mellon are to blame for the Great Depression of
the 1930s.

Mellon had hoped that Coolidge would reconsider his decision
not to run for reelection, and he and President Hoover had no love

for each other. But he continued as treasury secretary as Hoover took office in 1929. After the October stock market crash, Mellon believed that when speculation was wrung out of the system, the panic would be self-correcting. He advised patience, for example opposing Hoover's initiative in convening a conference of business leaders. In his memoirs, Hoover derided this advice, saying his treasury secretary offered "only one formula: liquidate labor, liquidate stocks, liquidate the farmers, liquidate real estate."

In the first months of 1930, it seemed that Mellon's view would be vindicated. The stock market rallied to 294 in April, against its 1929 low of 198 on November 13, the day Mellon announced that taxes would after all be cut by 1 percent. But looming over the "sucker's rally" was the issue of the tariff. Various sectoral interests, led by the farmers, were demanding protection from foreign imports. A petition of 1,028 economists urged Hoover to veto the bill; here was the occasion for presidential leadership. But Hoover signed; after dispatching Mellon to the Court of St. James in 1932, he also boosted taxes, taking the top marginal rate to 63 percent. The Dow Jones Industrial Average hit 41 a few months before Hoover's defeat by Franklin D. Roosevelt.

The tariff episode was archetypal of the failure to understand the international impact on the U.S. economy. The Versailles peace called on Germany to pay huge reparations, to be used by England and France to repay their war loans from the United States. John Maynard Keynes warned in *The Economic Consequences of the Peace* that this would not work, and would lead to untoward political ramifications. The point is that the only way Germany could pay for the financial transfers required by reparations was by running an equally huge surplus on the trade accounts. England and France, similarly, would need trade surpluses to finance debt repayment. The Smoot-Hawley Tariff, and the retaliatory duties it produced, closed down world trade, collapsed the international system, and plunged the world into depression.

Robert Mundell, who won the 1999 Nobel Prize in economics for his work on the international economy, has argued that the ultimate cause of the Depression was a shortage of world liquidity. Fed Chairman Benjamin Strong had more than an inkling of the problem, but he died in 1928, before the stock market crash. Mellon may or may not have understood; after passage of the tariff, he predicted that industry would adjust now that the uncertainty was ended. But Hoover, though an opponent of the German reparations, clearly didn't know what he was doing.

There is still a lingering sense that FDR led us out of the Depression. The notion seems to be that government-chartered cartels and the rest of the New Deal, if now recognized as bad economic policy, were good economic policy in the 1930s. At least, FDR's champions contend, he restored the national spirit. In the sense of anyone-but-Hoover, I certainly agree. But in fact, much of his spiritual uplift consisted of Jacksonian business bashing, encapsulated in his phrase "the Ishmaels and the Insulls." Chicago utilities magnate Samuel Insull was acquitted by three different juries.

The fact is that recovery did not come until World War II inflated world demand. An incipient recovery was aborted by a recession in 1938. Mundell has called my attention to some remarkable passages in the diaries of Treasury Secretary Henry Morgenthau as related by John Morton Blum. In late 1938 and early 1939, Morgenthau worried above all about business confidence, saying, "Of course we must have additional revenue, but in my opinion the way to make it is for businessmen to make more money." He brought the president a tax proposal that included repeal of the excess profits tax, reduction of corporate taxes, and a reduction in the top rate of individual income tax to 60 percent, from the 90 percent it had reached.

A "Mellon plan of taxation," FDR snorted to Morgenthau and Undersecretary John W. Haynes, adding, "This is a matter of politics." Morgenthau had a sign on his desk reading "Does It Contribute to Recovery?" The president declared this "very stupid." He said that the tax changes might help in the short term, but that assuming a pro-business stance would be a politically harmful reversal. Economic recovery, FDR suggested, was not worth the political price. The quote from Morgenthau's diary reads, "This would put a man in as President who, as he called it, would be controlled by a man on horseback, the way Mussolini and Hitler are. This lecture went on and on, he saying that this was going backwards and that this simply would mean that we would have a fascist President."

Happily, Morgenthau was not subject to presidential leadership on seemingly arcane issues of the international economy. A week after Pearl Harbor he ordered up a study of an inter-Allied stabilization fund, assigning the task to Harry Dexter White. White's studies ultimately resulted in the Bretton Woods Conference, with White and Keynes in the leading roles, which resulted in the ordering of a postwar financial world. At the same time, Secretary of State Cordell Hull was pressing for reciprocal trade agreements, and ultimately the General Agreement on Tariffs and Trade, to undo the damage of Smoot-Hawley. And of course General George C. Marshall made his name famous with the plan for reconstruction of Western Europe. It was a high mark of economic leadership, though Presidents Roosevelt and Truman were mostly in a passive role.

The Bretton Woods arrangements served well for a generation, facilitating a remarkable period of progress—a "golden age," in the words of Angus Maddison, the leading chronicler of world economic growth. But toward the end of the 1960s the exchange rate mechanism, with U.S. responsibility to maintain the price of gold at $35 an ounce, was starting to buckle. It might have been repaired for another generation, principally by increasing the gold price and thus providing more world liquidity. Instead, it was shattered by a dramatic act of presidential leadership.

On August 15, 1971, President Nixon descended from Camp David to announce his New Economic Policy. It included a ninety-day freeze on all wage and price increases, a study of more permanent wage-price controls, some targeted tax cuts, and a 10 percent surcharge on all imports. By the way, he also closed the gold window, unilaterally revoking the Bretton Woods obligation to redeem dollars from other central banks in gold at $35 an ounce. This lifted a restraint on inflation, while the controls suppressed price increases until the 1972 election, which Mr. Nixon won in a landslide.

It also set off a decade of mounting inflation, which the Ford and Carter administrations never understood. The Arab oil sheiks understood better than most what the floating dollar would do, and five weeks after August 15 the Organization of Petroleum Exporting Countries passed a resolution demanding oil price increases to offset the de facto devaluation of the dollar. There the "energy crisis" was born, and with it the decade of malaise, to borrow the word President Carter made famous.

This was finally resolved by what I'd regard as the stellar example of presidential leadership in economic policy, Ronald Reagan's tax cut and stalwart support of Fed Chairman Paul Volcker's tight money policy. The principles of the tax cut to spur economic activity were set out in the Reagan campaign's Policy Memorandum No. 1, drawn by Martin Anderson in August 1979. Volcker had started to tighten money when President Carter had more or less been forced to make him Fed chairman. But in February 1982, in the depths of recession for which the tax proposals were blamed and just after the Fed had announced yet-tighter money, Reagan proclaimed that he and the Fed agreed on not returning to "the fiscal and monetary policies of the past that have created the current conditions," and that "I have confidence in the announced policies of the Federal Reserve Board."

In the event, the Reagan-Volcker policies, the policy mix Robert Mundell recommended, did cure stagflation. While the tight money curbed inflation, the tax policies encouraged growth by increasing incentives. In 1983 a remarkable boom started; over the next twenty years, it was interrupted only by eight-month recessions starting in 1990 and 2001.

Perhaps business bashing has declined from the days of FDR and Jackson. Bill Clinton left business pretty much alone, and while he increased taxes, the boosts were modest compared with earlier in the century. His idol Jack Kennedy actually made an explicit decision to back off and woo business instead. His fight with Roger Blough over steel prices set the stock market swooning, but he deliberately reversed his stance toward business, starting with a notable speech at the Economic Club of New York. No recession eventuated, contributing to Paul Samuelson's crack that the market predicted nine of the last five recessions. (Sometimes the politicians get the message.) Eventually, this change of sentiment led to the Kennedy tax cuts, passed after the president's death.

Also, recent presidents have backed away from an earlier emphasis on regulation of business. The Microsoft antitrust case did not become another IBM suit, stretching ages and consuming whole law firms. The sparkplug for deregulation of airlines was Ralph Nader, a muckraker in the Upton Sinclair tradition. Teddy Roosevelt may not have been ready to upset Morgan's plans during a panic, but he was the major backer of the Hepburn Act of 1906, giving enforcement powers over railroad rates to the Interstate Commerce Commission, toothless when formally established in 1887. The ICC was the first of an alphabet soup of agencies to police business practices. A new generation of reformers abolished it in 1995, finding that competition was more effective than government regulation. In a broader sense, the ICC was rendered obsolete by another presidential initiative, President Eisenhower's Interstate Highway System.

So perhaps society, the government, and presidents are on something of a learning curve about economic management. Since the Federal Reserve Act, the record of presidential leadership compares poorly with the previous era of laissez-faire. It has two presidents, Hoover and Nixon, leading us into economic disaster. It features a Great Depression FDR could not control and a huge inflation Jimmy Carter couldn't begin to understand. But there's reason to hope that presidents are starting to get the hang of economic management.

The economy has a natural tendency to grow, and even to right itself. The main job of presidents consists not of hyperactive interventions, but of reducing artificial impediments, largely erected by previous generations of politicians for purposes other than advancing prosperity. When it comes to the economy, we can hope presidents are gradually learning that the secret of leadership is getting out of the way.

Mr. Bartley, who died in 2003, was editor emeritus of The Wall Street Journal. *He edited the* Journal's *editorial pages from 1972 to 2002.*

PRESIDENTIAL LEADERSHIP DURING WARTIME

by *Victor Davis Hanson*

Since its founding the United States has engaged in major wars—either defined by formal declaration or de facto by the large-scale deployment of troops abroad—over an aggregate of at least forty-six years, or about 20 percent of the life of our nation. Some fourteen presidents have guided the country through these national crises, which put 42 million Americans in battle and have cost the nation some 650,000 killed in action in addition to more than a million more wounded, missing, and dead abroad from sickness and disease.

If we include the so-called Indian Wars between 1819 and 1898, and an entire series of nineteenth- and twentieth-century "small wars" in places like Central America, the Caribbean, the Philippines, Korea, China, North Africa, and the Pacific Islands, then almost every one of our forty-two American presidents has overseen some use of American troops in battle. Jimmy Carter used to be proud that for most of his administration not a single American soldier had been killed in hostile action; but then in April 1980 he too eventually was faced with a national crisis, in which eight American servicemen died in a failed attempt to rescue by force fifty American hostages in Iran.

Controversy surrounds the nature of proper presidential leadership in war, not surprising when the United States draws on a tradition of civic militarism and civilian audit that goes back 2,500 years to the Greeks, whose public assemblies routinely fined, demoted, or executed their generals. Although our president is de jure commander in chief, Americans have neither a tradition of a uniformed leader replete with medals, sunglasses, and epaulettes arm-saluting phalanxes of goose-stepping troops, in the manner of a Mussolini, Tojo, Mao, Stalin, or Saddam Hussein, nor one of renegade officers—like the Greek colonels or a Manuel Noriega—seizing power and running the country through the military.

Nonetheless, Americans have always welcomed popular generals as their presidents—George Washington, Andrew Jackson, Zachary Taylor, Ulysses S. Grant, James Garfield, or Dwight Eisenhower—and political parties were especially eager to nominate combat veterans such as William Henry Harrison, Theodore Roosevelt, John F. Kennedy, and the elder George Bush. Their popularity arose not just because of past bravery and the approbation of a thankful citizenry, but also because such veterans were deemed to possess valuable expertise to lead the nation in the inevitable crises to come.

The contrast is equally true: When a president such as Bill Clinton was felt to have avoided military service and was uneasy with the armed forces, a gulf widened between the executive and the military. The former grew reluctant to rein in the latter, which had little confidence in the abilities of its president to lead it into war—resulting in incongruities like the secretary of defense forbidding the use of armor in Somalia or relatives of the fallen in Mogadishu publicly rebuking their commander in chief at a presidential commemoration.

There is always a degree of ambiguity about the proper military role and background of our presidents. On questions of war management there are two almost diametrically opposed schools of thought: Should presidents in detailed fashion oversee the military to such a degree as to approve, modify, or reject battlefield tactics; or should elected leaders state only broad war objectives, outline the parameters of forces necessary, and then leave questions of military management to the generals?

Perhaps one could counter that presidential leadership does not really matter all that much, since the U.S. has never lost a war except Vietnam. Despite the differing command styles of Madison, Polk, Lincoln, McKinley, Wilson, FDR, Truman, and Eisenhower, American forces usually defeated their opponents in such a dramatic manner that it was hard to calibrate to what degree presidential guidance was pivotal. An unknown and inexperienced Truman concluded FDR's inspired leadership of the Second World War in fine fashion, even as the old pro Eisenhower, the decorated five-star general, brought no magical expertise to improve on Truman's conduct of the stalemated Korean War.

Because the defeat in Vietnam was an anomaly in the American military experience, it naturally has become a focal point of what not to do when running a war. Critics fault Lyndon Johnson for arbitrarily selecting bombing targets in Vietnam from 1965 to 1968, and often putting restrictions on sending ground troops into the North. Indeed his five-year tenure as commander in chief is often cited as the classic case of an inept and inexperienced civilian micromanaging a war whose battlefield realities he knew nothing about. Yet as Eliot Cohen has pointed out in *Supreme Command*, the American military offered no alternate innovative plan of action that might have won the war within the larger political guidelines of confining the conflict to the Vietnamese peninsula.

Thus the problem was not just that Johnson sometimes capriciously interfered in military decision making, but that he intruded in a manner that abetted rather than interrupted the military's wrongheaded conduct of the war. Johnson rehashed the selection of bombing targets in the rural South where peasants suffered from collateral damage, rather than demanding systematic targeting of industrial and transportation hubs in the urban North. There was never presidential leadership that questioned flawed tactics like search-and-destroy missions, the abandonment of hard-won outposts like Khe Sanh, and emphasis on body counts, rather than organizing large attacks to capture, hold, and expand control of vital territory.

If we recognize that neither Kennedy, Nixon, nor Ford did much better in fashioning an innovative policy of stopping communist aggression in the South without incurring thousands of American casualties and tearing the country apart back home, it is difficult to single out Johnson as singularly inept. True, Nixon at least reenergized the military to increase its target list in the North, to chase enemy contingents across borders, and to reduce the presence of American ground troops without losing the South or involving China and Russia—but still at a terrible cost of another five years (1969–73) of American losses.

The key to presidential leadership seems instead to demand intrusion in military affairs to ensure that the nation's political objectives remain paramount and are achieved in their entirety through the commitment of commensurate force. Lincoln, despite a few weeks' service in a state militia during the Black Hawk War of 1832, had little more military experience than Lyndon Johnson—and far less than his Confederate counterpart, Jefferson Davis, who had served as a colonel in the Mexican War and as secretary of war in the Pierce administration. Yet Lincoln oversaw many of the details of the Union effort, from the grand strategy of the Anaconda Plan to the selection and removal of individual generals and the final winning formula of having Ulysses S. Grant face off with Robert E. Lee in Virginia while William Sherman ran amok in Georgia and the Carolinas. Lincoln, not Davis, proved the more adroit commander in chief. Clearly the problem was not civilian intrusion per se or the past battle experience of an American president, but rather the talent and skill through which a president directs the military in accordance with larger political objectives. Lincoln, remember, often advocated the use of more, not less, force in bringing the Civil War to its final resolution. "McClellan is not using the army," he famously said, referring to the general who would challenge him in the 1864 election. "I should like to borrow it for a while."

In the first Gulf War, President Bush left control of the theater almost entirely to General Norman Schwarzkopf and Joint Chiefs Chairman Colin Powell. Both accomplished a brilliant tactical defeat of Saddam Hussein's forces, but inexplicably had no real orders from their president concerning the nature of the armistice—and thus, besides not destroying the Republican Guard divisions, allowed defeated Iraqis subsequently to use airpower to help butcher thousands of Shiites and Kurds. The additional failure to resolve the conflict by taking Baghdad and removing Saddam Hussein led not only to thousands of innocent civilian deaths, and a subsequent twelve-year commitment of some 350,000 missions to patrol the no-fly zones, but indeed to a second Gulf War of March and April 2003. Although our first President Bush and his civilian staff (including National Security Adviser Brent Scowcroft, a retired lieutenant general) often intervened to urge Schwarzkopf to increase his efforts to find Scud missiles that posed no tactical danger of any magnitude but risked Israeli entrance into the war, no one advised the generals about the absolute necessity of destroying the Republican Guard if there was to be any hope of change in postwar Iraq—or at least the need for a formal postbellum humiliation of Saddam Hussein to preclude his efforts at reinventing himself as a pan-Arab phoenix who would arise intact from the inferno unleashed by America and its legion of allies.

In contrast, George W. Bush made it clear from the outset that the mission of the American military in Iraq during the 2003 war was the removal of Saddam Hussein. In addition, his cabinet instructed the military for political reasons to avoid both a long pre-battle bombardment and a huge deployment of American ground troops. Despite grumbling—especially by retired army generals—the military responded with an innovative plan that took Baghdad in three weeks. To conduct war, presidents should outline the ultimate objectives of the campaign, communicate the political boundaries under which the military must work, and then demand and carefully monitor a battle plan that fits just those criteria.

Conveying larger values and ideals is just as important as military supervision or apprising the generals as to the political stakes involved. It was the singular accomplishment of Lincoln to grasp that his initial reasons for using force to preserve the Union—the maintenance of a single nation—had to evolve into a larger moral vision of ending chattel slavery altogether. Unlike General McClellan, Lincoln saw that to maintain an effort of such cost in treasure and lives, the American people would require a transcendent, moral goal of extending freedom to the slaves, without whose liberation the country could never really be reunified. The result of the Emancipation Proclamation was not proof of political duplicity—Lincoln's critics charged that he had reneged on his earlier election pragmatism to save the Union at all costs—but the reality of spirited Union soldiers by autumn 1864 singing the "Battle Hymn of the Republic" as they marched 62,000 strong under Sherman through Georgia, freeing 40,000 slaves and targeting the plantations of the secessionists.

Both Woodrow Wilson and Franklin Roosevelt galvanized an often isolationist and skeptical public to stay the course in bloody wars abroad, not mainly through reminders of the national security interests of the United States, but rather by articulating that such sacrifice was needed to thwart odious ideologies—Prussian militarism, German Nazism, Italian fascism, Japanese militarism—that threatened the very premises of civilized society. Thus Wilson's Fourteen Points and FDR's Four Freedoms were rallying cries that emphasized America's moral obligations to defeat an enemy intent on envisioning a world that would exclude the very principles under which America was founded.

In this regard, despite rhetoric about the "axis of evil" and "weapons of mass destruction," President George W. Bush was mostly successful in imbuing the troops with the notion of liberation, that their four-hundred-mile race to northern Iraq—reminiscent of Epaminondas the Theban's great trek to free the Messenian Helots, Sherman's March to the Sea, or Patton's romp through central France in the summer of 1944—was aimed at ending oppression and freeing the enslaved.

Given the idealistic premises of American democracy, it is hard for presidents to conduct major wars of simple aggression over points of international law or long-term national interests without appeals to spreading democracy or help for captive peoples. It is no surprise that those wars in which American presidents were least successful in making such arguments—the Mexican War of 1846–48, the Spanish-American War of 1898–1902, and the Vietnam War between 1964 and 1975—remain our most controversial conflicts, with historians as divided now over their morality and utility as the general public was then.

Besides instructing the generals to find a battle plan that is both efficacious and consistent with American political objectives, and imbuing the American people with a sense of a moral conflict without cynicism and hypocrisy, a final trait is essential for wartime leadership: consistency and determination in the face of inevitable political and sometimes popular opposition. In this regard, we recall America's four difficult wars—the Civil War, World War II, Korea, and Vietnam—when the ultimate verdict was often in doubt.

In the first two conflicts, both Lincoln and FDR made it clear that

unconditional surrender of the enemy was the only acceptable con-
clusion to the conflict—and then remained unwavering in the face of
constant criticisms amid catastrophes like Bull Run, Cold Harbor,
Pearl Harbor, or massive B-17 losses, and either public rioting about
draft laws in New York in 1864 or general nonchalance in 1942 that
allowed East Coast cities to remain lit up at night, thus silhouetting
American ships to the joy of offshore German submariners.

In contrast, it was not altogether clear that any American president insisted on the abject defeat of either the North Koreans or
North Vietnamese. Instead, war aims seemed to vary with the perceived ebb and flow of battle, ranging from preserving an independent pro-Western country in the South to inflicting such
punishment on the North as to facilitate an eventual reunification
under American auspices. While one sympathizes with the array of
pressures that forced Lyndon Johnson to forgo a second term in
1968, he was in no worse position than was Lincoln in October
1864, who presided over an even bloodier stalemate in Virginia and
confronted a Copperhead opposition every bit as zealous as a
Eugene McCarthy. The difference was that Lincoln believed in his
cause, could articulate the stakes involved, and was willing to brave
fire until the battlefield turned around. Sherman's taking of Atlanta
in November was no more amazing than the lopsided American victory during the January 1968 Tet Offensive; but the former triumph
ensured Lincoln's reelection, while the latter win ended Johnson's
presidency.

If Lincoln and FDR could envision a clash of civilizations, in
which an American defeat would bring in a frightening new order,
Truman and the quartet of Vietnam-era presidents in a dangerous
era of mutually assured destruction were not altogether clear on
why or how the preservation of a noncommunist government in
distant Asia was vital to the safety of the American nation, much less
worth the lives of thousands of American soldiers in the theaters of
battle.

Their confusion may explain why Korea was our first negotiated
draw and Vietnam our first defeat. In sum, when the president of the
United States no longer can inspire the nation to take casualties,
believes a stalemate is as good as a triumph, and either cannot or will

not seek reelection in the middle of a war, then there is no reason why men in the field should continue to fight for victory—and quite understandably they sometimes don't.

Mr. Hanson is author of Carnage and Culture: Landmark Battles in the Rise of Western Power *(Anchor, 2002).*

PRESIDENTIAL LEADERSHIP AND THE JUDICIARY

by Robert P. George

When Justice Sherman Minton retired from the U.S. Supreme Court on September 7, 1956, President Eisenhower, with his sights fixed firmly on reelection that November, asked his aides to find a Catholic judge from a state court to fill the vacancy. Assistant Attorney General William Rogers suggested Justice William J. Brennan, Jr., of the New Jersey Supreme Court. Brennan had made a favorable impression on Rogers and Attorney General Herbert Brownell in a nonideological speech he had given earlier that year on ways of improving the federal judicial system.

"There's only one problem," Rogers said to Brownell, in a conversation recounted by Brennan biographer Kim Isaac Eisler. "Brennan is a Democrat."

"Eisenhower doesn't care about that," Brownell replied. "I want to make sure he's really a member of the Catholic Church."

Brennan's religious affiliation generated opposition from the National Liberal League, whose members feared that he would be a lawless judge who decided cases not in accordance with the Constitution, but rather on the basis of his religious beliefs. Their worry proved to be well founded. Ironically, though, the "religion" that guided Brennan's decisions over his thirty-four-year tenure on the court turned out not to be Catholicism but liberalism. In case after case, this appointee of a moderately conservative president managed to put together majorities to impose on the nation, under the guise of interpreting the Constitution, policies that reflected the prevailing social and moral dogmas of the liberal faith.

Eisenhower was far from the first president to nominate the kind of justice who seemed to fit the profile he had in mind only to find that his appointee followed a philosophy of judging that put him at variance with the president's own views. Nor would he be the last. President Reagan promised during his 1980 campaign to nominate the first woman to the Supreme Court. When Justice Potter Stewart retired in 1981, Reagan appointed Sandra Day O'Connor, a former Arizona legislator who at the time served as a state appellate judge. As it turned out, O'Connor played a decisive role in preserving the abortion license created in 1973 in *Roe v. Wade* and, later, in upholding the constitutionality of race discrimination in university admissions for the purpose of achieving "diversity" on campus. These are hardly achievements of which a president dedicated to the pro-life cause and the ideal of a color-blind Constitution could be proud.

By 1990, when Brennan retired, judicial involvement in social issues such as abortion and racial preferences had made Supreme Court appointments the hottest of political hot potatoes. President George H. W. Bush sought a "stealth" nominee—someone with no record of controversial publications or public statements that the president's liberal opponents could use to attack the nominee. On the advice of his trusted aide John Sununu, Bush nominated David Souter, a little-known judge who had served on a federal appeals court for just a few months and whom Sununu, as governor of New Hampshire, had appointed in 1983 to the state Supreme Court. The stealth strategy worked, at least insofar as the president was able to win easy confirmation of his nominee. Once on the court, however, Souter proved to be as consistent and doctrinaire a liberal judicial activist as Brennan had been. Like Eisenhower before him, Bush inadvertently appointed to a position of vast power and influence a judge who would use his office to advance the objectives of those on the opposite side of the ideological divide in American politics.

Although rarer, it is possible to think of justices who disappointed liberal presidents or their supporters. Byron White, a leading opponent of liberal judicial activism in cases involving abortion and homosexual conduct in the 1970s and 1980s, had been appointed to the Supreme Court by the moderately liberal President Kennedy. Of course, the issues that established White's reputation as something of a judicial conservative were not on the political—much less the judicial—radar screen when he was nominated by Kennedy in 1962.

Presidents often do succeed in appointing justices who do not disappoint them or their supporters. The same President Bush who appointed the liberal David Souter also gave us the conservative Justice Clarence Thomas. President Reagan appointed not only the socially liberal Sandra Day O'Connor, but also Antonin Scalia, the court's most forceful and articulate critic of the liberal judicial activism championed by Brennan in his day and Souter in ours. Reagan was, by every account, a "conviction politician," yet like many presidents before him he plainly sought to make Supreme Court appointments that would pay electoral dividends. Just as O'Connor was the first woman to be nominated to the highest court in the land, Scalia was the first Italian-American. (It must also be said that Scalia was a distinguished lawyer, legal scholar, and judge.)

An earlier conviction politician, Franklin D. Roosevelt, clashed repeatedly with a Supreme Court whose members were highly dubious of the constitutionality of many of his New Deal initiatives. His frustration at the resistance of the "nine old men" to the early New Deal led to the so-called court-packing plan—Roosevelt's proposal to expand the number of justices serving on the court according to a system that would have enabled him quickly to secure a majority for upholding New Deal legislation. Although the plan did not make it through Congress, Roosevelt soon got the opportunity to reconstitute the court by filling vacancies. While prudently honoring "Catholic," "Jewish," and "Southern" claims to seats on the court, Roosevelt left nothing to chance on the ideological front. He appointed reliable New Deal supporters, such as Hugo Black, Felix Frankfurter, William O. Douglas, and Frank Murphy.

Are nominations to the Supreme Court always in some sense politically motivated? Plainly political calculations of various sorts usually enter into a president's deliberation about whom he should appoint. (George Washington, for understandable political reasons, was careful to appoint a mix of Northerners and Southerners; and every one of his nominees was a loyal member of the Federalist Party.) This has never been considered scandalous, so long as the people appointed were widely believed to possess the talents and virtues required to serve on the nation's highest court. And there are cases in the historical record, admittedly rare, in which jurists appear to have been appointed purely on the basis of eminence or a reputation for brilliance in the law. Leading examples include Theodore Roosevelt's nomination of Oliver Wendell Holmes and Republican Herbert Hoover's appointment of Democrat Benjamin Cardozo.

Sometimes presidents see an advantage to themselves and, they surely suppose, to the public weal in appointing to the court lawyers who themselves possess broad political experience. Twentieth-century examples include William Howard Taft, a former president who was appointed chief justice by Warren Harding; Hugo Black, who had served in the U.S. Senate for a decade before his appointment, and in other political offices before that; Fred Vinson, a man of vast legislative and administrative experience who was appointed chief justice by President Truman; and Vinson's successor as chief justice, Earl Warren, an Eisenhower appointee, who had been governor of California and a plausible contender for the presidency in 1948 and 1952.

Presidents also sometimes look for opportunities to appoint their own trusted counselors to seats on the court. Lyndon Johnson, for example, cunningly persuaded Justice Arthur Goldberg to resign and accept an appointment as United Nations ambassador so that he could nominate his old friend and confidant Abe Fortas to Goldberg's seat (which was also considered at the time to be "the Jewish seat").

Many presidents both before and after FDR have come into conflict with the Supreme Court over the constitutionality of legislation favored by the president, and the corresponding question of the scope of judicial power to invalidate duly enacted laws as unconstitutional. President Jefferson famously disagreed with Chief Justice John Marshall over the powers Marshall claimed for the judicial branch in the 1803 case of *Marbury v. Madison*. Were the broad view of judicial powers to be accepted, the author of our nation's Declaration of Independence later wrote, it would have the effect of "placing us under the despotism of an oligarchy."

The Supreme Court in *Marbury* declared a piece of federal legislation to be unconstitutional. (The statutory provision in question was Section 13 of the Judiciary Act of 1789, which, according to the justices, expanded the original jurisdiction of the Supreme Court without constitutional warrant.) It would be more than fifty years before the justices would do it again. In the 1857 case of *Dred Scott v. Sandford*, Chief Justice Roger Brooke Taney, an appointee of President Jackson, invalidated the Missouri Compromise and declared the Congress to be without power to prohibit slavery in the federal territories.

When Abraham Lincoln was sworn in as president in 1861, he took the occasion of his inaugural address to challenge the authority of the Supreme Court to issue constitutional rulings that were binding on the other branches of the federal government, as the *Dred Scott* decision's supporters claimed it to be, beyond the particulars of the case at hand. According to Lincoln, *Dred Scott* was not merely incorrectly decided; considered as an attempt by the court to tie the hands of the president and Congress on the great and divisive issue of slavery, the ruling was a gross usurpation of the right of the people to rule themselves via the constitutionally established processes of republican government. No president before or since Lincoln has more starkly challenged the justices' claim to supremacy in matters of constitutional interpretation:

> If the policy of the government upon vital questions affecting the whole people is to be irrevocably fixed by decisions of the Supreme Court, the instant they are made in ordinary litigation between parties in personal actions, the people will have ceased to be their own rulers, having to that extent practically resigned their government into the hands of that eminent tribunal.

Yet in the end, judicial claims to supremacy have prevailed. In the 1958 case of *Cooper v. Aaron*, the Supreme Court asserted bluntly and without qualification that "the federal judiciary is supreme in the exposition of the law of the Constitution." President Eisenhower let the claim pass without significant comment. Sixteen years later, President Nixon (who had been Eisenhower's vice president) faced the consequences of presidential acquiescence to judicial supremacy. In hearings inquiring into the Watergate scandal, Congress and the public learned that Nixon possessed audiotape recordings of key conversations in the Oval Office. The office of the special prosecutor investigating the scandal sought to obtain the tapes by subpoena. When Judge John Sirica granted the subpoena, the stage was set for a showdown between the president and the Supreme Court over the judicial power to compel the president to release information and documents despite claims to executive immunity and privilege.

Nixon's position was that the courts were intruding into the internal affairs of the executive branch. The question of the tapes was, the president contended, a nonjusticiable "political" issue. For the Supreme Court to claim for itself the power to order a president to release tapes, his lawyers argued, would be to trench upon the constitutional authority of the executive as a coequal branch of the federal government. In a unanimous opinion written by Chief Justice Warren Burger—one of Nixon's own appointees—the court rejected the president's claims and ordered the tapes to be released. (The vote was 8–0; Associate Justice William H. Rehnquist, a former Nixon Justice Department official, did not participate in the case.) The question then became: Will the president comply with an order he believed the court had no constitutionally valid authority to issue? Politically enfeebled by the scandal, and under assault from the elite media, which had long despised him, Nixon gave up the tapes. Soon he was driven from office in disgrace.

Even in ordering release of the tapes, Chief Justice Burger acknowledged an especially wide scope for deference by the courts to executive branch claims of immunity and privilege in matters of defense and national security. This was in keeping with well-established practice. Presidents have always received greater deference from the Supreme Court on security matters than on issues of purely domestic relevance. So, for example, in a decision that most commentators rightly view as truly a black mark on the judicial (and executive) record, the Supreme Court in the midst of World War II went so far as to uphold as constitutionally legitimate President Roosevelt's War Relocation Authority, which effectively incarcerated innocent Japanese-Americans in assembly centers and then internment camps as possible security threats. In *Korematsu v. U.S.* (1944), Roosevelt appointee (and noted civil libertarian) Hugo Black wrote the opinion for the court, joined by fellow Roosevelt appointees (and noted civil libertarians) Felix Frankfurter and William O. Douglas, together with three others.

In view of the awesome power courts have come to wield in the American political system, and the fact that most judicial appointees will continue to serve long after the president who appoints them leaves office, presidents usually think carefully about whom they should nominate—especially when filling a vacancy on the Supreme Court. (Eisenhower's remarkably casual decision to appoint Brennan—"find a Catholic judge from a state court"—is the exception rather than the rule.) Often a president is then forced to spend significant political capital to secure confirmation of his nominee by the Senate. Yet, the historical record makes clear that a president and his supporters may nevertheless be deeply disappointed by their man's or woman's performance on the bench. Indeed, a president may himself run into profound conflict with his own appointees, as Nixon did in the tapes case.

Finally, what reflection, however brief, on presidents and justices would be complete without mentioning a Supreme Court decision that, in the end, settled a contested presidential election? In *Bush v. Gore,* seven of the nine justices were Republican appointees. Two of them—including one appointed by George W. Bush's father—joined the two Democrats in the minority. The others formed the majority whose order halted the recounts in Florida, leaving George W. Bush the narrow victor. This time, were the roles reversed? Did the justices "appoint" the president? Did "political" considerations intrude? These questions continue to be hotly debated. This much is clear, however: No president in the history of the republic has greater reason than George W. Bush to be cognizant of the future political significance of any Supreme Court appointments it may fall to him to make.

Mr. George is McCormick Professor of Jurisprudence and director of the James Madison Program in American Ideals and Institutions at Princeton University. He has served as a presidential appointee to the U.S. Commission on Civil Rights, and he currently serves on the President's Council on Bioethics. His most recent book is The Clash of Orthodoxies *(ISI Books, 2001).*

PRESIDENTIAL LEADERSHIP AFTER DISPUTED ELECTIONS

by James Taranto

In January 2001, just before George W. Bush took the oath as America's forty-third president, Jonathan Cohn of *The New Republic*—a magazine that had avidly supported Bush's opponent, Vice President Albert A. Gore, Jr.—weighed in with some advice for the new chief executive. Because of the unusual circumstances of the 2000 election, Cohn argued, Bush lacked "political authority." Cohn urged him to take a lesson from the past:

> In the nineteenth century, two presidents took office after finishing second in the popular vote. The first, John Quincy Adams, tried to govern as if he had a mandate to carry out his plans for the nation. He was met with robust opposition and resoundingly thrown out of office four years later—bested by Andrew Jackson, the man who had received the most votes in the previous race. The second, Rutherford B. Hayes, had more limited ambitions. Having come to office through a partisan battle not dissimilar from the one that took place this year [2000], he trimmed his sails, concentrating on civil service reform and vowing not to seek a second term (a promise he fulfilled). He didn't go down in history as a great president. But, then, he didn't have the support to be one, and he made the most of the support he had. [President Bush] would be wise to follow Hayes's lead.

It is fair to say that Bush declined to follow Cohn's advice. Not only did he seek a second term; he did so having pursued one of the more aggressive agendas among recent presidents. He persuaded

Congress to enact major tax cuts, to undertake a huge reorganization of the federal government (the creation of the Department of Homeland Security), to expand the Medicare entitlement, and to authorize a war of liberation in Iraq. He did all of these things over substantial Democratic opposition. In 2002 the president's party defied history by gaining seats in both houses of Congress and recapturing a majority in the Senate. Although bitterness over the election lingered on the Democratic left, Bush won an undisputed reelection in 2004, having succeeded in establishing a "legitimacy" and a degree of public support that eluded Adams and Hayes.

It's somewhat misleading to speak of John Quincy Adams as having failed to win a plurality of the popular vote. In 1824, when he was elected, only eighteen of the twenty-four states chose presidential electors by popular vote, and in only six of those states were all four major candidates on the November ballot. America had not yet established a stable two-party system (the Democratic Party would emerge four years later, the Republican Party in the 1850s), so the November election results resembled a crowded primary, a free-for-all among four men, all from the same (Democratic-Republican) party: Secretary of State Adams, General Andrew Jackson, House Speaker Henry Clay, and Treasury Secretary William Crawford. The result gave no one a majority, either in the Electoral College or in the aggregate popular vote:

	ELECTORAL VOTE	POPULAR VOTE
Jackson	99	41%
Adams	84	31%
Crawford	41	11%
Clay	37	13%

Although the lack of an Electoral College majority is a rare event—it hasn't recurred in the forty-five elections since 1824—resolving it was a straightforward matter of following the Constitution. The Twelfth Amendment, ratified in 1804, provides that when no candidate receives a majority in the Electoral College (131 votes in 1824), the House of Representatives chooses the president from among the top three finishers, under an unusual procedure in which each state's delegation casts a single vote and a candidate must win a majority of all states. Adams won the House vote with thirteen states, against seven for Jackson and four for Crawford.

Clay, who finished fourth, was not eligible, and he threw his support behind Adams. The three states he had carried in the Electoral College—Kentucky, Missouri, and Ohio—were just enough to give Adams a majority. Adams subsequently appointed Clay his secretary of state. Jackson's supporters campaigned relentlessly against Adams throughout the latter's term, denouncing what they called the "corrupt bargain" between Adams and Clay. In 1828 Jackson easily beat Adams, 178 electoral votes to 83, capturing nearly 56 percent of the popular vote. (By this time, twenty-two states chose their electors by popular vote, with Delaware and South Carolina the only holdouts.)

Fifty-two years later, America's political leaders had to improvise when a controversy developed that the Constitution's framers had not foreseen. The election of 1876 was a race between two governors, Ohio Republican Rutherford B. Hayes and New York Democrat Samuel J. Tilden. Tilden won 184 electoral votes, a single vote shy of a majority, but election results were disputed in three states—Florida, Louisiana, and South Carolina—with nineteen electoral votes among them. "In all three states," writes Hayes biographer Ari Hoogenboom, "Republicans had used fraud to counter Democratic fraud, violence, and intimidation." Hoogenboom believes Hayes would have won a fair election, but in the popular vote Tilden topped him 51 percent to 48 percent.

The dispute had even more twists and turns than the 2000 election would. Unofficial returns showed Hayes ahead in South Carolina, but Tilden led by 94 votes in Florida and 6,300 in Louisiana. "Visiting statesmen" from both parties went to the state capitals to lobby the election boards. All three boards, controlled by Republicans, ruled in Hayes's favor, but on December 6, electors from both parties submitted rival votes to Washington. One electoral vote from Oregon, a state Hayes carried, was also submitted twice, the Democratic governor having certified a Tilden elector on the grounds that the Hayes elector was constitutionally ineligible by virtue of having held federal office (he was a postmaster) at the time of the election.

The Constitution makes no provision for resolving such disputes. The Twelfth Amendment provides that the official electoral vote

count take place at a joint session of Congress: "The President of the
Senate shall, in the presence of the Senate and House of
Representatives, open all the certificates and the votes shall then be
counted." But it's unclear who has the authority to choose between
competing slates of electors. Hayes argued that this power belonged
to Senate President Thomas W. Ferry, a Michigan Republican.
Democrats, who controlled the House, urged a vote by the combined House and Senate, in which they would have had a majority.

Congress compromised and passed legislation setting up a fifteen-
member "electoral commission," consisting of five senators, five representatives, and five Supreme Court justices, to resolve the dispute.
The expectation was that the commission would consist of seven
members of each party, with Justice David Davis, a political independent, as the fifteenth member. But Davis did not serve, for the
Illinois legislature elected him to the U.S. Senate as the candidate of
the Greenback Party. Illinois Democrats "believed that by electing
Davis they had purchased his support, but they had made a monu-
mental miscalculation," Hoogenboom writes. "Because he was
beholden to the Democrats, Davis refused to serve on the commission. His place was filled by Justice Joseph P. Bradley, a Republican
from New Jersey."

In February 1877, on a series of 8–7 party line votes, the commission awarded Hayes all twenty disputed electoral votes, giving him a
185–184 majority. But the battle wasn't over. House Democrats
threatened to filibuster and did not relent until March 2, two days
before inauguration, and then only after a negotiating session called
the Wormley Conference, at which Republicans (Hayes himself did
not participate) promised Southern Democrats that Hayes would
withdraw federal troops protecting the Republican governments of
Louisiana and South Carolina.

Historians differ over the import of the Wormley agreement. The
conventional view is that it marked the end of Reconstruction, but
Hoogenboom disputes this, arguing that the days of Reconstruction
were coming to an end anyway. At the other extreme, the late C.
Vann Woodward believed that what he called the Compromise of
1877 was a turning point in postbellum America, one that "provided
a settlement for an issue that had troubled American politics for
more than a generation." In either case, Hayes's ultimate victory was

in part the product of political dealing with his partisan foes—and this sets it apart from the resolution of the election dispute 124 years later.

At first, the election of November 8, 2000, looked like a big win for the Democrats. Exit polls showed Vice President Gore carrying the crucial state of Florida, with twenty-five electoral votes. When Gore also won Michigan (eighteen electoral votes) and Pennsylvania (twenty-three), it appeared the presidency was his. But as the actual returns came in, it became clear that the exit polls had overstated Gore's strength in Florida. News organizations withdrew their projection of a Gore victory, then declared Governor Bush the victor. Bush had carried twenty-nine other states, and Florida would give him 271 electoral votes, with 270 needed to win. The vice president called the president-elect to concede.

But Gore was soon on the phone to the governor again, to withdraw his concession. Bush's margin of victory in Florida—under two thousand votes—was narrow enough to trigger an automatic recount. This closed Bush's margin to some one thousand votes. Gore sought "hand recounts" of punch card ballots in Florida's most heavily Democratic counties, and the local election boards obliged. This prompted a wave of litigation, and it also ate away at the Bush lead: By November 26, when Florida's Republican secretary of state certified that Bush had won, his margin was a razor-thin 537 votes out of just under six million.

Yet that didn't end the controversy, which would turn into a tug-of-war between the Florida Supreme Court and the U.S. Supreme Court. On November 21, the Florida court had unanimously overturned a trial judge's ruling and ordered the Gore re-recounts to continue. The U.S. Supreme Court—also unanimous—vacated this ruling on December 4 and ordered the Florida court to reconsider its ruling in light of an 1887 federal statute requiring that election disputes be resolved according to laws in place as of election day.

Back in Tallahassee, another case was making its way to the Florida Supreme Court, and on December 8 the court, this time divided 4-3, ordered more recounts. In a blistering dissent, Chief Justice Charles Wells opined that "the majority's decision cannot withstand the scrutiny which will certainly immediately follow under the United States Constitution." He was right. The case, called *Bush v. Gore*,

quickly landed in Washington, where it was overturned by a 5–4 ruling of the U.S. Supreme Court.

Seven of the nine justices agreed that the Florida ruling—which
provided for a patchwork of different counting standards depending
on the county, and sometimes within the same county—violated the
equal protection clause of the Fourteenth Amendment. Two of those
seven wanted to give the Florida Supreme Court more time to sort
things out, but a five-justice majority agreed that Florida law imposed
a statutory deadline for certifying electors as of December 12—the
day on which the high court ruled. Thus the election was over;
George W. Bush was president-elect. The next day Vice President
Gore conceded for real.

Gore had never led Bush in Florida, and subsequent examinations
of ballots by news organizations made clear that Bush would have
won any fairly conducted count. Even so, many on the Democratic
left remained bitter, insisting despite the evidence that the election
was stolen. This did not, however, turn out to be much of a political
hindrance to President Bush.

One reason is that it was the Supreme Court, a nonpolitical
branch of government, that resolved the election dispute. Thus Bush
was not forced into any bargains or compromises; he took office
beholden to no one but the 50 million or so Americans who voted
for him. Some on the left urged him to govern as a "centrist," but he
had learned the lesson of his father, who had lost reelection eight
years earlier in large part because he alienated his political base by
reneging on his emphatic pledge not to raise taxes.

In any event, those who refused to accept Bush's victory were not
centrist voters but those firmly on the Democratic left; they would
have opposed Bush even if he had won in a landslide. An ABC News
poll conducted December 3, 2000—at the height of the election
dispute—found that 73 percent of those surveyed said they'd accept
Bush as the legitimate winner, though the poll subjects, like the electorate, were about evenly divided (46 percent for Bush, 43 percent
for Gore) as to whom they'd prefer to see win.

The surprise attack on America of September 11, 2001, cemented
Bush's legitimacy. He benefited, obviously, from the country's natural tendency to rally around its commander in chief during wartime,

and from the successes of the military campaigns in Afghanistan and later in Iraq. But Bush was also fortunate in his domestic foes. A small, shrill antiwar movement developed, gaining strength as the debate progressed from Afghanistan to Iraq. Antiwar sentiment was inextricably bound up with anti-Bush sentiment, as was clear as early as September 12, 2001, when left-wing filmmaker Michael Moore wrote on his Web site about the previous day's attacks:

> This just is not right. They did not deserve to die. If someone did this to get back at Bush, then they did so by killing thousands of people who DID NOT VOTE for him! Boston, New York, DC, and the planes' destination of California—these were places that voted AGAINST Bush!

Eighteen months later, Moore was still at it, declaring at the Academy Awards that Bush was a "fictitious president" who owed his job to "fictitious election results" and was "sending us to war for fictitious reasons." The intervention in Iraq had begun a few days earlier, with the support of more than 70 percent of Americans. But while the Republican Party and most of the nation were united, the Democrats were badly divided between supporters and opponents of the war effort.

As the effort in Iraq ran into difficulties, Democrats increasingly gravitated toward Moore's mendacious and paranoid style of politics. In June 2004, enthusiastic Democratic lawmakers attended the Washington premiere of Moore's antiwar agitprop film *Fahrenheit 9/11*. "There might be half of the Democratic Senate here," said Senator Bob Graham of Florida. Among those in attendance was then-Minority Leader Tom Daschle of South Dakota, who was later forced to deny reports that he had *physically* embraced Moore. Twenty months earlier, Daschle had voted in favor of the Iraq war resolution.

In his first term, Bush's critics, like Jonathan Cohn, often argued that a majority of voters in 2000 rejected his conservative agenda, casting their ballots for either Gore or left-wing protest candidate Ralph Nader. But in 2004 he achieved a majority of the popular vote. He also had coattails; the GOP picked up a net four Senate and three House seats.

The president responded to victory by laying out an even more aggressive agenda for his second term. In his inaugural address, he promised to promote democracy worldwide, "with the ultimate goal of ending tyranny in the world." As for domestic policy, he proposed to alter fundamentally the bedrock program of the American welfare state by making personal investment accounts an element of Social Security.

The Michael Moore Democrats, meanwhile, descended into self-parody. Moore had opened *Fahrenheit 9/11* with scenes of House members in January 2001 futilely seeking a senator to join their challenge to the certification of Florida's electoral votes. Four years later, Bush's margin of victory in the decisive state of Ohio was 118,599 votes. There was no question that he had carried the state legitimately. Yet when Congress met to certify the election results, Senator Barbara Boxer rose to challenge Ohio's electoral votes. "Four years ago, I didn't intervene," she said. "Frankly, looking back on it, I wish I had." The Boxer rebellion failed. The House voted down her motion, 263–32; the Senate, 74–1.

If Bush had lost the election, he would have joined the ranks of one-termers John Quincy Adams, Rutherford Hayes, and Benjamin Harrison (whose election in 1888 was undisputed despite President Grover Cleveland's popular vote plurality, and who lost to Cleveland four years later). Instead he proved that it is possible for a "minority president" to win a popular mandate by governing as if he already has one.

Mr. Taranto is editor of OpinionJournal.com.

APPENDIX I
Methodology of Rankings

by James Lindgren

The reputations of presidents rise and fall. As experts on the presidency gain more perspective, their rankings of some presidents, such as Woodrow Wilson, have fallen, while their impressions of others, such as Dwight Eisenhower, have risen. Even some presidents long dead have taken reputational stumbles. For example, the presidencies of James Madison and John Quincy Adams are no longer as highly regarded as they were in the mid-twentieth century.

This study reports results from a survey of 85 experts on the presidency conducted in February and March 2005. It is in part a replication of an October 2000 survey of 78 academics, which was presented in the first edition of this book. Unlike most prior studies, these surveyed experts on presidential history and politics from the fields of law and political science, as well as from history. For the 2005 study, we added economists to the mix, including six Nobel laureates. Moreover, for both studies we balanced the group to be surveyed with approximately equal numbers of experts on the left and the right. Because political leanings can influence professional judgments, we think that the 2005 rankings are the most politically balanced estimates of presidential reputation yet obtained for American presidents.

To choose the scholars to be surveyed, in 2000 or 2005 we had four expert panels of two scholars in each field come up with a list of experts in their field. The eight scholars who consulted on the makeup of the sample were historians Alan Brinkley (Columbia University) and Forrest McDonald (University of Alabama), political scientists James W. Ceaser (University of Virginia) and Stephen Skowronek (Yale University), law professors Akhil Reed Amar (Yale University) and Steven G. Calabresi (Northwestern University), and economists David Henderson (Naval Postgraduate School and Hoover Institution, Stanford University) and Jeffrey Sachs (Columbia University).

We tried to choose approximately equal numbers of scholars who lean to the left and to the right. Our goal was to present the opinions of experts, controlling for political orientation. Another way to express this is that we sought to mirror what scholarly opinion might be on the counterfactual assumption that the academy was politically representative of the society in which we live and work. This study attempts to resolve the conflict between prior rankings of presidents done mostly by liberal scholars or mostly by conservative scholars,[1] but not by both together.

As in prior studies, George Washington, Abraham Lincoln, and Franklin Roosevelt continue to be the most esteemed presidents. Also like other studies, as a group Democratic and Democratic-Republican presidents tend to be rated higher than Republican, Whig, and Federalist presidents (though insignificantly so).

Overall, our response rate was a solid 65 percent (85 of 130 scholars surveyed responded), higher than our 59 percent response rate in 2000. Rates, however, varied by field: We obtained usable responses from 25 of 32 (78 percent) political scientists, 24 of 32 (75 percent) law professors, 19 of 30 (63 percent) historians, and 14 of 36 (39 percent) economists, plus three academics who participated anonymously.[2] Not every scholar rated every president. Of the 85

---

[1] Arthur M. Schlesinger, Jr., "Rating the Presidents: Washington to Clinton," 112 *Political Science Quarterly* 179 (1997) (mostly liberal scholars); William J. Ridings, Jr., and Stuart B. McIver, *Rating the Presidents: From the Great and Honorable to the Dishonest and Incompetent* (1997) (presumably mostly liberal scholars); Alvin S. Felzenberg, "There You Go Again: Liberal Historians and the *New York Times* Deny Ronald Reagan His Due," *Policy Review*, March-April 1997 (criticized by Schlesinger as "inviting the same suspicion" of political bias as his panel, though from the other side).

[2] These three scholars (all Democrats) were among those on our expert panel, but managed to avoid giving their names on the online version of the survey. If their contributions were omitted, there would be no major changes: John Adams would slightly overtake Grover Cleveland, and Franklin Pierce would slightly overtake Andrew Johnson.

respondents, every twentieth-century president except our current president, George W. Bush, was ranked by at least 80 academics. Overall, the mean number of rankings for each president was 80.2, with the lowest number of rankings for Zachary Taylor (67 scholars) and George W. Bush (68 scholars).

Each scholar was asked to rate each president[3] on a standard social-science 5-point scale from well below average to highly superior[4] and to name the most overrated and underrated presidents.[5] The scholars we surveyed were supposed to rate them as presidents, but undoubtedly other accomplishments sometimes affected the ratings. One economist suggested that Madison was underrated, citing his contributions to the creation of the Constitution. One 2000 respondent explicitly rejected this tendency: "Some of the low-ranking presidents [as he ranked them], such as John Quincy Adams, Martin Van Buren, and William Howard Taft, were able men who contributed a great deal to the nation, but not as president."

Unlike our 2000 survey, in 2005 we collected some political data on the scholars responding to the survey, which allows us to weight Republican and Democratic responses so that each makes an equal contribution to the overall ranking.

This strange modern genre of presidential rankings was initiated in 1948 by Arthur Schlesinger, Sr., who repeated his study in 1962.[6] In 1996 his son, Arthur Schlesinger, Jr., replicated the study.[7] Both our studies, in 2000 and 2005, found remarkably similar results, to each other and to the 1996 Schlesinger study. The correlation between ranks in our 2000 study and ranks in our 2005 study is .99. The corre-

[3] We excluded James Garfield and William Harrison because of their very brief terms in office.

[4] The scholars were asked: "Please rate each president. Please take into consideration the value of the accomplishments of his presidency and the leadership he provided the nation, along with any other criteria you deem appropriate."

[5] The scholars were asked: "Please identify the most Overrated or Underrated Presidents."

[6] See Arthur M. Schlesinger, Jr., "Rating the Presidents: Washington to Clinton," 112 *Political Science Quarterly* 179, (1997) (describing his father's studies for *Life* magazine in 1948 and *The New York Times Magazine* in 1962).

[7] Ibid. (Nineteen ninety-six study, results published first in *The New York Times Magazine* in 1996, followed by a scholarly paper published in 1997).

lations between the 1996 Schlesinger study and our ranks was .94 for the 2000 study and .91 for the 2005 study.[8] The main difference between the Schlesinger study and our 2005 study is that, while Ronald Reagan ranked 25th in Schlesinger's 1996 study, Reagan ranks 6th in our study (even Democrats in our study ranked him 14th).

Compared with the Schlesinger study, there are some methodological differences. Schlesinger surveyed 30 historians and 2 politicians (Mario Cuomo and the late senator Paul Simon). We surveyed 85 historians, economists, political scientists, and law professors. The ages of our respondents ranged from 29 to 92.

I. RANKING THE PRESIDENTS

Rating presidents is an odd practice. As Thomas Cronin and Michael Genovese have written, "Just as presidents cannot be experts on all areas of policy, historians cannot be experts on all presidents."[9] Many presidents (e.g., Ulysses Grant, Calvin Coolidge, and Warren Harding) are probably rated more on received wisdom than on assessments of their records. In 2000, the historian Robert Ferrell argued that once one goes beyond one's narrow area of expertise, there is "a rapid diminution of real authoritative judgment." Even someone who has written more than a dozen books on the presidency, Ferrell asserts, would "almost have to guess" for some of the presidents.

Some respondents reflected this cautiousness. Political scientist

---

[8] This result comes after correcting the Schlesinger ranks for arithmetical errors, some of which change ranks, some of which don't. Further, although his table purports to rank presidents by mean score, he inexplicably switches over to raw totals for poorly ranked presidents and then miscounts those total for two of them. Schlesinger appears not to have used a spreadsheet, since, e.g., the second category was weighted 2 points for some presidents and 1 point for most presidents. The correlations in the text reflect correcting errors in the Schlesinger ranks, but not recoding scores for the responses, which is also a problem. Besides arithmetical errors and changing the criteria for the ranking partway through one column, the Schlesinger study coded the bottom category in their 5-category scale –2, 3 points below the category just above it. With more conventional coding (an even 1-point spread between categories), the correlation is .96 with our ranks in the 2000 survey (with a stunning R^2 of .91) and .93 with our ranks in the 2005 survey. If we omit the one outlier, Ronald Reagan, the correlation between the Schlesinger ranks and our ranks is .97 in 2000 and .95 in 2005.

[9] Thomas E. Cronin and Michael A. Genovese, *The Paradoxes of the American Presidency* (2nd ed. 2004), p. 88.

Karen Hult noted in 2000 that rankings of U.S. presidents are problematic: "First, as summaries, they by necessity mask what may be important differences *within* administrations." Some presidents may be better at some tasks than others or better at different times within their administrations. "Second," she argues, "rankings of presidents appear to me to reinforce the too-frequent tendency in the United States to attribute more power to the individuals who occupy the Oval Office than they typically have (or had)." One historian this year made a similar point: "How do you rate a president with some great triumphs and a spectacular failure (i.e., Jefferson, whose first administration was dramatically more successful than his second)?"

Respondents used different criteria in ranking presidents. Many favored their own evaluations of the presidents' goals and accomplishments. Others, such as legal scholar Annette Gordon-Reed in 2000, emphasized the presidents' own goals: "I tried to make decisions based upon the extent to which each man was able to accomplish what he set out to do rather than relying only on my opinion of the worth of their efforts."

Taking a different approach, law professor Sandy Levinson explained in 2005 that he looked at presidents according to his own assessment of the direction they led the country: "I answered the questions by reference to my own normative views. If I were assessing 'greatness' on a more 'positivist' scale, i.e., looking at the impact of the presidents, I would have rated Ronald Reagan and (dare I say it) George W. Bush much higher than I did, since both have I believe for ill fundamentally transformed American politics in a way that say Bill Clinton did not."

Economist Kenneth Arrow noted correctly that rankings such as ours often collapse performances that vary from area to area, "The one-dimensional ranking obscures the fact that the same president can belong to both ends of the scale. I am thinking particularly of L. B. Johnson and Nixon." Or as a historian put it, "For presidents such as FDR and Kennedy, who combined such extremes of the best and the worst, I found myself in the awkward situation of having to say that they were average. Of course, there was nothing average about these men, but this was the only way I could capture their very mixed qualities."

Expressing discomfort with rating presidents, one law scholar thus argued, "I'm a bit dubious about this rating exercise. Is it really possible to compare the performances of Monroe, Cleveland, and George H. W. Bush?" According to political scientist Andrew Busch, in most rankings there are systematic biases to favor particular sorts of presidents:

> Traditionally, ratings of presidents have inflated "progressive" presidents by overplaying the importance of "activism" and underplaying the questions of (a) whether the policies were successful and beneficial in the short or long term, and (b) whether the presidency advanced American constitutional principles or undermined them. Taking these questions into account, Wilson, Johnson, and Kennedy (and even FDR) do not look as good.

The problems that a president faces can reflect on his reputation. As political scientist William Connelly wryly observes about Madison (whom Connelly considers underrated): "It is hard to look good while the British are sacking Washington, D.C."

A. The Best Presidents

"The plain fact is that over half of our presidents have been mediocrities," wrote the late historian Robert Rutland in his response to our 2000 study. That same year Thomas Cronin was more sanguine: "At least two dozen individuals have served with distinction; only a few have been grossly inadequate." Some presidents were ranked highly by almost everyone in our study.

The 10 presidents ranked highest in this survey all made it into Schlesinger's top 10 except Ronald Reagan. (They are presented here in Table 1.) George Washington ranked 1st, while Abraham Lincoln and Franklin Roosevelt came in 2nd and 3rd respectively. As historian Steven Gillon remarks simply in his comments on the survey, "Washington, Lincoln, and Franklin Roosevelt belong in a class of their own. They are the only really 'great' presidents."

Compared with the 2000 survey, fewer respondents in 2005 give Lincoln the highest rating of 5. As one historian explains, "My problem with President Lincoln concerns his *means*, not his ends. Unlike Martin Luther King, who insisted that 'the means we use must be as pure as the ends we seek,' Lincoln countenanced 'any means necessary' to achieve his goal: preservation of the union."

Just a step below Washington, Lincoln, and Roosevelt is Thomas Jefferson (4th). Indeed, because Franklin Roosevelt's scores dropped from 2000 to 2005, the gap between FDR and Jefferson has closed considerably. One could make the case for restoring Jefferson to the category of "great" presidents, a characterization that he held in the 1948 and 1962 rankings by Arthur Schlesinger, Sr. All 4 of these presidents averaged well above 4.0 on a 5-point scale.

Some scholars might have thought that Jefferson's reputation was slipping, partly because of an increase in discussions of his slave-holding in general and his probable fathering of children with Sally Hemings. In 2000, political scientist David Mayhew's comment expressed this concern, "Jefferson is getting downgraded these days, but after reading Henry Adams's volumes recently, I see him as first-rate."

Rounding out the top 10 are Theodore Roosevelt (5th), Ronald Reagan (6th), Harry Truman (7th), Dwight Eisenhower (8th), James Polk (9th), and Andrew Jackson (10th), all scoring above 3.5, with a rating of 4 being the median ranking for all 4 men. Between 2000 and 2005, Andrew Jackson dropped 4 places from 6th to 10th, and Ronald Reagan climbed 2 slots from 8th to 6th.

TABLE 1: THE 10 BEST U.S. PRESIDENTS
(RANKED BY WEIGHTED MEAN SCORE)

1. George Washington	4.94
2. Abraham Lincoln	4.67
3. Franklin Roosevelt	4.41
4. Thomas Jefferson	4.23
5. Theodore Roosevelt	4.08
6. Ronald Reagan	4.03
7. Harry Truman	3.95
8. Dwight Eisenhower	3.67
9. James Polk	3.59
10. Andrew Jackson	3.58

Feb.-March 2005 Survey of Professors of Economics, History, Politics, and Law
N=76–85 scholars

B. *The Worst Presidents*

According to the 85 experts on our panel, the worst president was James Buchanan (ranked 40th), followed by Warren Harding (39th) and Franklin Pierce (38th). Buchanan and Pierce are usually blamed for doing little to head off the impending Civil War.

Of those presidents in the bottom 10, 5 did not serve even one full term: Harding, Andrew Johnson (37th), Millard Fillmore (36th), John Tyler (35th), and Zachary Taylor (33rd). In addition, Richard Nixon (32nd) was forced from office, and Andrew Johnson was impeached. Compared with the 2000 survey, Herbert Hoover (now 31st) replaces Ulysses Grant (now 29th) in the bottom 10.

In the past few decades Grant has been enjoying a reappraisal. As one law professor contended, "Grant's civil rights record is exemplary, rivaled only by Lincoln, Truman, and Lyndon Johnson; and Grant helped ensure decades of future prosperity by moving the country to hard money." Grant has climbed from next to the bottom in Schlesinger's 1948 and 1962 surveys to 12th from the bottom in 2005.

In our latest survey Jimmy Carter has slipped a few places (from 30th to 34th), probably because the attacks of September 11, 2001, reminded scholars of his poor handling of Islamic fundamentalism—a shortcoming that he shares with most or all of his successors. Nonetheless, Carter has his supporters, such as political scientist Karen Hult, who considers him underrated because of scholars' "tendency to focus only on the initial part of [his] term, overlooking the learning that took place later in the term." Likewise, politics professor Mary Stuckey sees Carter as underrated: He "had more success governing in a difficult political context than he gets credit for." Political scientist Erwin Hargrove sounds a similar note: "Carter is underrated, because his achievements, especially in foreign policy, were good, despite his failures in domestic politics."

TABLE 2: THE 10 WORST U.S. PRESIDENTS
(RANKED BY WEIGHTED MEAN SCORE)

31. Herbert Hoover (10th worst)	2.50
32. Richard Nixon	2.40
33. Zachary Taylor	2.30
34. Jimmy Carter	2.24

35. John Tyler	2.23
36. Millard Fillmore	1.85
37. Andrew Johnson	1.75
38. Franklin Pierce	1.73
39. Warren Harding	1.64
40. James Buchanan	1.31

Feb.-March 2005 Survey of Professors of Economics,
History, Politics, and Law
N=67–85 respondents

C. Grouping the Presidents

It has been traditional to group the presidents as "great," "near great," and so on. While any such classifications are arbitrary, we can group using our scores in something like these traditional categories. Remember, however, that our respondents did not use these particular characterizations; these are applied after the fact to group the results.

There may be some surprises here. Perhaps because of the extravagant eulogies after his death, in 2005 Ronald Reagan moved up 2 places to 6th. Although Woodrow Wilson retained his 11th place, his ratings dropped enough that he was better grouped with the "above average" category.

Our three most recent presidents all fall in the "average" category. Nonetheless, Bill Clinton (22nd) jumped over 3 presidents (Hayes, Van Buren, and John Quincy Adams), bringing him just 2 places behind his spot in the 1996 Schlesinger survey.

Carter and Nixon both had low median ratings of 2.0. In 2000 Carter was ranked 3 spots higher than Nixon, but he is now 2 spots behind Nixon. In Nixon's case, this low rating reflects what many scholars believe to be his mostly disastrous domestic, international, and economic policies, not to mention the corruption of his administration. Nonetheless, 12 respondents considered him underrated, including political scientist Bert Rockman, who said:

Richard Nixon—yes, he was responsible for a regime crisis, and for an effort to unbalance our constitutional system. But he also was responsible for much regulatory reform (so considered in his era), for attacking pollution, and for proposing what would today be considered rad-

ical initiatives. He also had a theory about foreign policy, which may
have been dead wrong, but it was thought through. A man of genuine
intellectual virtues, but flawed moral sense.

TABLE 3: RANKING OF PRESIDENTS BY WEIGHTED MEAN SCORE

	MEAN	MEDIAN	STD. DEV.
GREAT			
1. George Washington	4.94	5.00	0.28
2. Abraham Lincoln	4.67	5.00	1.02
3. Franklin Roosevelt	4.41	5.00	1.01
NEAR GREAT			
4. Thomas Jefferson	4.23	4.00	0.71
5. Theodore Roosevelt	4.08	4.00	0.89
6. Ronald Reagan	4.03	4.00	0.98
7. Harry Truman	3.95	4.00	0.76
8. Dwight Eisenhower	3.67	4.00	0.63
9. James Polk	3.59	4.00	1.31
10. Andrew Jackson	3.58	4.00	1.03
ABOVE AVERAGE			
11. Woodrow Wilson	3.41	4.00	1.08
12. Grover Cleveland	3.34	3.00	1.15
13. John Adams	3.33	3.00	0.96
14. William McKinley	3.32	3.00	1.17
15. John Kennedy	3.25	3.00	0.78
16. James Monroe	3.24	3.00	0.98
AVERAGE			
17. James Madison	3.07	3.00	1.07
18. Lyndon Johnson	3.05	3.00	1.07
19. George W. Bush	3.01	3.50*	1.58
20. William Taft	2.97	3.00	0.84
21. George H. W. Bush	2.95	3.00	0.64

22. Bill Clinton	2.93	3.00	0.97
23. Calvin Coolidge	2.77	3.00	1.11
24. Rutherford Hayes	2.73	3.00	1.09

BELOW AVERAGE

25. John Quincy Adams	2.66	3.00	0.99
26. Chester Arthur	2.65	3.00	1.07
27. Martin Van Buren	2.63	3.00	1.05
28. Gerald Ford	2.61	3.00	0.62
29. Ulysses Grant	2.57	3.00	0.87
30. Benjamin Harrison	2.54	3.00	0.91
31. Herbert Hoover	2.50	3.00	0.84
32. Richard Nixon	2.40	2.00	0.98
33. Zachary Taylor	2.30	2.00	1.08
34. Jimmy Carter	2.24	2.00	0.88
35. John Tyler	2.23	2.00	1.08

FAILURE

36. Millard Fillmore	1.85	2.00	0.88
37. Andrew Johnson	1.75	1.75*	0.90
38. Franklin Pierce	1.73	2.00	0.97
39. Warren Harding	1.64	1.00	0.84
40. James Buchanan	1.31	1.00	0.65

* These are split medians. For George W. Bush, equal numbers of respondents chose 4 and higher and 3 and lower. For Andrew Johnson, 1 respondent indicated a rating between 1 and 2 (i.e., 1.5), which led to a split median of 1.5 and 2.
Feb.-March 2005 Survey of Professors of Economics, History, Politics, and Law
N=67–85 respondents, weighted equally between political parties

D. The Presidents with the Most Variable Ratings

Several presidents had highly variable ratings. As historian Alonzo Hamby noted, "I don't believe George W. Bush can be properly evaluated until his presidency can be completed." Perhaps not surprisingly, in our 2000 survey Bill Clinton had the highest variation in our ratings and in 2005 George W. Bush has that dubious honor. Yet Bush's variability in 2005 is substantially higher than Clinton's in 2000. As political scientist Andrew Busch noted, "G. W. Bush could wind up at anywhere from 1 to 5 depending on events." Indeed, Clinton and Reagan, whose ratings were highly variable last time, were somewhat less so in 2005.

Other presidents with high variability in their ratings include James Polk and William McKinley. While in the 2000 study the presidents with high variability tended to be the most controversial (Clinton, Wilson, Reagan, Nixon, and Lyndon Johnson), except for the current President Bush in 2005 the highest variability seemed to be in the rankings of presidents for which some respondents might lack information—Polk, McKinley, Cleveland, Coolidge, Hayes, Taylor, and Tyler.

TABLE 4: THE PRESIDENTS WITH THE MOST VARIABLE RANKINGS (STANDARD DEVIATIONS IN RANKINGS ON A 1–5 SCALE)

1. George W. Bush	1.58
2. James Polk	1.31
3. William McKinley	1.17
4. Grover Cleveland	1.15
5. Calvin Coolidge	1.11
6. Rutherford Hayes	1.09
7. Zachary Taylor	1.08
8. John Tyler	1.08
9. Woodrow Wilson	1.08
10. James Madison	1.07
11. Chester Arthur	1.07
12. Lyndon Johnson	1.07
13. Martin Van Buren	1.05
14. Andrew Jackson	1.03
15. Abraham Lincoln	1.02
16. Franklin Roosevelt	1.01

Feb.-March 2005 Survey of Professors of Economics, History, Politics, and Law
N=67–85 respondents

E. The Most Overrated and Underrated Presidents

We asked the scholars surveyed to list the most overrated and underrated presidents. Because this question refers to an unstated baseline reputation, the results are not terribly meaningful. Moreover, one professor listed Franklin Roosevelt as both overrated (for his handling of the economy) and underrated (for his handling of World War II). Enough of our respondents (16) cited Ronald Reagan as underrated that he ties Calvin Coolidge for the most underrated president, but nearly as many respondents (15) listed him as overrated.

There were two presidents who were listed as overrated by more than a third of our respondents: John Kennedy and Woodrow Wilson. About Kennedy, political scientist Colleen Shogan argues, "John Kennedy is heralded as a remarkable modern president, but most of his contributions were symbolic rather than institutional." Mary Stuckey agrees—"Kennedy did considerably less than people think"—as does economist Murray Weidenbaum: "Kennedy's major accomplishment was oratory." Political scientist Bruce Miroff goes further: "The much-vaunted sophistication of the New Frontier concealed some stale formulae for governance, driving the Cold War to dangerous heights, and prompting a cold and belated response to the civil rights revolution." Nonetheless, Kennedy has his defenders. Finding him underrated, historian David Burner notes that Kennedy "balanced caution and aggressiveness in foreign policy."

Woodrow Wilson had nearly as many scholars listing him as overrated as did Kennedy. Law professor Annette Gordon-Reed sounds a note echoed by some other respondents, particularly legal scholars: "Wilson let his personal racial prejudices intrude upon his role as the leader of all Americans. He came to Washington and brought Jim Crow with him. His moralism in foreign affairs, making the world safe for democracy, when he did not believe in it for all Americans, undermined his strength as a true moral leader."

Along similar lines, political scientist Stephen Knott explained why he considers Wilson overrated: "An important figure and thus 'above average' but a sanctimonious prig. It's difficult not to see him as a hypocrite—preaching to the world about human rights while sanctioning blatant racism at home." According to law professor Sandy

Levinson, there is a "tendency to brush aside [Wilson's] racism." And as law professor John McGinnis explained, "Wilson's racial policies were unenlightened even by the standards of his time."

Some criticized Wilson for other policies. Economist Kenneth Arrow offered this explanation for viewing Wilson as overrated: "His great domestic accomplishments and the entry into the war are canceled by his excessive moralism and his failure to compromise on the League of Nations." Law professor Gary Lawson was harsher in his assessment: "Between World War I and the Progressive agenda, Woodrow Wilson may have done more national damage than any other president." Political scientist William Connelly offers a cynical explanation for Wilson's high ranking: "Woodrow Wilson is overrated because intellectuals, especially political scientists, love him. It didn't hurt that he was president of the APSA [American Political Science Association] before being president of the United States." As one prominent historian noted about Wilson, "People remember the idealism but forget the weakness of his political capacities." Economist Murray Weidenbaum said simply, "He lost the peace."

The third most often listed as overrated is Ronald Reagan. Political scientist Mary Stuckey explains: "Ronald Reagan gets more credit than he deserves for ending the Cold War, and not enough blame for the economic problems and positions on race." Arguing that Reagan is underrated, Gary Lawson offers this explanation: "There is a movement afoot to create a conventional wisdom that Russia simply gave up the Cold War and that Reagan deserves no credit. That is rewriting history. I never voted for the guy, but history proved him right."

Politics professor Bruce Buchanan makes the same criticism of Reagan as he does of Kennedy: Their high rankings are an "overreaction to rhetoric and style relative to achievement." Political scientist Peri Arnold offers one of the more interesting comments on why Reagan is overrated: "He is properly credited with substantial accomplishments in reducing marginal tax rates and tax reform as well as fostering positions that exacerbated the Soviet Union's instabilities. However, the current virtual industry of pamphleteers pumping up Reagan's record and accomplishments have tended to . . . bloat

Reagan's reputation while simultaneously reducing attention to the substance of his real accomplishments."

TABLE 5: THE MOST OVERRATED PRESIDENTS
(NUMBER OF 85 SCHOLARS CITING A PRESIDENT AS OVERRATED)

1. John Kennedy	33
2. Woodrow Wilson	30
3. Ronald Reagan	15
4. Andrew Jackson	11
4. Franklin Roosevelt	11
6. Bill Clinton	10
7. Thomas Jefferson	9
8. Theodore Roosevelt	8
9. George W. Bush	7
10. Abraham Lincoln	6
10. Lyndon Johnson	6

Feb.-March 2005 Survey of Professors of Economics, History, Politics, and Law

The scholars we surveyed list fewer presidents as underrated than overrated. Ronald Reagan and Calvin Coolidge are cited by more respondents as underrated than any other president—though ranked 6th in this survey, he cannot be underrated here. Coolidge, on the other hand, is cited by 16 scholars as underrated, yet his overall scores in our survey place him near the bottom of the "average" category. As political scientist Colleen Shogan argues: "Calvin Coolidge made great contributions regarding the plebiscitary capacities of the office, which are rarely noted." In the same vein, law professor John McGinnis asserts: "Coolidge cleaned up scandals at the White House, pursued policies for lean yet effective government, and projected the modesty befitting a republican leader."

Economist David Henderson notes that Coolidge (along with Cleveland and Van Buren) "tried, somewhat successfully, to rein in a powerful central government and even shrunk government. In doing so, they paid attention to the Constitution [and] . . . avoided major wars."

TABLE 6: THE MOST UNDERRATED PRESIDENTS
(NUMBER OF 85 SCHOLARS CITING A PRESIDENT AS UNDERRATED)

1. Calvin Coolidge	16
1. Ronald Reagan	16
3. Richard Nixon	12
4. George W. Bush	11
5. Dwight Eisenhower	10
6. Herbert Hoover	8
7. James Polk	7
7. Lyndon Johnson	7
9. (eight presidents tied)	6
James Madison	
John Adams	
John Quincy Adams	
William McKinley	
Harry Truman	
Gerald Ford	
Jimmy Carter	
Bill Clinton	

Feb.-March 2005 Survey of Professors of Economics, History, Politics, and Law

II. PREDICTORS OF HIGH PRESIDENTIAL RATINGS

In this section, we briefly explore differences in ratings within our sample and possible variables that might explain them. We examined whether the presidential ratings were higher before Andrew Jackson opened up the process of nominating presidents. Before Jackson, candidates were usually chosen by slate-making in the congressional caucus. With Jackson's encouragement, political parties moved to choosing candidates in national party conventions. This corresponded with a Jacksonian revolution in extending the franchise to wider segments of the adult white male population. Counting Jackson as a product of the older era, the 6 presidents picked before the populist era of national party conventions rated an insignificant .54 points higher than the later presidents.

Presidents who served parts of two terms (or more) rated a full point higher (1.04) than presidents who served just one term or part of a term. Two-term presidents are today rated much higher than one-term presidents. Thus, while John Kennedy ranks only 15th (in the "above average" group), he is first among presidents serving less than one full term and third among presidents serving only one term. (James Polk and John Adams are the two one-term presidents ahead of him.) By contrast, Bill Clinton, ranked 22nd overall, is rated lower than all presidents serving two full terms except Ulysses Grant.

III. COMPARING THE RESPONSES OF SCHOLARS IN ECONOMICS, HISTORY, LAW, AND POLITICAL SCIENCE

Scholars in different fields see the world somewhat differently. Although we observed few large field-specific differences in ranking U.S. presidents, there were several. In this study, the economics scholars were usually the outliers. Indeed, the correlated with ranks in the other fields at .75–.80. The rankings in politics, history, and law correlate with one another at .94–.95.

For example, while the other three fields ranked Ronald Reagan from 5th to 7th place, economists ranked him 16th. While Andrew Jackson was ranked 8th to 11th by other fields, he was ranked 19th by economic professors. Economists also ranked George W. Bush 35th, well below the other fields (which ranked him 15th to 19th)— probably because of the high government spending and the recession in Bush's first term.

But the biggest difference was the ranking of William McKinley, who was ranked 36th by economists, compared with 10th to 12th in the other three fields. Since none of the economists lists McKinley as overrated, the reason for his low rating is a mystery. One would think his eventual reduction of tariffs would have been popular with economics respondents. Since economists rated Ulysses Grant (who put the United States on the gold standard) higher than did other academic fields, it seems unlikely that the economists favored William Jennings Bryan's call for easier money, but with gold's apparent role in the Great Depression of the 1930s, perhaps McKinley's support for gold is the explanation.

Perhaps the most plausible explanation for McKinley's low rating by economists comes not from an economist, but from political scientist Peri Arnold:

McKinley's historical reputation rests heavily on the rise of nationalist chauvinism after the Spanish-American War along with the expansion of government activities during his slightly over four years in office. However, McKinley was also a politician of little imagination who was largely inattentive to problems of his day that ought to have been addressed by his government, but were not put firmly on the government agenda until Theodore Roosevelt was in office.

Political scientists differ little from the other fields, though they rank George W. Bush and Lyndon Johnson a bit higher, perhaps because of Bush's and Johnson's aggressive use of presidential power. And political scientists rank Ulysses Grant a bit lower, probably because of political corruption in his administration. Historians also differed little from those in other academic disciplines, except that they rank Calvin Coolidge at least 10 places lower than every other field, and Benjamin Harrison a bit higher. Law professors rank presidents much like political scientists and historians, though they rank Lyndon Johnson and Woodrow Wilson a bit worse and William Taft a bit better, in Taft's case perhaps because he subsequently served as chief justice.

In the 2000 study, though Washington took the top spot, the politics and history professors ranked him second to Lincoln. In 2005, all four fields rank Washington first. When I pointed out this result to law professor Philip Hamburger, he said wistfully, "Although we have had only two truly great presidents, Washington and Lincoln, we have had only one *profound* president—Lincoln."

TABLE 7: RANKING OF PRESIDENTS BY SCHOLARLY FIELD

PRESIDENT (OVERALL RANK)	ECONOMICS RANK	MEAN	HISTORY RANK	MEAN	LAW RANK	MEAN	POLITICS RANK	MEAN
George Washington (1)	1	4.89	1	5.00	1	4.95	1	4.94
Abraham Lincoln (2)	3	4.33	3	4.57	2	4.79	2	4.91

PRESIDENT (OVERALL RANK)	ECONOMICS RANK	ECONOMICS MEAN	HISTORY RANK	HISTORY MEAN	LAW RANK	LAW MEAN	POLITICS RANK	POLITICS MEAN
Franklin Roosevelt (3)	4	3.80	2	4.64	3	4.43	3	4.72
Thomas Jefferson (4)	2	4.47	6	4.00	4	4.25	4	4.28
Theodore Roosevelt (5)	5	3.80	4	4.31	6	4.07	5	4.27
Ronald Reagan (6)	16	3.27	7	3.85	5	4.24	6	4.22
Harry Truman (7)	7	3.71	5	4.23	7	3.92	7	4.04
Dwight Eisenhower (8)	10	3.48	9	3.72	9	3.66	10	3.79
James Polk (9)	14	3.38	8	3.85	11	3.40	11	3.63
Andrew Jackson (10)	19	2.84	11	3.46	8	3.77	8	3.87
Woodrow Wilson (11)	12	3.43	14	3.31	18	3.08	9	3.85
Grover Cleveland (12)	6	3.80	13	3.38	16	3.14	16	3.26
John Adams (13)	8	3.60	12	3.42	13	3.34	17	3.11
William McKinley (14)	36	2.17	10	3.66	10	3.43	12	3.51
John Kennedy (15)	15	3.32	15	3.30	14	3.23	14	3.36
James Monroe (16)	9	3.56	17	3.14	12	3.38	19	2.94
James Madison (17)	11	3.44	18	2.97	20	2.94	20	2.94
Lyndon Johnson (18)	24	2.61	16	3.30	23	2.84	13	3.43
George W. Bush (19)	35	2.19	19	2.92	19	3.08	15	3.29
William Taft (20)	17	2.96	21	2.85	15	3.23	24	2.82
George H. W. Bush (21)	28	2.48	23	2.85	17	3.13	18	3.11
Bill Clinton (22)	13	3.42	20	2.85	21	2.94	22	2.91
Calvin Coolidge (23)	23	2.71	33	2.33	22	2.93	21	2.92
Rutherford Hayes (24)	37	2.13	25	2.84	25	2.74	23	2.84
John Quincy Adams (25)	20	2.79	27	2.57	27	2.59	28	2.67
Chester Arthur (26)	21	2.75	24	2.84	29	2.49	26	2.72
Martin Van Buren (27)	22	2.75	26	2.68	30	2.41	27	2.71
Gerald Ford (28)	25	2.58	32	2.41	26	2.70	25	2.82
Ulysses Grant (29)	18	2.94	29	2.52	24	2.75	34	2.21
Benjamin Harrison (30)	27	2.53	22	2.85	33	2.25	30	2.55
Herbert Hoover (31)	26	2.56	31	2.43	28	2.55	29	2.61
Richard Nixon (32)	29	2.48	28	2.57	31	2.41	31	2.36
Zachary Taylor (33)	33	2.25	30	2.49	32	2.26	35	2.18
Jimmy Carter (34)	31	2.44	34	2.26	34	2.15	33	2.27
John Tyler (35)	32	2.30	35	2.23	35	2.06	32	2.30

(continued on next page)

TABLE 7: RANKING OF PRESIDENTS BY SCHOLARLY FIELD (continued)

PRESIDENT (OVERALL RANK)	ECONOMICS RANK	ECONOMICS MEAN	HISTORY RANK	HISTORY MEAN	LAW RANK	LAW MEAN	POLITICS RANK	POLITICS MEAN
Millard Fillmore (36)	39	1.88	36	2.15	38	1.54	36	1.85
Andrew Johnson (37)	34	2.21	38	1.61	37	1.65	37	1.72
Franklin Pierce (38)	30	2.46	37	1.72	39	1.46	38	1.71
Warren Harding (39)	38	1.89	39	1.58	36	1.74	39	1.35
James Buchanan (40)	40	1.71	40	1.34	40	1.24	40	1.18

Feb.-March 2005 Survey of Professors of Economics, History, Politics, and Law
N=64–82 respondents, weighted equally by political party within each field

IV. COMPARING THE RESPONSES OF DEMOCRATS AND REPUBLICANS

The rankings in this chapter are computed by averaging the ranks for each president given by respondents who lean toward the Republicans with the ranks given by respondents who lean toward the Democrats. Unlike our 2000 survey, in 2005 we collected political data on the scholars responding to the survey, which allows us to weight Republican and Democratic responses so that each makes an equal contribution to the overall ranking.

We asked three political questions: which candidate they voted for or favored in the 2000 and 2004 presidential elections and "If you had to choose, which of the two major parties would you feel closer to?" Most respondents answered all three questions in a Republican or Democratic direction; among those who split their answers, the majority answer was used as their affiliation. Of the 80 respondents who disclosed their party or voting preferences, 43 leaned Democratic and 37 leaned Republican.

For the 5 respondents who gave no indication of their political leanings, we developed a simple scale to predict their political leaning. We averaged ratings of Presidents Clinton, Carter, Lyndon Johnson, Kennedy, Franklin Roosevelt, Wilson, and Jackson; then we subtracted the average rating of Presidents George W. Bush, Reagan, Coolidge, and Harding. A high score suggested that a scholar leaned Democratic and a low score suggested that a scholar leaned

Republican. Applying this scale to the 80 respondents who disclosed their politics predicted their political orientation with 94 percent accuracy. Four of the 5 who did not disclose their politics were easily classified with this scale, because among the other 80 scholars, everyone with their score or a more extreme one was on the same side of the political spectrum. Only one respondent was close enough to the center on the index that classifying him as leaning Republican even overlapped with any Democrats with lower scores, in this case two Democrats with slightly lower scores. Among all 85 respondents, then, 46 leaned Democratic and 39 leaned Republican.

As Table 8 reveals, political background has a major influence on the evaluations of presidents.

TABLE 8: RANKING OF PRESIDENTS BY POLITICAL PARTY OF RESPONDENTS

PRESIDENT (OVERALL RANK)	REPUBLICAN		DEMOCRAT	
	RANK	MEAN	RANK	MEAN
George Washington (1)	1	4.95	2	4.93
Abraham Lincoln (2)	3	4.36	1	4.98
Franklin Roosevelt (3)	5	3.88	3	4.93
Thomas Jefferson (4)	4	4.08	5	4.39
Theodore Roosevelt (5)	7	3.74	4	4.41
Ronald Reagan (6)	2	4.51	14	3.54
Harry Truman (7)	9	3.72	6	4.17
Dwight Eisenhower (8)	8	3.74	12	3.59
James Polk (9)	10	3.58	11	3.60
Andrew Jackson (10)	16	3.21	8	3.95
Woodrow Wilson (11)	23	2.74	7	4.07
Grover Cleveland (12)	15	3.26	15	3.41
John Adams (13)	11	3.50	18	3.15
William McKinley (14)	13	3.31	16	3.32
John Kennedy (15)	20	2.85	10	3.65
James Monroe (16)	14	3.28	17	3.21
James Madison (17)	17	3.15	19	2.98

(continued on next page)

TABLE 8: RANKING OF PRESIDENTS BY POLITICAL PARTY
OF RESPONDENTS (*continued*)

PRESIDENT (OVERALL RANK)	REPUBLICAN		DEMOCRAT	
	RANK	MEAN	RANK	MEAN
Lyndon Johnson (18)	31	2.38	9	3.72
George W. Bush (19)	6	3.88	35	2.14
William Taft (20)	19	3.03	20	2.91
George H. W. Bush (21)	18	3.05	21	2.85
Bill Clinton (22)	34	2.28	13	3.59
Calvin Coolidge (23)	12	3.32	33	2.22
Rutherford Hayes (24)	22	2.81	25	2.66
John Quincy Adams (25)	21	2.82	28	2.51
Chester Arthur (26)	29	2.52	23	2.78
Martin Van Buren (27)	26	2.59	24	2.67
Gerald Ford (28)	25	2.62	26	2.61
Ulysses Grant (29)	24	2.74	30	2.40
Benjamin Harrison (30)	28	2.55	27	2.53
Herbert Hoover (31)	27	2.58	29	2.41
Richard Nixon (32)	30	2.49	31	2.30
Zachary Taylor (33)	33	2.30	32	2.30
Jimmy Carter (34)	39	1.69	22	2.78
John Tyler (35)	32	2.31	34	2.15
Millard Fillmore (36)	35	2.03	36	1.67
Andrew Johnson (37)	37	1.92	37	1.58
Franklin Pierce (38)	38	1.91	38	1.55
Warren Harding (39)	36	2.03	39	1.25
James Buchanan (40)	40	1.44	40	1.19

Feb.-March 2005 Survey of Professors of Economics, History, Politics, and Law
N=67–85 respondents

There are some stunning differences. Among Democrats, Lyndon Johnson and John Kennedy are ranked 9th and 10th, while among Republicans, they are ranked 31st and 20th respectively. Woodrow Wilson is in 7th place among Democrats, but in 23rd place among

Republicans. Democrats rank Bill Clinton 13th, while Republicans rank him 34th.

Even more stunning are the ranks for presidents favored by Republican scholars. Ronald Reagan ranks 2nd.[10] George W. Bush ranks 6th, which would put him in the "near great" category. This compares to a respectable 14th place for Reagan as rated by Democrats, and a very low ranking of 35th for George W. Bush, which would place him between the "below average" and "failure" categories. And Calvin Coolidge fares 21 places better among Republicans than Democrats.

Most of the rankings of presidents are quite close between scholars from different political parties, but where there are meaningful differences, the gaps are sometimes huge. Accordingly, for some presidents—Wilson, Coolidge, Kennedy, Reagan, Clinton, and especially George W. Bush—the ratings one obtains in a survey reflect more the political makeup of one's panel of experts than the accomplishments or failures of the president being evaluated. It is, moreover, crucial to collect political information to assess what is really being measured by questions trying to discern rankings of presidents. As historian Alonzo Hamby argues: "Too much traditional political history has been, and continues to be, shamelessly partisan. We need to try to put some space between ourselves and the past, evaluate presidents with a sense of context, and realize that both parties have their virtues."

---

[10] Law Professor Michael Rappaport offers his opinion that Reagan is the greatest president of the twentieth century:

> Reagan's accomplishments were tremendous in both the domestic and foreign spheres, and they were not undermined by any significant failures. In the domestic sphere, Reagan inherited an economy plagued by stagflation and bequeathed one with both low inflation and strong economic growth. In foreign affairs, Reagan took a nation that was paralyzed by Iranian students and transformed it into one that persuaded the Soviet Union that it could never win the Cold War. Reagan's failures, such as trading arms for hostages, pale in comparison.
>
> Perhaps President Reagan's greatest accomplishment was that he achieved these goals even though elites, especially liberal elites, regarded his policies as dangerous if not absurd. The elites claimed he practiced voodoo economics, and in 1982–1983 in the midst of a severe recession, lesser men would have despaired. But the president's courage and wisdom prevailed, and the Reagan boom soon emerged.

V. CONCLUSION

Ranking U.S. presidents is much more than a parlor game for academics and much less than a full assessment of the myriad successes and failures of the men who have held our highest office. Global measures, such as "above average" or "average," make sense only in comparative terms—and even then they are severely reductionist. Nonetheless, educating the public (as well as other scholars) about current assessments of presidents can contribute to understanding the history of the office, as well as give some perspective for evaluating the recent inhabitants of that office.

In this 2005 survey, Ronald Reagan continues his rise within the "near great" category to 6th place, and since 2000 Bill Clinton has moved ahead of 3 other presidents, though he is still in the middle of the pack at 22nd. George W. Bush, moreover, debuts in the "average" category at 19th, with ratings that place him just barely in the top half of presidents, a few spots in front of his father and Bill Clinton. Ulysses Grant continues his climb out of the cellar to 29th, while Jimmy Carter slips a few places into the middle range of the bottom 10 presidents, at 34th.

Of one thing we can be certain: Presidential reputations will change. The reputations of controversial recent presidents—Ronald Reagan, Bill Clinton, and George W. Bush—are particularly likely to either grow or lessen as we get more perspective on their accomplishments and failures. Being president is a tough job. Only one president in each century is rated high enough for us to call him "great": George Washington in the eighteenth century, Abraham Lincoln in the nineteenth century, and Franklin Roosevelt in the twentieth century. Perhaps sometime in this new century, we will have another.

Mr. Lindgren is Benjamin Mazur Research Professor of Law at Northwestern University.

APPENDIX 2
Survey Participants

The following scholars participated in the 2005 *Wall Street Journal/* Federalist Society survey rating the presidents (affiliations listed are as of 2005).

HISTORIANS

Joyce Appleby, University of California, Los Angeles
Paula M. Baker, Ohio State University
Alan Brinkley, Columbia University
David Burner, SUNY, Stony Brook
Robert Dallek, Boston University
Robert A. Divine, University of Texas
Joseph J. Ellis, Mount Holyoke College
Ronald P. Formisano, University of Kentucky
Elizabeth Fox-Genovese, Emory University
Steven M. Gillon, University of Oklahoma Honors College
Alonzo L. Hamby, Ohio University
Michael Kazin, Georgetown University
Pauline Maier, Massachusetts Institute of Technology
Forrest McDonald, University of Alabama
Robert V. Remini, University of Illinois
Arthur Schlesinger, Jr., The Graduate Center, CUNY
Joel H. Silbey, Cornell University
Raymond R. Wolters, University of Delaware
Gordon S. Wood, Brown University

Political Scientists
Peri E. Arnold, Notre Dame University
Joseph M. Bessette, Claremont McKenna College
Bruce Buchanan, University of Texas
Andrew Busch, Claremont McKenna College
James W. Ceaser, University of Virginia
William F. Connelly, Jr., Washington and Lee University
Thomas E. Cronin, Whitman College
George C. Edwards III, Texas A&M University
Richard J. Ellis, Willamette University
Michael A. Genovese, Loyola Marymount University
Gary L. Gregg, University of Louisville
Erwin C. Hargrove, Vanderbilt University
Karen Hult, Virginia Tech University
Charles O. Jones, University of Wisconsin, Madison
Stephen F. Knott, University of Virginia
David R. Mayhew, Yale University
Sidney Milkis, University of Virginia
Bruce Miroff, SUNY, Albany
James W. Pfiffner, George Mason University
Bert A. Rockman, Ohio State University
Colleen Shogan, George Mason University
Stephen Skowronek, Yale University
Mary Stuckey, Georgia State University
Jeffrey K. Tulis, University of Texas-Austin
Philip D. Zelikow, University of Virginia

Law Professors
Bruce Ackerman, Yale Law School
Steven G. Calabresi, Northwestern University School of Law
Daniel A. Farber, University of California, Berkeley-Boalt Hall
Michael J. Gerhardt, William & Mary School of Law
Mary Ann Glendon, Harvard Law School
Joel Goldstein, Saint Louis University School of Law
Annette Gordon-Reed, New York Law School
Philip Hamburger, University of Chicago School of Law
Douglas Kmiec, Pepperdine University School of Law

Harold J. Krent, Chicago-Kent College of Law
Gary Lawson, Boston University School of Law
Sanford Levinson, University of Texas Law School
James Lindgren, Northwestern University School of Law
Michael W. McConnell, U.S. Court of Appeals, Tenth Circuit
John O. McGinnis, Northwestern University School of Law
Geoffrey Miller, New York University School of Law
Michael Stokes Paulsen, University of Minnesota School of Law
H. Jefferson Powell, Duke University School of Law
Saikrishna Prakash, University of San Diego School of Law
Stephen B. Presser, Northwestern University School of Law
Michael B. Rappaport, University of San Diego School of Law
Peter M. Shane, Ohio State University School of Law
Cass R. Sunstein, University of Chicago School of Law
John Choon Yoo, University of California, Berkeley-Boalt Hall

Economists
George Akerlof, University of California, Berkeley
Kenneth J. Arrow, Stanford University
Alan Blinder, Princeton University
James Buchanan, George Mason University
Harold Demsetz, University of California, Los Angeles
Jeffrey Frankel, Harvard University
Milton Friedman, Stanford University
David R. Henderson, Naval Postgraduate School
James C. Miller III, CapAnalysis
Jeffrey A. Miron, Boston University
Edward C. Prescott, Arizona State University
Robert Solow, Massachusetts Institute of Technology
Murray Weidenbaum, Washington University, St. Louis
Walter E. Williams, George Mason University

APPENDIX 3
Election Data
1789–2004

NOTES ON ELECTORAL VOTES

In the elections of 1789 through 1800, each elector cast two votes. The candidates with the highest and second-highest number of votes were elected president and vice president, respectively. In the event of a tie (or if no one received votes from the majority of electors), the House chose the president, with each state's delegation getting one vote and a majority of all states required for victory. In 1800 an equal number of votes were cast for Thomas Jefferson and Aaron Burr, so the House decided the election.

Under the Twelfth Amendment, ratified June 15, 1804, each elector casts separate votes for president and vice president. The House still chooses the president if no one receives a majority of electoral votes, and it did so in 1824.

In 1789, three of the original thirteen states did not participate in the election. New York's legislature failed to agree on a slate of electors, and North Carolina and Rhode Island had not yet ratified the Constitution. The states of the Confederacy (Alabama, Arkansas, Florida, Georgia, Louisiana, Mississippi, North Carolina, South Carolina, Tennessee, Texas, and Virginia) did not vote in the 1864 election. Mississippi, Texas, and Virginia did not vote in the 1868 election. In 1872 Congress refused to count electoral votes from Arkansas and Louisiana owing to disruptive conditions during Reconstruction. Electoral votes from Florida, Louisiana, Oregon, and South Carolina were disputed in 1876 and from Florida in 2000; see "Presidential Leadership After Disputed Elections," page 241, for details.

The charts below show all candidates who received at least one electoral vote.

NOTES ON POPULAR VOTES

Although some states chose presidential electors by popular vote as early as 1789, no national popular vote records exist for the years prior to 1824. While popular voting was the norm in most states by 1824, the following states did not choose presidential electors by popular vote: Georgia, Louisiana, New York, and Vermont (1824); Delaware (1824–28); South Carolina (1824–56); Florida (1868); and Colorado (1876).

The charts show all candidates who received at least 1 percent of the aggregate nationwide popular vote.

PARTY ABBREVIATIONS

D   Democrat

DR   Democratic-Republican

F   Federalist

NP   No party

R   Republican

W   Whig

Sources: *Presidential Elections, 1789–2000* (Congressional Quarterly Press, 2002), *David Leip's Atlas of U.S. Presidential Elections* (http://uselectionatlas.org).

1789	ELECTORAL VOTES
George Washington (NP)	69
John Adams (NP)	34
John Jay (NP)	9
Robert Harrison (NP)	6
John Rutledge (NP)	6
John Hancock (NP)	4
George Clinton (NP)	3
Samuel Huntington (NP)	2

1789	ELECTORAL VOTES
John Milton (NP)	2
James Armstrong (NP)	1
Benjamin Lincoln (NP)	1
Edward Telfair (NP)	1

1792	ELECTORAL VOTES
George Washington (F)	132
John Adams (F)	77
George Clinton (DR)	50
Thomas Jefferson (DR)	4
Aaron Burr (DR)	1
Votes not cast*	6

*Two electors from Maryland and one from Vermont did not vote.

1796	ELECTORAL VOTES
John Adams (F)	71
Thomas Jefferson (DR)	68
Thomas Pinckney (F)	59
Aaron Burr (DR)	30
Samuel Adams (F)	15
Oliver Ellsworth (F)	11
George Clinton (DR)	7
John Jay (F)	5
James Iredell (F)	3
John Henry (DR)	2
Samuel Johnston (F)	2
George Washington (F)	2
Charles Pinckney (F)	1

1800	ELECTORAL VOTES	HOUSE VOTE
Thomas Jefferson (DR)	73	10
Aaron Burr (DR)	73	4
John Adams (F)	65	
Charles Pinckney (F)	64	
John Jay (F)	1	
Votes not cast*		2

*The Delaware and South Carolina delegations did not vote.

1804	ELECTORAL VOTES
Thomas Jefferson (DR)	162
Charles Pinckney (F)	14

1808	ELECTORAL VOTES
James Madison (DR)	122
Charles Pinckney (F)	47
George Clinton (DR)	6
Votes not cast*	1

*One elector from Kentucky did not vote.

1812	ELECTORAL VOTES
James Madison (DR)	128
DeWitt Clinton (F)	89
Votes not cast*	1

*One elector from Ohio did not vote.

1816	ELECTORAL VOTES
James Monroe (DR)	183
Rufus King (F)	34
Votes not cast*	4

*One elector from Delaware and three from Maryland did not vote.

1820	ELECTORAL VOTES
James Monroe (DR)	231
John Quincy Adams (DR)	1
Votes not cast*	3

*One elector each from Mississippi, Pennsylvania, and Tennessee did not vote.

1824	ELECTORAL VOTES	POPULAR VOTE	HOUSE VOTE
John Quincy Adams (DR)	84	30.92%	13
Andrew Jackson (DR)	99	41.35%	7
William Crawford (DR)	41	11.17%	4
Henry Clay (DR)	37	12.99%	

1828	ELECTORAL VOTES	POPULAR VOTE
Andrew Jackson (D)	178	55.97%
John Quincy Adams (National Republican)	83	43.63%

1832	ELECTORAL VOTES	POPULAR VOTE
Andrew Jackson (D)	219	54.23%
Henry Clay (National Republican)	49	37.42%
John Floyd	11	0*
(Independant Democrat)		
William Wirt (Anti-Masonic)	7	7.78%
Votes not cast**	2	

*Floyd's 11 electors were appointed by the South Carolina legislature.
**Two electors from Maryland did not vote.

1836	ELECTORAL VOTES	POPULAR VOTE
Martin Van Buren (D)	170	50.83%
William Henry Harrison (W)	73	36.63%
Hugh White (W)	26	9.72%
Daniel Webster (W)	14	2.74%
Willie Mangum (W)	11	0*

*Mangum's 11 electors were appointed by the South Carolina legislature.

1840	ELECTORAL VOTES	POPULAR VOTE
William Henry Harrison (W)	234	52.88%
Martin Van Buren (D)	60	46.81%

1844	ELECTORAL VOTES	POPULAR VOTE
James K. Polk (D)	170	49.54%
Henry Clay (W)	105	48.08%
James Birney (Liberty)	0	2.30%

1848	ELECTORAL VOTES	POPULAR VOTE
Zachary Taylor (W)	163	47.28%
Lewis Cass (D)	127	42.49%
Martin Van Buren (Free Soil)	0	10.12%

1852	ELECTORAL VOTES	POPULAR VOTE
Franklin Pierce (D)	254	50.84%
Winfield Scott (W)	42	43.87%
John Hale (Free Soil)	0	4.91%

1856	Electoral votes	Popular vote
James Buchanan (D)	174	45.28%
John Fremont (R)	114	33.11%
Millard Fillmore (American)	8	21.53%

1860	Electoral votes	Popular vote
Abraham Lincoln (R)	180	39.82%
John Breckenridge (Southern Democrat)	72	18.10%
John Bell (Constitutional Union)	39	12.61%
Stephen Douglas (D)	12	29.46%

1864	Electoral votes	Popular vote
Abraham Lincoln (R)	212	55.10%
George McClellan (D)	21	44.90%
Votes not cast*	1	

*One Lincoln elector from Nevada did not vote.

1868	Electoral votes	Popular vote
Ulysses S. Grant (R)	214	52.66%
Horatio Seymour (D)	80	47.34%

1872	Electoral votes	Popular vote
Ulysses S. Grant (R)	286	55.61%
Horace Greeley (D)	0*	43.82%
Thomas Hendricks (D)	42	0*
B. Gratz Brown (D)	18	0*
Charles Jenkins (D)	2	0*
David Davis (D)	1	0*
Votes not counted**	17	

*Greeley died November 29, 1872, before the Electoral College met. Sixty-three of his 66 electors voted for Hendricks, Brown, Jenkins, or Davis.
**Congress did not count 3 Georgia electors' votes for Greeley, or 14 Grant electors' votes from Arkansas and Louisiana.

1876	Electoral votes	Popular vote
Rutherford B. Hayes (R)	185	47.95%
Samuel Tilden (D)	184	50.98%

1880	ELECTORAL VOTES	POPULAR VOTE
James Garfield (R)	214	48.30%
Winfield Hancock (D)	155	48.21%
James Weaver (Greenback)	0	3.32%

1884	ELECTORAL VOTES	POPULAR VOTE
Grover Cleveland (D)	219	48.87%
James Blaine (R)	182	48.25%
John St. John (Prohibition)	0	1.50%
Benjamin Butler (Greenback)	0	1.34%

1888	ELECTORAL VOTES	POPULAR VOTE
Benjamin Harrison (R)	233	47.82%
Grover Cleveland (D)	168	48.61%
Clinton Fisk (Prohibition)	0	2.19%
Alson Streeter (Union Labor)	0	1.29%

1892	ELECTORAL VOTES	POPULAR VOTE
Grover Cleveland (D)	277	46.01%
Benjamin Harrison (R)	145	42.97%
James Weaver (Populist)	22	8.49%
John Bidwell (Prohibition)	0	2.24%

1896	ELECTORAL VOTES	POPULAR VOTE
William McKinley (R)	271	51.10%
William Jennings Bryan (D)	176	45.82%

1900	ELECTORAL VOTES	POPULAR VOTE
William McKinley (R)	292	51.67%
William Jennings Bryan (D)	155	45.50%
John Woolley (Prohibition)	0	1.50%

1904	ELECTORAL VOTES	POPULAR VOTE
Theodore Roosevelt (R)	336	56.41%
Alton Parker (D)	140	37.60%
Eugene Debs (Socialist)	0	2.98%
Silas Swallow (Prohibition)	0	1.91%

1908	ELECTORAL VOTES	POPULAR VOTE
William Howard Taft (R)	321	51.58%
William Jennings Bryan (D)	162	43.05%
Eugene Debs (Socialist)	0	2.82%
Eugene Chafin (Prohibition)	0	1.70%

1912	ELECTORAL VOTES	POPULAR VOTE
Woodrow Wilson (D)	435	41.84%
Theodore Roosevelt (Progressive)	88	27.39%
William Howard Taft (R)	8	23.18%
Eugene Debs (Socialist)	0	5.99%
Eugene Chafin (Prohibition)	0	1.38%

1916	ELECTORAL VOTES	POPULAR VOTE
Woodrow Wilson (D)	277	49.24%
Charles Evans Hughes (R)	254	46.11%
Allan Benson (Socialist)	0	3.18%
James Hanley (Prohibition)	0	1.19%

1920	ELECTORAL VOTES	POPULAR VOTE
Warren G. Harding (R)	404	60.34%
James Cox (D)	127	34.12%
Eugene Debs (Socialist)	0	3.42%

1924	ELECTORAL VOTES	POPULAR VOTE
Calvin Coolidge (R)	382	54.04%
John Davis (D)	136	28.82%
Robert LaFollette (Progressive)	13	16.59%

1928	ELECTORAL VOTES	POPULAR VOTE
Herbert Hoover (R)	444	58.24%
Alfred E. Smith (D)	87	40.77%

1932	ELECTORAL VOTES	POPULAR VOTE
Franklin D. Roosevelt (D)	472	57.41%
Herbert Hoover (R)	59	39.65%
Norman Thomas (Socialist)	0	2.25%

1936	ELECTORAL VOTES	POPULAR VOTE
Franklin D. Roosevelt (D)	523	60.78%
Alf Landon (R)	8	36.53%
William Lemke (Union)	0	1.95%

1940	ELECTORAL VOTES	POPULAR VOTE
Franklin D. Roosevelt (D)	449	54.89%
Wendell Willkie (R)	82	44.83%

1944	ELECTORAL VOTES	POPULAR VOTE
Franklin D. Roosevelt (D)	432	53.39%
Thomas Dewey (R)	99	45.89%

1948	ELECTORAL VOTES	POPULAR VOTE
Harry S. Truman (D)	303	49.51%
Thomas Dewey (R)	189	45.12%
Strom Thurmond (States' Rights Democrat)	39	2.40%
Henry Wallace (Progressive)	0	2.38%

1952	ELECTORAL VOTES	POPULAR VOTE
Dwight D. Eisenhower (R)	442	54.88%
Adlai Stevenson (D)	89	44.38%

1956	ELECTORAL VOTES	POPULAR VOTE
Dwight D. Eisenhower (R)	457	57.38%
Adlai Stevenson (D)	73	41.95%
Walter Jones (D)	1	0*

*One Stevenson elector from Alabama cast his vote for Jones.

1960	ELECTORAL VOTES	POPULAR VOTE
John F. Kennedy (D)	303	49.72%
Richard M. Nixon (R)	219	49.55%
Harry Byrd (D)	15	0*

*Six unpledged electors from Alabama, 8 unpledged electors from Mississippi, and 1 Nixon elector from Oklahoma cast their votes for Byrd.

1964	ELECTORAL VOTES	POPULAR VOTE
Lyndon B. Johnson (D)	486	61.05%
Barry Goldwater (R)	52	38.47%

1968	ELECTORAL VOTES	POPULAR VOTE
Richard M. Nixon (R)	301	43.42%
Hubert Humphrey (D)	191	42.72%
George Wallace	46	13.53%
(American Independent)		

1972	ELECTORAL VOTES	POPULAR VOTE
Richard M. Nixon (R)	520	60.69%
George McGovern (D)	17	37.53%
John Hospers (Libertarian)	1	0*
John Schmitz	0	1.41%
(American Independent)		

*One Nixon elector from Virginia cast his vote for Hospers.

1976	ELECTORAL VOTES	POPULAR VOTE
Jimmy Carter (D)	297	50.06%
Gerald R. Ford (R)	240	48.00%
Ronald Reagan (R)	1	0*

*One Ford elector from Washington state cast his vote for Reagan.

1980	ELECTORAL VOTES	POPULAR VOTE
Ronald Reagan (R)	489	50.75%
Jimmy Carter (D)	49	41.01%
John Anderson (National Union)	0	6.61%
Ed Clark (Libertarian)	0	1.06%

1984	ELECTORAL VOTES	POPULAR VOTE
Ronald Reagan (R)	525	58.77%
Walter Mondale (D)	13	40.56%

1988	ELECTORAL VOTES	POPULAR VOTE
George Bush (R)	426	53.37%
Michael Dukakis (D)	111	45.65%
Lloyd Bentsen (D)	1	0*

*One Dukakis elector from West Virginia cast her vote for Bentsen.

1992	ELECTORAL VOTES	POPULAR VOTE
Bill Clinton (D)	370	43.01%
George Bush (R)	168	37.45%
Ross Perot (NP)	0	18.91%

1996	ELECTORAL VOTES	POPULAR VOTE
Bill Clinton (D)	379	49.24%
Bob Dole (R)	159	40.71%
Ross Perot (Reform)	0	8.40%

2000	ELECTORAL VOTES	POPULAR VOTE
George W. Bush (R)	271	47.87%
Al Gore (D)	266	48.38%
Ralph Nader (Green)	0	2.74%
Votes not cast*	1	0

*One Gore elector from the District of Columbia did not vote.

2004	ELECTORAL VOTES	POPULAR VOTE
George W. Bush (R)	286	50.73%
John Kerry (D)	251	48.26%
John Edwards (D)	1	0*

*One Kerry elector from Minnesota cast his vote for Edwards.

ACKNOWLEDGMENTS

Steven Calabresi, a professor of law at Northwestern University and a scholar of executive power, came up with the idea of developing a new survey of scholars to rank the presidents—one that, unlike previous surveys, tries to balance for the political biases of academia.

James Lindgren, a Northwestern law professor and distinguished statistician, designed the 2005 survey of scholars and analyzed the results, taking care to make it even more rigorous than the one in 2000. Kenneth Wiltberger of the Federalist Society assisted in gathering the data.

Brendan Miniter, assistant editor of OpinionJournal.com, *The Wall Street Journal*'s editorial page's Web site, oversaw the publication of the original survey on the site in November 2000. (It is still available, at www.OpinionJournal.com/hail/.)

Jessica King ably assisted us in coordinating the solicitation, completion, and submission of the essays on each of the presidents.

Kate LaVoie of *The Wall Street Journal* assembled the artwork for this volume, a *Journal*-style line drawing of each president.

Thanks to all at the *Journal*—especially former Deputy Managing Editor Steve Adler, Editorial Page Editor Paul Gigot, Editor Emeritus Robert Bartley, and Associate Editorial Page Editor Melanie Kirkpatrick—for their support and enthusiasm. Thanks to Fred Hills, our editor at Simon & Schuster, and his assistant, Kirsa Rein, for all their help and patience as we organized the contributions of more then four dozen authors. And thanks above all to those authors, a group of uncommon distinction whose work we are proud to collect here.

—*James Taranto and Leonard Leo*

INDEX

abolitionist movement, 36, 69, 74, 100, 108

Achtenberg, Roberta, 204

Adams, Abigail, 23–24, 27, 40

Adams, Charles Francis, 43

Adams, George Washington, 42

Adams, Henry, 98

Adams, John, 17, 19, 20–24, 27, 42, 277, 278
  ranking of, 11, 20, 258, 264, 265, 267, 296

Adams, John Quincy, 24, 35, 37, 39–43, 241, 242–43, 248, 279
  ranking of, 12, 249, 251, 259, 264, 267, 270

Adams, Louisa Catherine, 41

Adams, Samuel, 21, 278

Adams-Onis Treaty, 37

Afghanistan, 191, 196, 210, 247

Agnew, Spiro T., 184

Alabama claims, 96, 97–98

Albany Regency, 49

Alien and Sedition Acts (1798), 27

al Qaeda, 212

Amendments, Constitutional:
  Eighteenth, 134
  Fifteenth, 96, 103
  Fourteenth, 96, 103, 246
  Nineteenth, 144
  Seventeenth, 133
  Sixteenth, 133, 137, 220
  Thirteenth, 85
  Twelfth, 242, 243–44, 276
  Twenty-fourth, 162

American Colonization Society, 36

American Revolution, 17, 18, 20, 31, 45, 232

Americans with Disabilities Act (1990), 201

American System, 35

Anaconda Plan, 229

Anderson, John, 285

Anderson, Martin, 224

Arafat, Yasser, 212

arbitration, binding, 98

Armstrong, James, 278

Army, U.S., 21

American Party, 70

Arthur, Chester Alan, 107–10, 219
  ranking of, 12, 107, 259, 260, 267, 270

Articles of Confederation, 31

atomic bomb, 160

Atwater, Lee, 210

Babcock, Orville, 98
Baker, Howard, 7, 179
Baker, James, 7
Bank of the United States, 35,
    45–46, 50, 218, 219
Belknap, William, 98
Bell, John, 281
Bennett, William J., 7
Benson, Allan, 283
Benton, Thomas Hart, 43
Bentsen, Lloyd, 285
Berlin Airlift, 161
Berlin Decree (Napoleon), 28
Berlin Wall, 170–71, 196, 200
Biddle, Nicholas, 46, 219, 220
Bidwell, John, 282
"Billion Dollar Congress," 117
Bill of Rights, 31, 32
Birney, James, 280
Black, Hugo, 236, 237, 239
Black Hawk War, 229
Blacks, 96, 98, 100, 110
Blaine, James G., 110, 282
Blair, Tony, 203
Bland-Allison Act (1878), 102
Blough, Roger, 224
Board of War and Ordnance, 21
Boers, 123
Bolivar, Simón, 53
Booth, John Wilkes, 87
Bosnia, 192
Boston Massacre, 21
Boutwell, George, 97
Bowers, Lloyd, 132–33
Boxer, Barbara, 248
Bradley, Joseph P., 244
Breckinridge, John C., 281
Brennan, William J., Jr., 234, 235,
    236, 240
Bretton Woods Conference, 223

Breyer, Stephen, 8
Brezhnev, Leonid, 185, 191
Brown, B. Gratz, 281
Brownell, Herbert, 234
Brown v. Board of Education, 167
Bryan, William Jennings, 136, 282,
    283
Buchanan, James, 72, 75–79, 281
    ranking of, 12, 75, 256, 257, 259,
        268, 270
Buena Vista, Battle of, 65
Bull Run, Battle of, 232
Bunker Hill, Battle of, 40
Bureau of the Budget, U.S., 142
Burger, Warren, 181, 239
Burr, Aaron, 23, 180, 276, 278
Bush, George Herbert Walker, 49,
    175, 198–201, 227, 229, 235,
    236, 240, 285, 286
    ranking of, 12, 198, 258, 267, 270
Bush, George Walker, 1, 41, 121,
    140, 175, 208–13, 230, 231,
    240, 241–42, 245–47, 253–54,
    286
    ranking of, 251, 258, 259–60,
        263, 264, 265, 266, 267, 270,
        271, 272
Bush, Prescott, 199
Bush Doctrine, 212
Bush v. Gore, 240, 245–46
Butler, Benjamin, 282
Byrd, Harry, 284

Calhoun, John C., 41
Cardozo, Benjamin, 237
Carter, James Earl, Jr., 121, 140,
    175, 186, 187, 188–92, 223,
    224, 225, 226, 285
    ranking of, 12, 188, 256, 257,
        259, 264, 267, 270, 272

Casey, William J., 7
Cass, Lewis, 280
Castro, Fidel, 170
Ceausescu, Nicolae, 190
Central Intelligence Agency, 199
Chafin, Eugene, 283
Cheney, Richard, 186
Chesnut, Mary, 85
China, 165, 166, 176, 191, 228
Churchill, Winston S., 157, 212
Civilian Conservation Corps, 154
civil rights, 96, 102, 110, 116, 162,
    167, 171, 174, 175–76
Civil Rights Act (1875), 110
Civil Rights Act (1964), 162, 174
Civil Service Reform Act (1978), 109
civil service system, 108, 109–10,
    126, 162
Civil War, U.S., 36, 65, 70, 74, 81,
    83–86, 95, 97, 106, 108, 123,
    219, 229, 231, 232, 256
Clark, Ed, 285
Classification Acts (1923, 1949), 109
Clay, Henry, 32, 36, 41, 42, 56, 58,
    68, 242–43, 279, 280
Clayton Antitrust Act (1914), 137
Cleveland, Stephen Grover, 111–14,
    116, 118, 218–19, 248, 282
  ranking of, 11, 111, 258, 260,
    267, 269
Clifford, Clark, 170, 195
Clinton, DeWitt, 279
Clinton, George, 277, 278, 279
Clinton, Hillary Rodham, 204, 205
Clinton, William Jefferson, 8, 142,
    175, 179, 194, 202–7, 209,
    210, 220, 224, 227, 253, 286
  ranking of, 12, 202, 257, 259,
    260, 263, 264, 265, 267, 270,
    271, 272

Cohn, Jonathan, 247
Cold Harbor, Battle of, 84, 232
Cold War, 191, 197, 261, 262
Compromise of 1850, 66, 69, 77
Compromise of 1877, 244
Confederacy, 59, 78, 84, 276
Congress, U.S., 5–7, 8, 9, 16, 28,
    142, 242–44, 276
  see also House of
    Representatives, U.S.; Senate,
    U.S.
Conkling, Roscoe, 108
Constitution, U.S., 5–10, 16, 31, 32,
    56, 58–59, 93, 243–44, 276
  see also Amendments,
    Constitutional
Constitutional Convention, 32
containment, 161–62
Continental Congress, 21, 24
Cooke, Jay, 218
Coolidge, John Calvin, 140, 146–50,
    220, 283
  ranking of, 12, 146, 252, 259,
    260, 261, 263, 264, 266, 267,
    270, 271
Cooper v. Aaron, 238
courts, federal, 9
Cox, Archibald, 179, 180
Cox, James, 283
Coxey's Army, 114
Crawford, William, 242–43, 279
Crédit Mobilier, 218
Cuba, 37, 78, 122, 191
Cuban Missile Crisis, 176
Custer, George Armstrong, 97

Dana, Francis, 40
Darman, Richard, 201
Daschle, Tom, 247
Daugherty, Harry, 148

Davis, David, 244, 281
Davis, Jefferson, 65, 74, 229
Davis, John, 283
Debs, Eugene V., 139, 282, 283
Declaration of Independence, 21,
    26, 29, 116
Defense of Marriage Act (1996), 8
Democratic Party, 7, 8, 47, 49, 51,
    61
Democratic-Republican Party, 18,
    22, 23, 35, 57
Depression, Great, 148, 151,
    152–54, 156–57, 220–22, 225,
    265
Dewey, Thomas E., 284
Dirksen, Everett, 174
Dole, Robert, 286
Douglas, Stephen, 281
Douglas, William O., 236, 239
Douglass, Frederick, 2
Dred Scott v. Sandford, 76, 238
détente, 185, 191, 195–96
Dukakis, Michael, 285
Dupont de Nemours, Pierre-
    Samuel, 29

Edwards, John, 286
Egypt, 167, 192
Eisenhower, Dwight David, 8, 154,
    163–67, 176, 225, 227, 228,
    234–35, 237, 238, 240, 284
    ranking of, 11, 163, 249, 255,
    258, 264, 267, 269
Elders, Joycelyn, 204
elections, national, 5–7, 10
    voting data for, 276–86
Electoral College, 242–43, 276
Ellsworth, Oliver, 278
Emancipation Proclamation, 85,
    230

Embargo Act (1807), 28–29
energy crisis, 223–24
Era of Good Feelings, 34, 35
executive privilege, 180–81

Fall, Albert, 144, 148
Federalist, The, 5–7, 8, 32, 59,
    159–60, 161
Federalist Party, 18, 22, 23, 35, 236
Federal Reserve, 137, 218, 220, 224,
    225
Federal Trade Commission, 137
Ferry, Thomas W., 244
Fillmore, Millard, 66, 67–70, 281
    ranking of, 12, 67, 256, 257, 259,
    268, 270
Fisk, Clinton, 282
Fisk, Jim, 97
Fitzgerald, John F., 170
Floyd, John, 280
Force Bill, 57
Ford, Gerald Rudolph, 7, 183–87,
    189–90, 223, 228, 285
    ranking of, 12, 183, 259, 264,
    267, 270
Fortas, Abe, 237
Fort Sumter, 76, 78, 80–81, 100
Four Freedoms, 231
Fourteen Points, 138, 231
France, 17–18, 23, 28, 138, 139,
    143, 166–67, 221
Frankfurter, Felix, 236, 239
Franklin, Benjamin, 2
Fremont, John C., 281
French Revolution, 17–18, 22, 23
Frick, Henry Clay, 114
Fugitive Slave Act (1850), 69, 74

Gadsden Purchase, 74
Galbraith, John Kenneth, 220

Garfield, James Abram, 103–6, 107, 108–9, 218–19, 227, 282
General Accounting Office, 142
General Agreement on Tariffs and Trade, 223
Genet, Edmond-Charles, 18
George III, king of England, 19
Germany, 123, 129, 138, 143, 153, 157, 221
Gettysburg, Battle of, 84
Gierek, Edward, 190
Ginsburg, Ruth Bader, 8
Glass-Steagall Act (1934), 153
Goldberg, Arthur, 237
gold standard, 102, 114, 121
Goldwater, Barry, 175, 194, 285
Gorbachev, Mikhail, 196, 200
Gore, Albert A., Jr., 241, 245–46, 286
Gould, Jay, 97
Gould, Lewis, 123
Government Performance and Result Act (1993), 109
Graham, Bob, 247
Grant, Ulysses Simpson, 2, 84, 94–98, 108, 110, 218–19, 227, 229, 281
   ranking of, 12, 94, 252, 256, 259, 265, 266, 267, 270, 272
Great Britain, 18, 28, 37, 62, 96, 97–98, 123, 138, 139, 143, 157, 166–67, 221
Great Society, 157, 174–75, 176
Great Strike (1877), 102
Greeley, Horace, 83, 281
Greenback Era, 219
Greenback Party, 244
Greenspan, Alan, 186
Guiteau, Charles Julius, 105, 109
Gulf War, see Persian Gulf War, First

Haig, Alexander, 184
Hale, John, 280
Halpin, Maria, 112–13
Hamilton, Alexander, 17, 18, 23, 26, 32, 57, 218, 219
Hancock, John, 277
Hancock, Winfield Scott, 105, 282
Hanley, James, 283
Hanna, Mark, 120–21
Harding, Warren Gamaliel, 72, 76, 131, 139, 141–45, 148, 152, 203, 237, 283
   ranking of, 12, 141, 252, 253, 256, 257, 259, 267, 268, 270
Harrison, Benjamin, 115–18, 130–31, 218–19, 248, 282
   ranking of, 12, 115, 259, 266, 267, 270
Harrison, Robert, 277
Harrison, William Henry, 49, 51, 52–54, 56, 105, 115, 116, 227, 280
Hartmann, Robert, 187
Hayes, Rutherford Birchard, 41, 96, 99–103, 108, 218–19, 241, 242, 243–44, 248, 281
   ranking of, 12, 99, 259, 260, 267, 270
Hayne, Robert, 46
Haynes, John W., 222
Hearst, William Randolph, 122
Helsinki Accords, 185
Hemings, Sally, 255
Hendricks, Thomas, 281
Henry, John, 278
Hepburn Act (1906), 225
Hill, James J., 218
Hodel, Donald, 7
Holmes, Oliver Wendell, Jr., 156, 237

Homeland Security, Department of, 242

Homestead Act (1862), 218

Homestead strike, 114

Hoover, Herbert Clark, 39, 142, 151–54, 220–21, 222, 225, 237, 277
    ranking of, 12, 151, 256, 259, 264, 267, 270

Hospers, John, 285

House of Representatives, U.S., 5–7, 8, 242–43, 244, 276

Housing and Urban Development Department, U.S., 175

Houston, Sam, 61

Huerta, Victoriano, 137

Hughes, Charles Evans, 142, 143, 283

Hull, Cordell, 223

human rights, 185, 189–91

Humphrey, Hubert H., 285

Huntington, Samuel, 277

Hussein, Saddam, 200, 210, 212, 229

impeachment, 89, 92–93, 96, 142, 179, 206

income tax, 137, 220, 221, 222

Independent Treasury Act (1840), 51

Insull, Samuel, 222

International Trade Commission, 143

Interstate Commerce Commission, 128, 225

Interstate Highway System, 167, 225

Iran, 190

Iran-contra affair, 197

Iraq, 200, 209, 210, 212, 229–30, 231, 242, 247
    see also Persian Gulf War, First; Persian Gulf War, Second

Iredell, James, 278

Israel, 167, 192, 230

Jackson, Andrew, 35, 37, 41, 42, 44–47, 49–50, 56, 57–58, 61, 76, 218, 219, 220, 227, 238, 241, 242–43, 279, 280
    ranking of, 11, 44, 255, 258, 260, 263, 264, 265, 267, 269

Jacksonian democracy, 38

Jackson-Vanik amendment (1974), 189

Japan, 70, 74, 143, 150, 157, 160–61

Japanese-Americans, 239

Jay, John, 32, 277, 278

Jefferson, Thomas, 2, 16, 17, 18, 21, 22, 23, 24, 25–29, 31, 35, 36, 56, 57, 180, 218, 237, 253, 276, 278, 279
    ranking of, 11, 25, 255, 258, 263, 267, 269

Jeffersonian Republicans, see Democratic-Republican Party

Jenkins, Charles, 281

Johnson, Andrew, 88–93, 95, 98, 142, 203
    ranking of, 12, 88, 256, 257, 259, 268, 270

Johnson, Lyndon Baines, 51, 157, 173–77, 228, 229, 232, 237, 253, 254, 280
    ranking of, 12, 173, 258, 260, 263, 264, 266, 267, 270

Johnston, Samuel, 278

Jones, Walter, 284

Jordan, Hamilton, 121

Juárez, Benito, 95
judiciary, federal, 9
Judiciary Act (1789), 237–38
Justice Department, U.S., 144

Kansas-Nebraska Act (1854), 74
Karadzic, Radovan, 192
Kelley, Virginia, 203
Kellogg-Briand Pact, 140
Kennedy, John Fitzgerald, 2, 37, 43,
    168–72, 174, 176, 200, 205,
    220, 224, 227, 228, 235–36,
    253, 254, 284
  ranking of, 12, 168, 258, 261,
    263, 265, 267, 269, 271
Kennedy, Joseph P., 170
Kerry, John, 286
Keynes, John Maynard, 221
Khrushchev, Nikita S., 170, 171, 172
Kim Il Sung, 192
King, Martin Luther, Jr., 171
King, William Rufus, 77, 279
Kissinger, Henry, 184, 185, 188,
    191, 195
Know-Nothing Party, 70
Korean War, 163, 164, 165, 228,
    231, 232
Korematsu v. U.S., 239
Ku Klux Klan, 96
Kuwait, 200

Labor Department, U.S., 133
Lafayette, Marquis de, 18
LaFollette, Robert, 283
laissez-faire, 51, 207, 225
Landon, Alf, 157, 284
League of Nations, 139, 143, 144,
    156, 262
Lee, Robert E., 65, 84, 86, 95, 229
Lemke, William, 284

Liberia, 36
Limited Test Ban Treaty, 176
Lincoln, Abraham, 2, 3, 70, 76, 77,
    78, 79, 80–87, 91, 95, 97, 108,
    123, 218, 227, 229, 230,
    231–32, 238, 281
  ranking of, 11, 80, 250, 254, 258,
    260, 261, 266, 269, 272
Lincoln, Benjamin, 278
Lincoln, Mary Todd, 85
Livingston, Robert, 36
Lodge, Henry Cabot, 139, 199
Log Cabin Bill, 58
Louisiana Purchase, 28, 36, 37, 61,
    218
Lusitania, S.S., 138

MacArthur, Douglas, 164
McCarthy, Eugene, 232
McCarthy, Joseph R., 166
McCarthyism, 164, 166, 176
McClellan, George B., 70, 83, 229,
    230, 281
McGovern, George, 194, 285
McKinley, William, 100, 119–24,
    125, 218–19, 227, 282
  ranking of, 11, 119, 258, 260,
    263, 265–66, 267, 269
McKinley Tariff, 117, 118
McNary-Haugen Bill, 147
Madison, James, 2, 5–6, 8, 19, 29,
    30–33, 36, 39, 56, 57, 65, 227,
    251, 254, 279
  ranking of, 11, 30, 249, 258, 260,
    264, 267, 269
Maine, U.S.S., 122
Mangum, Willie, 280
Manifest Destiny, 78
Marbury v. Madison, 181, 237–38
Marshall, George C., 164, 223

Marshall, John, 29, 237
Marshall Plan, 223
Maximilian, emperor of Mexico, 95
Mayaguez, S.S., 185
Medicaid, 175
Medicare, 175, 211, 242
Meese, Edwin, 7
Mellon, Andrew, 22, 142, 152, 220–21
Mexican War, 62–63, 65, 229, 231
Mexico, 58, 62–63, 74, 137, 138
Milan Decree (Napoleon), 28
Milton, John, 278
Minton, Sherman, 234
Missouri Compromise, 35, 36, 238
Mondale, Walter, 285
Monroe, James, 34–38, 40, 56, 279
    ranking of, 12, 34, 258, 267, 269
Monroe Doctrine, 37–38, 40, 128–29
Moore, Michael, 247, 248
Morgan, J. Pierpont, 217, 218, 220, 225
Morgenthau, Henry, 222–23
Morrill Act (1862), 218
Morris, Richard, 209
Moyers, Bill, 175
Moynihan, Daniel Patrick, 189, 195
Mundell, Robert, 221, 222, 224
Murphy, Frank, 236

Nader, Ralph, 224–25, 286
Napoleon I, emperor of France, 28
Napoleonic wars, 19
National Endowments for the Arts and the Humanities, 175
National Liberal League, 234
National Public Radio, 175
National Security Council, 166

Native Americans, 16, 41, 46–47, 96, 97
Navy, U.S., 21, 110, 129
New Deal, 8, 157, 174, 236
New Orleans, Battle of, 45
New York Anti-Slavery Society, 108
New York Customhouse, 103, 105, 108
New York draft riots, 84, 232
Nicaragua, 197
Nixon, Richard Milhous, 177, 178–82, 184, 185, 194, 203, 204, 223, 225, 228, 238–39, 240, 284, 285
    ranking of, 12, 178, 256, 257–58, 259, 260, 263, 267, 270
Noriega, Manuel, 227
North Atlantic Treaty Organization, 161, 165
Northwest Territory, 53
nullification, 46

O'Connor, Sandra Day, 235, 236
Office of Management and Budget, 143, 201
Orders in Council (Great Britain), 28
Oregon Territory, 37, 62, 63
Organization of Petroleum Exporting Countries, 223
Ostend Manifesto, 78
O'Toole, Tara, 204

Paine, Thomas, 18, 21–22
Palestine Liberation Organization, 192
Palmer, A. Mitchell, 139
Palmer Raids, 139
Panama Canal, 129, 186
Pan-American Conference, 117

Panic of 1819, 35
Panic of 1857, 76
Panic of 1873, 97, 100
Panic of 1893–96, 219–20
Panic of 1907, 217–18
Paris Peace Conference, 138
Parker, Alton, 282
Patton, George S., 231
Pearl Harbor attack, 157, 223, 232
Pendleton Act (1883), 103, 108, 109
Permanent Court of International
    Justice, 143
Perot, H. Ross, 286
Perry, Matthew, 70
Pershing, John J., 138, 164
Persian Gulf War, First, 192, 200,
    229–30
Persian Gulf War, Second, 210, 212,
    229, 230, 231, 242, 246–47
Philippines, 122, 131
Pickett's Charge, 84
Pierce, Franklin, 71–74, 77, 280
    ranking of, 12, 71, 72, 256, 257,
    259, 268, 270
Pinckney, Charles, 278, 279
Pinckney, Thomas, 278
Point Four Program, 161
Polk, James Knox, 35, 58, 60–63,
    227, 280
    ranking of, 11, 60, 255, 258, 260,
    263, 264, 267, 269
Populist Party, 114
Powell, Colin, 210, 229
preemption, 212
presidency, presidents, 8–10
    best, ranking of, 254–55
    disputed elections and leader-
    ship of, 241–47
    economic leadership of, 217–25
    first elections for, 16

grouping of, 257–59
judiciary and leadership of,
    234–40
leadership issues of, 47, 215
most overrated and underrated,
    261–64
most variable ratings, 259–60
rankings of, 11–12, 249–72
Virginia succession of, 35, 40
wartime leadership of, 226–33
worst, ranking of, 256–57
see also specific presidents
Progressive Era, 149
Prohibition, 134
Public Broadcasting System, 175
Pulitzer, Joseph, 122
Pullman strike, 114
Pure Food and Drug Act (1906),
    128
Putin, Vladimir, 209

Quay, Matt, 117

Radical Republicans, 85, 89, 100
rankings, presidential:
    high, predictors of, 264–65
    methodology of, 66, 249
    by political party of respon-
    dents, 268–71
    by scholarly fields, 65, 266–68
    survey participants of, 273–75
Reagan, Ronald Wilson, 2, 3, 7–8,
    49, 140, 148, 186, 191,
    193–97, 199, 200, 203, 220,
    224, 235, 236, 253, 285
    ranking of, 11, 193, 252, 254,
    255, 257, 258, 260, 261,
    262–63, 264, 265, 267, 269,
    271, 272
Reaganomics, 196–97

Reconstruction, 89, 96–97, 100, 101, 244, 276

Reconstruction Finance Corporation, 153

Red Scare, 144

Rehnquist, William H., 239

Republican Party, 7, 70, 108
see also Radical Republicans; Stalwart Republicans

Resumption Act (1875), 97

Richardson, Elliott, 180

Rockefeller, Nelson A., 184, 199

Roe v. Wade, 235

Roosevelt, Franklin Delano, 2, 120, 140, 154, 155–58, 194, 221, 222–23, 225, 227, 228, 229–30, 231–32, 236, 239, 283, 284
ranking of, 11, 155, 250, 253, 254, 255, 258, 260, 261, 263, 267, 269, 272

Roosevelt, Theodore, 2, 49, 112, 114, 120, 122, 131–32, 136, 140, 225, 227, 237, 266, 282, 283
ranking of, 11, 255, 258, 267, 269

Roosevelt Corollary, 128–29

Rove, Karl, 121, 210

Ruckelshaus, William, 180

Rumsfeld, Donald, 186, 210

Rush, Benjamin, 24

Russia, 37, 62, 139
see also Soviet Union

Russo-Japanese War, 129

Rutledge, John, 277

St. John, John, 282

Sakharov, Andrei, 190

Samuelson, Paul, 224

Santa Anna, Antonio López de, 65

"Saturday Night Massacre," 180

Scalia, Antonin, 236

Schmitz, John, 285

Schwarzkopf, Norman, 229, 230

Scott, Dred, 76, 238

Scott, Thomas, 102

Scott, Winfield, 62–63, 73, 81, 280

Scowcroft, Brent, 200, 212, 229–30

Scranton, William, 199

Senate, U.S., 5–7, 244

September 11, see World Trade Center and Pentagon attack

Seward, William, 81

Sheridan, Philip, 95, 97

Sherman, William Tecumseh, 84, 85, 229, 230, 231, 232

Sherman Antitrust Act (1890), 117

Sherman Silver Purchase Act (1890), 117

Shultz, George, 7

Sirica, John, 238

Six Day War, 192

slavery, 36, 46, 53, 58, 65–66, 68, 77–78, 81, 85, 100, 230, 238

Smith, Adam, 51

Smith, Alfred E., 283

Smith, William, 42

Smoot-Hawley Tariff, 148, 221, 223

Social Security, 199, 211

Solzhenitsyn, Alexander, 185

Somalia, 227

Souter, David, 235, 236

Soviet Union, 157–58, 160, 161–62, 164, 165, 166, 176, 185, 189, 190, 191, 195–96, 199–200, 228

Spain, 37, 122

Spanish-American War, 120, 122–23, 231, 266

Specie Circular, 50

spoils system, 45, 108, 117
Stalin, Joseph, 157–58
Stalwart Republicans, 108, 109
Stamp Act (1765), 21
Stanton, Edwin M., 79, 93, 96
State Department, U.S., 18
Stevenson, Adlai, 284
Stowe, Harriet Beecher, 69
Strategic Defense Initiative, 196
Streeter, Alson, 282
Strong, Benjamin, 221–22
Suez Canal crisis, 167
Sullivan, Mark, 152
Sumner, Charles, 85
Sununu, John, 201, 235
supply side economics, 196–97
Supreme Court, U.S., 8–10, 92, 110,
    118, 131, 132, 133–34, 157,
    167, 179, 180–82, 220,
    234–40, 245–46
Swallow, Silas, 282

Taft, William Howard, 39, 49, 117,
    130–34, 142, 220, 237, 283
    ranking of, 12, 130, 251, 258,
    266, 267, 270
Taliban, 212
Taney, Roger Brooke, 83, 238
Tariff Commission, 143
"tariff of abominations," 46
Taylor, Zachary, 64–66, 68, 227, 280
    ranking of, 12, 64, 251, 256, 259,
    260, 267, 270
Teapot Dome scandal, 144, 148
Tecumseh, 53
Telfair, Edward, 278
terrorism, 1, 210, 212
Tet offensive, 232
Texas, 58–59, 62–63, 65–66, 69
Thomas, Clarence, 236

Thomas, Norman, 283
Thurmond, J. Strom, 284
Tilden, Samuel Jones, 101, 243–44,
    281
Tippecanoe, Battle of, 53
Tito, Josip Broz, 190
Trail of Tears, 47
Transportation Department, U.S.,
    175
Treasury Department, U.S., 17, 61,
    211
Tripartite Declaration, 167
Truman, Harry S., 49, 140, 142, 154,
    159–62, 177, 212, 223, 227,
    228, 232, 237, 284
    ranking of, 11, 159, 255, 258,
    264, 267, 269
Tyler, John, 53, 54, 55–59
    ranking of, 12, 256, 257, 259,
    260, 267, 270

Underground Railroad, 69
United Nations, 158, 165, 199, 200,
    210, 212
Upper California, 62–63

Van Buren, Martin, 46, 48–51, 53,
    58, 280
    ranking of, 12, 251, 259, 260,
    267, 270
Vance, Cyrus, 191
Versailles, Treaty of, 139, 221
veto, 57, 59, 186
vice presidency, 5, 8, 276
Vietnam, 191
Vietnam War, 176–77, 183, 185, 227,
    228, 231, 232
Villa, Pancho, 138
Vinson, Fred, 237
Virginia Statute (Jefferson), 29

Volcker, Paul, 224
Volstead Act (1919), 134
Voting Rights Act (1965), 175

Wade, Benjamin, 85
Wagner, Robert F., 153
Wallace, George C., 285
Wallace, Henry A., 284
Wallace, William, 116
War Department, U.S., 21
War of 1812, 32, 40, 219
War on Poverty, 174–75
War Relocation Authority, 239
Warren, Earl, 237
Washington, George, 2, 5, 15–19,
    23, 27, 35, 36, 56, 95, 218,
    227, 236, 277, 278
  farewell address of, 18, 19
  ranking of, 11, 15, 250, 254, 258,
    266, 267, 272
Washington Naval Conference,
    143–44
Watergate affair, 179–82, 183,
    238–39
Waxman, Seth, 133
Weaver, James, 282
Webb, Lucy Ware, 100
Webster, Daniel, 53, 219, 280
Weinberger, Caspar, 7

Welles, Gideon, 81
Wells, Charles, 245
Whig Party, 47, 51, 53, 56, 65–66
Whiskey Rebellion, 17
White, Byron, 235–36
White, Harry Dexter, 223
White, Hugh, 280
White League, 96
Wilderness, Battle of the, 84
Willkie, Wendell, 284
Wilmot, David, 65
Wilmot Proviso, 65–66
Wilson, Thomas Woodrow, 27, 120,
    131, 135–40, 144, 152, 156,
    220, 227, 230–31, 254, 283
  ranking of, 11, 135, 249, 257,
    258, 260, 261–62, 263, 266,
    267, 269, 270–71
Wirt, William, 280
Woolley, John, 282
World Trade Center and Pentagon
    attack, 1, 210, 212, 246
World War I, 138, 156, 220
World War II, 156, 157, 160–61, 164,
    165, 169, 199, 223, 231, 232,
    239
Wormley Conference, 244

Yalta Conference, 157–58

About the Editors

JAMES TARANTO has been Editor of OpinionJournal.com, the Web site of *The Wall Street Journal*'s editorial page, since its inception in 2000. He writes the popular "Best of the Web Today" column for the site. He previously served as Deputy Editorial Features (op-ed) Editor for the *Journal*.

LEONARD LEO is Executive Vice President of the Federalist Society, an organization of 25,000 libertarians and conservatives dedicated to restoring the rule of law. He collaborated with Professor Steven Calabresi, Chairman of the Federalist Society, on a new ranking of presidents that led to this book.